E. Michael Iba / Thomas L. Johnson

The German Fairy Tale Landscape

Bibliografische Information der Deutschen Nationalbibliothek
Die Deutsche Nationalbibliothek verzeichnet diese Publikation in der Deutschen Nationalbibliografie; detaillierte bibliografische Daten sind im Internet über http://dnb.d-nb.de abrufbar.

Photo credits
p. 434–438

Map of the German Fairy Tale Route
With the approval of "Deutsche Märchenstraße e. V.", Kassel

Cover
Sababurg Castle: Home of Sleeping Beauty
p. 434

Manufacturing and designing
CW Niemeyer Buchverlage GmbH

Printing
Quedlinburg Druck GmbH, Quedlinburg

ISBN
978-3-8271-9139-7

Internet: www.deutsche-maerchenstrasse.com

E. Michael Iba / Thomas L. Johnson

The German Fairy Tale Landscape

The storied world of the Brothers Grimm

CW Niemeyer
Buchverlage

This book is dedicated to an American-German friendship that has lasted for more than forty years and has survived Cold War, globalization and economic recession.

Table of Contents

The fifty-three member communities of the German Fairy Tale Route

and the two Brothers Grimm locales Göttingen and Berlin:

Sagas – Legends – Songs

Brothers Grimm: Children's and Household Tales

The German Fairy Tale Route

Invitation to Discovery

Founded in the council chamber of the historic town hall of Steinau an der Straße on April 11, 1975 to honor the Brothers Grimm, the German Fairy Tale Route has become, with its over sixty cities, towns, villages and counties, one of the oldest and most revered vacation itineraries in Germany.

This fabulous route has guided the traveler since then through the lovely landscapes of Hesse and the Weser region as far as the mouth of the Weser River in Bremerhaven through a number of nature parks with forests and fields including the old **beech forest** (41,000 acres) of the Kellerwald-Edersee National Park that was designated a **UNESCO World Natural Heritage Site** in 2011. The route wends through architectural highlights located in the towns and cities of Marburg, Alsfeld, Homberg, Fritzlar, Kassel (**Mountain Park Wilhelmshöhe: a UNESCO World Heritage Site**, since 2013), Bad Hersfeld, Hann. Münden, Hamelin, Buxtehude, Bremen and others. Since 2004, **Bremen's City Hall** – as well as the **Roland Statue** on the market place are UNESCO World Heritage Sites. Corvey Castle, a **UNESCO World Heritage Site** since 2014, is located alongside the Weser River and the **UNESCO World Natural Heritage Site**, Wadden Sea, lies just outside Bremerhaven.

Knowledge about fairy tales and sagas alike can be gathered in museums and collections such as the **GRIMMWORLD** in Kassel (its gem is the **UNESCO World Document Heritage**: the Brothers Grimm first edition of the **Children's and Household Tales**, 1812) and the *Museum Brothers Grimm House* in Steinau or the *German Fairy Tale and Weser Saga Museum* in Bad Oeynhausen.

We are genuinely pleased that this volume will communicate much that is worth knowing about the Brothers Grimm and the stages of their lives to English-speaking audiences. Both of the authors, E. Michael Iba and Professor Emeritus Thomas L. Johnson, have known the German Fairy Tale Route for decades and have followed it closely since its founding in 1975. They and the publisher as well as our former intern Annika Ludwig and all participating members and partners deserve great thanks that we have suc-

Fairy Tale characters gather at Trendelburg Castle

cessfully completed this book and can present it in time on the occasion of the 40th anniversary of this theme route in April of 2015.

May this volume also help make a trip on the **German Fairy Tale Route** more instructive and simultaneously more enjoyable. Our wish is that you might discover aspects or a part of Germany that you might not have previously known.

We welcome you, dear reader, to the book and to **the German Fairy Tale Route**.

Benjamin Schäfer
General Manager of
German Fairy Tale Route
(registered association)

Uwe Schmidt
President of the German Fairy Tale Route
Head of the Kassel County District

Kurfürstenstr. 9
34117 Kassel
Germany
www.deutsche-maerchenstrasse.com

The German Fairy Tale Landscape: a brief background "Where do fairy tales come from?" A reader wonders.

The answer will likely be expressed in geographical or biographical terms: *From the Brothers Grimm, from Perrault, from Hans Christian Anderson, from France, from Denmark, from Germany, especially Germany.* If the reader objects, saying that is not what was really meant at all, there is a second-level answer: fairy tales come from something called oral tradition, the simple telling of stories within and between generations. The conventional wisdom holds that the famous collectors of fairy tales transcribed them as recited by anonymous sources on their deathbeds. And there is at least one instance where that was at least the intention. In 1823, when Clemens Brentano mentioned to Wilhelm Grimm that an old woman at St. Elizabeth Hospital in Marburg had told him several fairy tales, Wilhelm paid this woman in declining health a visit hoping to hear fairy tales from her but failed in the end as the *oracle* wouldn't speak.

This volume starts with a far simpler assumption. Fairy tales come from many sources and places, but in the end they become either localized because some intrinsic content is localizable or because of the tradition that has grown around a fairy tale as it has resided in a specific region or area. Within the Grimm tradition that is at the heart of this volume, we have rare localized tales such as *the Bremen Town Musicians* (who, incidentally, never reach Bremen in the tale) or *The Hare and the Hedgehog* (Buxtehude), and many more localized sagas like that of the *Pied Piper of Hamelin.* Indeed, it was localization that Jacob Grimm introduced as one of the key distinctions between the fairy tale and saga. While fairy tales are only occasionally localized, sagas almost always are.

Over time, however, specific fairy tales become tied to certain places through one of two means: *tradition or intervention.* The *Sleeping Beauty* fairy tale spans a century in the life of an unnamed castle surrounded by a dense thicket. Eventually, however, this originally unlocalized tale is linked by tradition to the beautiful *Sababurg Castle* near Hofgeismar. Readers of the Grimms found the partial ruin of *that castle* a convincing *home* for the sleeping

UNESCO World Natural Heritage Site:
Germany's old beech forest (Kellerwald-Edersee National Park)

princess. Several of the tales, *Snow White* and *Rapunzel* among them, are actually claimed also by different places.

Sometimes it is a single striking detail that leads to the localizing of a fairy tale. As part of their historical folk costume, unmarried young women in the Schwalm district wear a red bonnet on their heads reminiscent of that of *Little Red Riding Hood* in the beloved Grimm Fairy Tale. For this reason, tradition allows Schwalmstadt to lay claim to that tale in declaring itself the capital of *Little Red Riding Hood Territory.*

Promoting the rich cultural and geographical tradition of the fairy tale is at the heart of the work of the **Association of the German Fairy Tale Route** that has its headquarters in downtown Kassel. In the last forty years, it has established the *German Fairy Tale Route* as a touristic venture stretching from Hanau to Bremerhaven with ties to the scores of communities that belong to the association. While purists occasionally resist this effort for its sometimes artificial attempts to localize certain tales, the association remains true to the spirit of the Brothers Grimm, as attested to in their itinerary and choice to be headquartered in what is essentially the adopted home city of the Grimms: Kassel.

Format of the Book

This volume is organized by locales running from south to north, we have chosen to include both sagas and fairy tales, along with some other German authors but predominantly from Jacob and Wilhelm Grimm or their forgotten brother, Ferdinand. We have occasionally added a rare local tale by an anonymous or traditional author. There are 53 member communities (cities, towns and villages) of the German Fairy Tale Route. Each is described in detail with their fairy tales, sagas or literary references and with their historic events (History) and sights (What to See and Do). In addition

UNESCO World Heritage Site: Mountain Park Kassel-Wilhelmshöhe: Devil's Bridge (Teufelsbrücke) and Waterfall

to these 53 member communities of the Fairy Tale Route, Berlin and Göttingen are also included in this volume, because each played an important role in the life and work of the Brothers Grimm. Beyond the descriptions of these 55 locations, the book is comprised of a number of representative fairy tales, legends, songs, as well as many sidebars (i.e. German Romanticism, What is the Huguenot tradition? – Happy endings/Sad endings: Which are better? – What is a Hanseatic City?) to develop key ideas or questions that this voyage introduces.

Preceding this main section is a prolonged summary of the life and work of the Brothers Grimm. Following it is a fairy tale section of twelve of the favorite tales of the Brothers Grimm with enchanting illustrations by Markus Lefrançois. Concluding sections include a Web-index (web addresses of place and information on population), an extensive bibliography, a short biography of authors, photo credits, an alphabetical listing of locations and a current map featuring the route of the German Fairy Tale Route from Hanau to Bremerhaven.

N.B. Spelling in German:
ae = ä / oe = ö / ue = ü / ss = ß

The Brothers Grimm

Although the name of the Brothers Grimm is linked worldwide with the memory of their *Children's and Household Tales*, the Grimm Brothers are known for much more than merely as collectors of fairy tales and sagas. Jacob and Wilhelm Grimm were the founders of German antiquity studies, German linguistics, and German philology. They were personalities of the highest intellectual order who conducted research in the fields of literature, linguistics, folklore, history, religion and law, and who mastered approximately a dozen languages including Latin, classical Greek, English, French, Provençal, Spanish, Swedish, Russian, and, of course, German. Their work extended far beyond the borders of Germany and led to activities with individual languages and folk poetry in countless European lands and to a brisk international scientific exchange.

There is a crucial distinction to be made at the outset. Although there were five brothers and one girl who grew into adulthood in the Grimm household, it is only Jacob and Wilhelm, indivisible in both their lives and their work, whom we mean when we refer to the Brothers Grimm. Indeed, this volume will include works written by Ferdinand Grimm and make numerous references to the artist brother, Ludwig Emil Grimm. Neither, however, are considered Brothers Grimm – that title is reserved for the two eldest, Jacob and Wilhelm.

Jacob Grimm was born in Hanau on January 4, 1785 as was Wilhelm on February 24, 1786. The family Grimm moved from Hanau to Steinau an der Straße in 1791 when their father returned to his birthplace to assume the prestigious position of district magistrate in the administrative and judicial districts of Steinau and Schlüchtern. The Grimms moved into the roomy and stately half-timbered Steinau magistrate's house that today is a significant Grimm museum. Here in Steinau, where their sister Charlotte (Lotte) was born on March 10, 1793, the Grimm children lived a carefree, unburdened, and happy childhood that came to an abrupt end with the unexpected death of their father of a virulent lung infection on the

10th of January, 1796. Steinau is currently the location on the German Fairy Tale Route that has the most authentic Grimm sites preserved.

Philipp Wilhelm Grimm's (1751–96) death brought about a dramatic decline in the material situation of the family, allowing financial need to determine much of the further course of their lives. During these difficult years, the family Grimm received financial support from Henriette Zimmer, a sister of Mrs Grimm who lived at the court of Kassel. Her beneficence allowed her nephews Jacob

The Brothers Grimm of Kassel, alias Stefan Becker and Carlo Ghiradelli behind the Brothers Grimm Monument in Kassel

and Wilhelm to visit secondary school (Lyceum Fridericianum) in Kassel and later to attend the University of Marburg where they both studied law before branching out into other research areas. In 1803, the three other Grimm brothers, Carl, born April 24, 1787, Ferdinand, born December 18, 1788, and Ludwig Emil, born March 14, 1790, also resettled to Kassel, followed two years later by Lotte and their mother.

In the Marburg Chapter, we will discuss the importance of the Brothers Grimm Marburg years (1802–06) and, in particular, their friendship with the young professor Friedrich Carl von Savigny

(1779–1861) upon the development of the Grimms. Without doubt, however, the thirty years that the Brothers Grimm spent in Kassel formed the focal point in their life and work. Initially unemployed or underemployed, they eventually found positions as librarians and produced a substantial scholarly output.

After the death of their mother on May 27, 1808, the heavy burden of supporting the whole family fell more on the eldest, Jacob, than on his sickly brother, Wilhelm. Encouraged to do so by Clemens Brentano, they had begun to collect fairy tales in 1806. Their principal contacts for fairy tales in Kassel and its surroundings were the families Wild, Hassenpflug, and the Ramus siblings, who introduced the Brothers Grimm to Dorothea Viehmann from nearby Niederzwehren, the dragoon constable Krause in neighboring Hoof, Friederike Mannel and Ferdinand Siebert from the Schwalm region. Indeed, Wilhelm married Dorothea (Dortchen) Wild, a major contributor to their fairy tale texts. Jacob Grimm remained a bachelor throughout his life.

Passed over for advancement in the Elector's Library in Kassel, the brothers moved to Göttingen in 1829 where they served as both professors and librarians for eight years until the new King of Hanover, Ernst August, violated the legal constitution and dissolved parliament, bringing the Brothers Grimm to sign, along with five other noteworthy professors, the protest of the *Göttingen Seven*, an act that led to their firing and banishment from Göttingen. They returned to Kassel and moved in with their brother Ludwig Emil and began work leading to the German Dictionary in the two years of their unemployment.

By now in their mid 50's, Jacob and Wilhelm moved from Kassel to Berlin in 1841 to go on with their work on the German Dictionary, where they received commensurate salaries and enjoyable work conditions. Eventually they died, Wilhelm on December 16, 1859, and Jacob on September 20, 1863. Their final resting place is in the cemetery of the Matthäus Community in Berlin-Schöneberg.

Finally, in June 2005, the Children's and Household Tales of the Brothers Grimm were officially registered among 120 worldwide texts as part of the UNESCO Memory of the World register.

The Brothers Grimm of Hanau, alias Ulrich Lüer and Wolfgang Kamberg in front of the Brothers Grimm National Monument in Hanau

Chronology of the Brothers Grimm

1785	Jacob Grimm born on January 4 in Hanau
1786	Wilhelm Grimm born on February 24 in Hanau
1787	Carl Grimm born on April 24 in Hanau
1788	Ferdinand Grimm born on December 18 in Hanau
1790	Ludwig Emil Grimm born on March 14 in Hanau
1791	Grimm family moves to Steinau
1793	Charlotte (Lotte) Grimm born on March 10 in Steinau
1796	Father Philipp Wilhelm Grimm dies January 10
1798	Jacob and Wilhelm move to Kassel and enter school (Lyceum Fridericianum)
1802	April, Jacob goes to Marburg to study law at Philipps University
1803	April, Wilhelm joins Jacob at Marburg
1806	The Brothers Grimm begin to collect fairy tales
1808	Their mother, Dorothea Grimm, dies on May 27 in Kassel
1812	Volume One of the Children's and Household Tales is published

1815	Volume Two of the Children's and Household Tales is published
1814/15	Jacob in the Electoral Hessian delegation at the Congress of Vienna, afterwards in Paris
1816	Brothers Grimm publish the first volume of the German Sagas
1818	Brothers Grimm publish the second volume of the German Sagas
1819	Jacob Grimm, German Grammar, volume I
1819	Jacob and Wilhelm Grimm awarded honorary doctorates in Marburg
1825	Wilhelm marries Dorothea (Dortchen) Wild, a major contributor of fairy tale texts
1826	Jacob Grimm, German Grammar, volume II
1829	Brothers Grimm accept a call to Göttingen
1831	Jacob Grimm, German Grammar, volume III
1837	Jacob Grimm, German Grammar, volume IV
1837	Protest of the Göttingen Seven ends the brothers' Göttingen careers
1840	Brothers Grimm called to Berlin to complete the German Dictionary
1845	Ferdinand Grimm dies on January 6 in Wolfenbüttel
1848	Jacob serves in the Parliament in Frankfurt as an advocate for democracy in the National Assembly that met in St. Paul's Church (Frankfurt)
1854	Brothers Grimm, German Dictionary, volume I
1857	Seventh edition of Children's and Household Tales; source of many English translations
1859	Wilhelm Grimm dies on December 16 in Berlin
1860	Brothers Grimm, German Dictionary, volume II
1863	Ludwig Emil Grimm dies on April 4 in Kassel
1863	Jacob Grimm dies on September 20 in Berlin
1961	Completion of the complete sixteen volumes German Dictionary the Brothers Grimm began in 1838
2005	Children's and Household Tales named to UNESCO'S Memory of the World register

2012 Two hundred years of Children's and Household Tales:
International Conference
"Märchen, Mythen und Moderne",
(Fairy Tales, Myths and Modern Times),
December 17–20, University of Kassel

Brothers-Grimm-City Hanau

Fairy Tale Hanau: Birthplace of the Brothers Grimm

Like any good story, a Fairy Tale Route needs both a beginning and an ending. The simple fact that Hanau is the birthplace of Jacob (1785–1863) and Wilhelm (1786–1859) Grimm and most of their siblings would seem to make Hanau a perfect place to begin our journey. Most fairy tales, however, have that moment when perfect beginnings are sidetracked or even destroyed; Hanau is no different. On March 19, 1945, just two months before the end of World War II, allied bombers destroyed over 80 per cent of the city of Hanau including many of the sites that were central to the Grimm family story. The birthplace of the Brothers Grimm, for instance, is gone except for a plaque with pictures and text at the former site of their birthplace. There is, nevertheless, a feeling of good beginnings when one stands facing the New City Hall and its German National Monument to the Brothers Grimm.

Ludwig Emil Grimm: The Brothers Grimm

Starting Point of the German Fairy Tale Route

As the birthplace of the Brothers Grimm, Hanau is the natural starting point for the German Fairy Tale Route that begins at the Brothers Grimm National Monument in front of the New

The Brothers Grimm National Monument

City Hall. It ends more than 400 miles away in Bremerhaven where the Weser River flows into the North Sea.

Jacob (1785–1863) and Wilhelm Grimm (1786–1859) as well as their brothers Carl (1787–1852), Ferdinand (1788–1845), who also collected sagas, as well as the painter and drawer Ludwig Emil Grimm (1790–1863) were all born in Hanau. Additionally, Hanau is where Jeanette and Marie Hassenpflug, who contributed such well-known tales as *Little Red Riding Hood, Puss in Boots, Brother and Sister* or *Sleeping Beauty* to the Grimms' Children's and Household Tales, spent their childhoods.

The Brothers Grimm got their first instruction from Aunt Schlemmer, the sister of their father and from their maternal grandfather, Johann Hermann Zimmer (1709–98). Early on they learned French. In his memoirs, Wilhelm

Philippsruhe Castle: Location of the Hanau History Museum and of the Hanau History Association 1844

Grimm recalls how he walked hand-in-hand with Jacob across the market of the New Town (Neustadt) to a French teacher who lived near the Wallonian church.

The Brothers Grimm National Monument was erected in the marketplace of the New Town in 1896. Ever since, Jacob Grimm has to stand on the pedestal while Wilhelm Grimm makes himself comfortable on a chair and leafs through a thick volume. Rumor has it, however, that the brothers change places in the witching hour to give Jacob some time to rest.

Hanau's Brothers Grimm Festival, which takes place each year in the months of May to July in the amphitheater of Philippsruhe Castle, is esteemed by both locals and visitors. The beautiful Philippsruhe Castle contains a remarkable Grimm Collection (memorabilia and drawings of L. E. Grimm) and is the residence of the tradition-rich Hanau History Society, founded in 1844.

History

Many of the towns and cities we will visit on the Fairy Tale Route began with a castle; Hanau is no exception. In 1143, the construction of moat-encircled Hanau castle was documented in Mainz. In 1168, the castle passed into the hands of the masters of Dorfelden – later the lords and counts of Hanau. In 1303, King Albrecht I (1298–1308) granted a municipal charter for the village that had sprung up around the castle to Master Ulrich I. After 1436, the town became the regular residence of the counts of Hanau, whose most famous representative is Philipp Ludwig II of Hanau-Münzenberg (1580–1612).

Market day on the large square in front of the New Town Hall

A town often will have a critical moment when something takes place that forever changes its course. In the centuries before 1945, it was the so-called Hanau Capitulation of June 1, 1597, when the reformed Count Philipp Ludwig II signed a pact giving reformed Calvinists from the Spanish Netherlands the right to establish a new town (Neustadt) outside the gates of the old town of Hanau. With the arrival of these exiled craftsmen and businessmen, Hanau developed a reputation for luxury goods.

The German Goldsmith House

In 1661, the town saw the establishment of the first German faience (specialized ceramic) factory and Hanau attained a position of prominence in both the textile industry and goldsmithing. After the counts of Hanau died out in 1736, the town, along with its county of Hanau-Münzenberg, passed over to the landgrave of Hesse-Kassel because of succession agreements. With the arrival of railroads in the nineteenth century, Hanau developed into a significant distribution hub.

Hanau today is a modern, bustling city that still retains many of its traditional industries like gold and silver conversion and the gemstone trade as well as those of any modern industrial city situated just eleven miles from the transportation hub, Frankfurt am Main. Enough of pre-war Hanau has been preserved or lovingly restored to allow the visitor to appreciate both what the city was before the war and what it is afterwards.

What to See and Do

Note: A visit to all the sites of Hanau will involve more travel than in most towns of the Fairy Tale Route as the key sites are spread around the city and its immediate surroundings.

1. **Brothers Grimm National Monument** (1896). This imposing sculpture of Jacob and Wilhelm Grimm stands in the large square in front of the **New City Hall** (Neustädter Rathaus, 1723–33). It is the perfect first step for a journey covering the German Fairy Tale Route.

Brothers Grimm Festival: scene from King Thrushbeard (Drosselbart)

2. **Philippsruhe Castle.** The castle Philippsruhe (1701–12), is an impressive structure built in the style of the Palace of Versailles that houses the **Hanau History Museum** and its noteworthy Grimm Collection. The amphitheater of the castle serves as a backdrop for **Brothers Grimm Festival** that runs from May to July.

3. **The Wallonian-Dutch Church** (1600–08), the 1st Reformed Church building in Germany. The bombed out exterior of the Wallonian church today remains a commemorative site and an

Wilhelmsbad State Park – the best preserved cure and bath installation of the 18th century in Germany

impressive reminder of the destructive effects of World War II.

4. German Goldsmith House (1538–50), former Hanau Town Hall of the Old Town, this famous half-timbered building honors Hanau's gold crafts. Across from it is the St. Mary's Church (14th–15th centuries).

5. Wilhelmsbad State Park (1777–82), once the summer residence of the Hessian landgraves, features the best-preserved example of cure and bath installations of the 18th century in Germany.

6. Hanau-Steinheim. This picturesque old town is a reminder of what all of Hanau once looked like. Worth a visit to see its Tower (1430) and the Steinheim Castle with its museum. The town features half -timbered houses from the 15th and 16th centuries and St. John the Baptist Church from the 14th and 15th centuries.

7. Several miles east of Hanau sits the ancient **Trages Estate** (1370), now a golf course with a restaurant in a romantic environment (most of the other historical buildings are private). This is

Steinheim (Platz des Friedens): Beautiful timber-framed houses

where leaders of the German Romantic Movement, including Clemens and Bettina Brentano, Achim von Arnim, Caroline von Günderrode, and Jacob and Wilhelm Grimm were invited by the owner of the estate, the legal historian and professor at Marburg University, Friedrich Carl von Savigny (1779–1861).

German Romanticism

For many English speakers, the words Romantic or romanticism evoke the great English romantic tradition where poets like William Wordsworth, Samuel Taylor Coleridge, John Keats, Mary and Percy Bysshe Shelley and Lord Byron rediscovered nature and the power of the sublime and took issue with the artistic conventions of classicism or the enlightenment. In Germany, however, there was a vigorous period in art, music, and literature that is clearly romantic in its emphasis on organic, creative, perception-based expression. Like the English Romantic Movement, it engaged in what historian Paul Johnson calls the open battle between classicism-reason, on the one hand, and romanticism-unreason on the other. The German Romantics, however, tended more often to look both inwards and backwards, building both a lyrical tradition and rediscovering the pre-classical German past.

Are the fairy tales of the Brothers Grimm an expression of Romanticism? Yes. Throughout this book you will see references to other authors often engaged in the same sort of monumental project as were the Brothers Grimm. The collection, The Boy's Wonderhorn (1805–08) by Clemens Brentano and Achim von Arnim, for example, is typical of these encyclopedic projects that seek to uncover the ethnic folk expression in its purest forms and is commonly considered among the most distinctive pieces of Romanticism in Germany. (see Marburg)

For Jacob and Wilhelm Grimm, it was their exposure to the young professor Friedrich Carl von Savigny at Marburg that brought them into contact with Brentano and von Arnim, for whom they began collecting the tales that eventually led to their own monumental project, the Children's and Household Tales. The particular group with whom they associated during these years is called the High Romantics and includes E.T.A. Hoffmann, Joseph Eichendorff and Adelbert von Chamisso. One of the unfortunate outcomes of this great creative period in German culture is the extent to which the Nazis willingly embraced many of the same feelings for those folk expressions of German heritage. Yet, it is the resiliency of the fairy tale form that gives the Brothers Grimm both a place within the Romantic literary movement but also a stature that transcends that movement.

Brothers-Grimm-Town Steinau an der Straße

Ludwig Emil Grimm: The Brothers Grimm

The Museum Brothers Grimm House

Fairy Tale and Saga References

The particular and enduring appeal of *Steinau an der Straße* (Steinau on the road) is that this delightful town is where the Grimm children spent their somewhat painful but likely enchanting formative years. Unlike most of the larger locales that figure in their biography, Steinau retains the look and feel that it had more than two centuries ago in 1791 when Jacob (6) and Wilhelm (5) moved to their father's birthplace from Hanau, which they left in 1798.

It is in this quiet town then that Jacob, Wilhelm and their brothers Carl, Ferdinand, and

Ludwig Emil Grimm spent a carefree, uncomplicated and happy childhood, in the dignified and roomy half-timbered Steinau Administrative Building (1652) with a stair tower and surrounded by barns, stalls, vegetable and fruit gardens. In addition to the Grimms, the widowed sister of the father, Juliane, called *Aunt Schlemmer* also lived in the house. Steinau is where their father, Philipp Wilhelm Grimm (1751–96), was born. Trained as a lawyer, he later worked in his hometown as an appointed district magistrate until his sudden and premature death in 1796, an event that radically altered the fortunes of the family Grimm. The only Grimm sister, *Lotte* (short for Charlotte, 1793–1833), was born in Steinau. Historically, ancestors as far back as the grandfather of the Grimms, Friedrich Grimm (1707–77), who worked for 47 years as a reformed pastor in Steinau, had lived there and fourteen people bearing the name Grimm are buried in Steinau.

Museum Brothers Grimm House: Interior

Museum Brothers Grimm House: Interior

In the Reformed Protestant School, whose successor sits next to the town hall and the Catherine's Church, the Brothers Grimm were placed under the strict control of the dreaded town preceptor, Zinckhan, who taught violin, piano, arithmetic, religion, and Latin. He taught all six children of the Grimm family although Lotte attended only in the summer months.

Brother Ludwig Emil Grimm gave a detailed description of the Steinau years in his *Memories from My Life.*

History

The name Steinau refers to rocks, probably those in the Kinzig River. Around the year 900, Steinau belonged to the monastery of Fulda, which decided to build a castle to protect trade and that later became the fief of the mighty

An aerial photograph shows the circular design of the town

counts of Rieneck. In 1272, the castle and the surrounding territory passed to Ulrich I of Hanau as a dowry. King Rudolf I of Habsburg granted Steinau municipal status in 1290. Steinau prospered in the Middle Ages due to its strategic position on the major trade route between Frankfurt and Leipzig. In the 15th and 16th centuries, the town became the centerpiece of the upper County of Hanau and the occasional residence of the counts of Hanau.

What to See and Do

1. Visit the picturesque **Museum Brothers Grimm House.** The historic judge's residence and home of the Grimm family includes extensive exhibits from the life and effects of the Brothers Grimm:

Four Generations of the Grimm Family, Life in Steinau, the Cabinet of Ludwig Emil Grimm, Origin of Fairy Tales, the Fairy Tales of the Brothers Grimm, the International Diffusion of Fairy Tales, etc.

Opposite the *Brothers Grimm Museum* is a huge barn, today the residence of the *Steinau Museum* which features, among other topics,

Steinau Castle

the significance of Steinau on the important trade route between Frankfurt and Leipzig.

2. **Steinau Castle** has stood since 1278 but was reconfigured between 1528–60, giving it an eclectic combination of both Renaissance and medieval architecture. It has a *Castle Museum* and a Grimm collection with personal memorabilia of the Grimm family and with marionettes set into tableaus representing various fairy tales including *Rumpelstiltskin*, *Hansel and Gretel*, and *the Bremen Town Musicians.* The puppet theater *Die Holzköppe*, (wooden heads), renowned for the performance of Grimms' fairy tales, is located in the old stables of the castle.

3. Walk around **historic Steinau** and stop in at *Catherine's Church* (1481–1511), *Town Hall* (1561) and other places the Brothers Grimm lived or knew such as the *Reformed Protestant School, Reformed parsonage*, built in 1690,

residence of the grandparents and birthplace of their father, *Hutten Hospital, Old Wine Cellars, Reinhard Church* (1724), the former Guest House White Horse (*Weißes Ross*) and the favorite places of the Grimm boys, the *town well* and *town wall.*

4. Visit the **Devil's Cave**, a public cave located about two miles north of Steinau. Legends have this cave being discovered when a cow crashed through into its largest dome in 1584.

Ferdinand Grimm

Born on December 18, 1788, Ferdinand Philipp Grimm is most widely known as the unknown Brother Grimm. Of course, he barely stands a chance when compared to Jacob and Wilhelm but even younger brother Ludwig Emil is known for his artistic output. Like his middle brother Carl Friedrich and little sister Lotte Ferdinand died relatively young and largely undistinguished.

Moving to Steinau in his third year, he later attended school with Ludwig at the Secondary School in Kassel earning grades ranging from *relatively studious* to *inattentive, playful,* and *not studious enough.* He left school to write, but was unable to nourish himself as a writer.

We get a more complete portrait of Ferdinand by listening to what others said of him: „Lotte and Ferdinand don't do anything evil, but also nothing good, at least not against the others of us but succumb to indescribable laziness." This was Jacob's complaint while Wilhelm simply said: „With Ferdinand, who often says nothing for several days, there's no way to start anything."

His brother Wilhelm and most probably Achim von Arnim intervened with their publisher, Reimer, to get Ferdinand a position as a proofreader and correspondence clerk in Berlin. The family hoped that he would finally be on the right track as he became acquainted with many interesting individuals (von Savigny, Ernst Moritz Arndt, Hoffmann von Fallersleben, and Heinrich Heine).

Soon enough, however, the news from Berlin grew troubling as Ferdinand was unable to survive on his salary and touched up friends and wrote begging letters. The brothers reached into their pockets and the family reputation was again at risk.

In addition to their annoyance with his spendthrift ways, the brothers harbored another concern: Ferdinand as a writer. As early as 1815, Arnim had alerted Jacob and Wilhelm that Ferdinand had published a pair of poems in a Swiss journal. They exhibited no joy at the success of their brother and made no attempt to enlist him as a partner in their own work. Ferdinand provided simple assistance making copies of folk song texts and collecting saga and fairy tale materials. His services in this role were acknowledged in the preface to the first volume of German Sagas. Ferdinand, who had his own ambitions, must have found that too little so he collected his own sagas and published them under a pseudonym:

1) 1820 in Leipzig: Volkssagen und Märchen der Deutschen und Ausländer (Folk Tales and Fairy Tales of the Germans and Foreigners), published by Lothar.
2) 1838 in Zeitz: Volkssagen der Deutschen (Folk Tales of the Germans), published by Philipp von Steinau.
3) 1846 in Wolfenbüttel: Burg- und Bergmärchen (Mountain and Castle Fairy Tales), (posthumous) collected by Friedrich Grimm.

His elder brothers continued to pitch in with payments before he finally fell apart in Berlin. In March 1834, they invited their sick and failing brother to Göttingen where he seemed to recover remarkably from his sickness. Eventually, his laziness brought Jacob to kick him out in 1836. He died in poverty in Wolfenbüttel in 1845 while his brothers in Berlin were still over a decade away from issuing their final version of the Children's and Household Tales (1857). While Ferdinand turned to the simple people for his sagas, a fact that shows up in his transcripts, his more famous brothers chose to associate generally with more affluent and educated raconteurs.

Interestingly, the modern play Der unbekannte Bruder Grimm (The unknown Brother Grimm) by Hartmut Mechtel has made Ferdinand better known to at least theater-goers.

Freiensteinau

Saga References

Theodor Bindewald (see Herbstein) collected many sagas from the Vogelsberg district where Freiensteinau is a community comprised of twelve villages. Three of the sagas, namely *The Christ Child's Cradle, The Goblin in the March Bush* (Märzenstrauch) as well as *Naxburg* take place in the region of Freiensteinau.

Historic Administrative Center (Riedeselscher Amtshof 1689) and Church of Freiensteinau

History

Mentioned in a document from the year 930 as *mosah,* the most likely reference is to Moos, one of the communities constituting Freiensteinau. The courts of Freiensteinau and Moos were acquired around 1400 by the lords of Eisenbach whose line died out in 1428 to be replaced by the Riedesels of Melsungen. In the 15th to 17th centuries there was fierce fighting for the predominance of the Vogelsberg area between the Prince-Abbot of Fulda, the Land-

Tourist Center at Nieder-Mooser See

grave of Hesse, and the Riedesel barons of Eisenbach. Freiensteinau also was called Blue Corner (Blaues Eck) from the time between 1618–48 when it was part of Bavaria under the rule of Duke Maximilian. In the treaties of 1684 with Fulda and 1713 with Hesse-Darmstadt, the Riedesels were able to preserve the major part of their ownership. In 1806, Freiensteinau joined Hesse when Napoleon incorporated the entire Vogelsberg area into the Grand Duchy of Hesse.

What to See and Do

1. Clearly visible on a hill are the parish church of **Freiensteinau** (with noteworthy baroque gravestones in the cemetery) that was built in 1721–24 and the administrative center (Amtshof) of the Riedesels from the year 1689. A number of half-timbered houses of Hessian-Thuringian style have been preserved as well as a stone draw-well from 1688 in front of the parsonage.

Church of Nieder-Moos

2. The church of **Nieder-Moos** (Lower-Moos) was built in the years 1784–90 by Johann

The ornamental Rococo organ in Nieder-Moos Church

Georg Linck of Brückenau. A piece of particular value located there is the richly decorated Rococo organ (1790–91) of Johann-Markus Oestreich that is noted primarily for the purity of its tones. Concerts are regularly staged in the church.

3. Attracting seekers of rest and relaxation is the tourist center at **Nieder-Mooser See** (Lake) with camping grounds as well as the nearby favorite of nature-lovers, the **Ober-Mooser See** (Upper-Mooser Lake) with a rich selection of animal and plant species, the Rodebach Pond, the Reichloser Pond as well as the region of the High Vogelsberg mountains with their wandering paths.

Facilities of Herbstein's Vulcan Baths

Herbstein

Fairy Tale and Saga References

Many sagas and fairy tales of the Vogelsberg region find their origins in Herbstein and its surroundings. The collection *Herbstein, The Town On the Mountain: Sagas, Fairy Tales, Stories* (Die Stadt auf dem Berge: Sagen – Märchen – Schwänke – 1993) by the folklorist and teacher Ulrich Benzel (1925–99) has special significance.

In addition, the pastor Theodor Bindewald (1829–80), best known for his locally collected *Upper Hessian Saga Book* (Oberhessisches Sagenbuch – 1873), an impressive number of upper Hessian vernacular sagas from the area of Vogelsberg, was born in the section of town called Altenschlirf.

History

Wood–carved Figure of St. Jacob inside the parish church

The town of Herbstein, recognized for its climatic and therapeutic spas, was first mentioned as *heribrahteshusun* in the second half of the 10th century when acreage was transferred to the Abbey of Fulda in a deed of gift. Around 1260, Abbot Henry IV from Fulda built a castle and weir system making Herbstein the base and cornerstone of the western flank of the Abbey of Fulda.

Herbstein, whose first documented mention as a town was in the year 1262, belonged to the Abbey of Fulda over the centuries. After the dissolution of the abbey of Fulda in 1802, the town passed over into the property of Prince William of Nassau-Orange. From 1806 until 1810 Herbstein belonged to the Grand Duchy of Frankfurt and was French. It fell to Hesse-Darmstadt in November of the year 1810.

During the Thirty Years War, Herbstein was besieged and shelled resulting in a partial destruction of the castle and the encircling wall. Two major fires, the first in 1540 and the second in 1907, destroyed large parts of the town but the medieval configuration of the town with its circular pattern of streets centered around the Catholic church has been preserved.

What to See and Do

1. Have a look at the restored parts of the 13th century **town wall** with three defensive towers and the underground vault of the former castle.

Parish church (ca. 1400) and the restored parts of the 13th century town wall

2. The parish church, a late Gothic hall church with its particularly high central nave, was erected around 1400. The interior holds valuable late-Gothic wall paintings, a Gothic Pieta from around 1460, a series of wood-carved figures, a baptismal font from the 16th century as well as a Baroque pulpit.

3. The half-timbered houses of Herbstein originated in the 16th through 20th centuries. The half-timbered **Town Hall** re-built after the fire of 1907 is a masterpiece of carpentry.

4. In the Stockhausen subdivision, one can visit the neo-Romanesque parish church of 1845–49 as well as the **palace** (built between 1790 and 1807) with its Baroque palace park.

5. The tradition-rich **Herbstein Shrovetide** (called *Foeselt*) and the **Straße der Ehe** (marriage street), a birch-lined boulevard at the spa park

Herbstein Shrovetide

where marital pairs plant trees in commemoration of their marriages, are widely known.

6. The child and family-friendly **Herbstein Vulcan Baths**, a large thermal physiotherapy pool, invites users to relax.

Alsfeld

Alsfeld is one of the most picturesque stops on the Fairy Tale Route. The town was selected by the European Council as one of 51 European model towns in the Monument Protection Year of 1975.

Fairy Tale and Literary References

Built in 1628, the Alsfelder Märchenhaus (Fairy Tale House) draws young and old into the realm of fairy tales, myths and legends. The colorful rooms are decorated in fairy tale style with each

Alsfeld Fairy Tale House

Alsfeld: Gateway to the Little Red Riding Hood Country

Grabbrunnen (grave well) where legend has is it that the stork delivers new-born babies

designed to honor a single fairy tale. In the story room, a storyteller keeps her audience spellbound with fairy tales and sagas. On the top floor of the Alsfelder Märchenhaus is a large collection of historical dolls and dollhouses.

Another idyllic spot is the grave well with its old fountain basin. According to legend, newborn children are delivered here by the stork.

Also steeped in legend is the witch's dance floor on the Bechtelsberg near the the Berfa subdivision, where witches are said to cavort on Walpurgis Night at the end of April.

The poet Johanna Merck (1737–73), a precursor of German Classicism, is remembered with a gravestone in Alsfeld's cemetery. The dramatist and lyricist Karl Weiser (1848–1913, *Hutten*), and the writer, local dialect poet and prolific publisher Karl Brodhäcker (1919–2013) were both born in Alsfeld.

Alsfeld Town Hall and Alsfeld Regional Museum

History

Alsfeld dates from as early as the 8th and 9th centuries when it was founded as a Carolingian royal seat and developed by the landgraves of Thuringia. Called *adelsfelt* as early as 1069, it was already minting its own coins between 1180 and 1190. It received its municipal charter in 1222 and passed over into Hessian ownership in 1247 due to a conflict over an inheritance. Its favorable position on the road *"through the short Hesse,"* an old trade route that stretched from Frankfurt to Leipzig, made the town wealthy during the 14th through 16th centuries. Most of the key buildings of the town were built during this era. For some time Alsfeld served as the residence of the Hessian Landgrave, Hermann the Learned; a split inheritance landed Alsfeld in Hesse-Marburg in 1567 and in Hesse-Darmstadt in 1604.

The Thirty Years War (1618–48) hit Alsfeld particularly hard, unleashing starvation, plundering, plague, and eventual occupation. By the war's end, the town had lost much of its previous stature as well as its population base.

What to See and Do

Just a short distance from the Autobahn A5, Alsfeld allows the day-tripper easy access to its historic town center.

1. Meriting a visit is the **Alsfeld Fairy Tale House** (Märchenhaus) located in a cozy, half-timbered building, where a fairy tale teller greets her guests. Not far away is the grave well, where legend has it that the stork delivers new-born babies.

In addition, the *Gothic Cemetery Chapel* that was once drawn by Ludwig Emil Grimm is above the town on the Frauenberg.

Schwalm Fountain, reminiscent of Little Red Riding Hood

2. Go to the **Tourist Center** and pick up the handy map with a 60 minute walking tour of the picturesque old town, featuring many of these sites: The late Gothic **Town Hall** (1512–16), one of the most important half-timbered buildings in Germany with noteworthy murals in its council chambers; the **Walpurgis Church** (13th–15th centuries) which demonstrates how complicated a building's history can become when stretched across centuries. Then

Tombstone and Leonhardsturm

just follow the map, stopping at the **Hochzeitshaus** (Wedding House, 1564-71), the **Stumpf-Haus** (1609) and the **Bücking-Haus** (around 1515).

3. Two patrician homes, the **Minnigerode-Haus** (1687) and the **Neurath-Haus** (1688) accommodate the nicely maintained **Regional Museum** that focuses attention on the degree to which Alsfeld has given its historical core a modern focus.

4. About two kilometers from the town center is the **Altenburg Castle** and castle church from the 18th century, built on the remains of a medieval site on a hill overlooking the Schwalm.

5. Visitors who make the 6 km car trip to nearby **Romrod** will discover its castle, castle church, half-timbered houses and its cultural center in the former synagogue.

What is Walpurgis Night?

If you have read this chapter closely, you may have noticed that both Alsfeld's Gothic church and the night when the groom from Berfa dabbles in witchcraft are named Walpurgis. What is Walpurgis Night and how might it relate to Walpurgis church?

Technically, Walpurgis Night on the evening of April 30 is celebrated very much like Halloween, the night preceding All Saints' Day. Unique to both Halloween and Walpurgis Night is the feeling of two traditions colliding, one pagan and one Christian. When Goethe, for instance, allows Faust to be taken by Mephistopheles to the highest peak of the Harz, the Brocken, he is brought into the midst of a purely Wiccan event, a witch's ball.

What are the witches celebrating?

In the pagan procession of seasons, April 30 is the night when the forces of summer (and light) abolish those of spring with its remnant of wintry darkness. In a very understandable way, one cavorts with the witches and forces of darkness less to join them than to ward off their evil. Like Halloween, rituals arise in this drama of good versus evil. Above all, Walpurgis Night is a time of noise. You should not be surprised to hear clattering and hollering on this one night. In some places it is a time for youthful pranks.

All of this brings us back to the original question: where does the church enter in? In fact, the very name refers back to one of the early saints of the church, St. Walburga, abbess and missionary of the group of St. Boniface (see Fritzlar) in the 8th century. After her death in 779, her relics were felt to have healing powers and it just so happens that the date that those relics were taken to Eichstätt (Bavaria) was April 30. After this, the name Walpurgis was applied to a number of churches throughout Germany and Belgium. Go figure. Go celebrate.

The Bridegroom from Berfa

(Johann Heinrich Schwalm – English version: Thomas L. Johnson)

A lad from Berfa was ready for marriage and had picked out a bride whom he visited often. This story took place on Walpurgis Night when he discovered that his intended had already made plans to visit a witch's dance on top of the Bechtels Mountain near Alsfeld-Berfa. She covered herself with a balm and recited the chant: "I smear myself with witch's balm and avoid every corner and crease." She immediately went up the chimney and then to Bechtels Mountain. In her great hurry, however, the little witch had forgotten the jar full of witch's balm.

The astonished bridegroom covered himself with the magic balm just like she had and recited, because he had not heard it well in his fear, "I smear myself with witch's grease and run into every corner and crease." Then he traveled up the chimney but smacked into every corner and wall and reached the witches on Bechtel's Mountain after a very harrowing ride.

Once there, he was accepted immediately as a musician and directed to play for the witch's dance. His instrument was a beautiful new trumpet into which he was supposed to blow: "I blow, I blow the hair away, from behind the hair of the cat away." When the dance finally ended, he received the trumpet as a gift in addition to a pack of Berliner donuts. His riding horse, however, was a three-legged billy-goat.

While riding the billy-goat, he was instructed to neither think nor speak. Eventually he came to a large body of water. "Man, if I were just across that water," he thought. In that exact moment, the goat launched himself on a church-steeple-high jump and our rider was deposited unceremoniously onto the other shore. His steed, however, was off and out of there. After all the excitement, he became hungry. He opened the package in order to enjoy the gift of donuts but was shocked by what he found. Inside was horse manure, not donuts and, instead of a trumpet, a dead cat whose hair had been completely removed. So shocked and saddened was he that he trotted all the way home by foot.

He had scarcely put himself into bed, however, when the furniture started to travel around the room causing him to slam his head hard against the wall. He cried out desperately: "Whoever wants to go can go, but I am no longer going with!" Finally, the strange vehicle stood still and the witch's magic was at an end.

Marburg

University Home of the Brothers Grimm

Plaque on the Brothers Grimm Marburg Residence (Barfüßerstr. 35)

Fairy Tale and Literary References

Visitors who want to wander through Marburg on the trail of the Brothers Grimm need to direct their attention toward the Castle of the Landgraves, the Forest Home of Carl von Savigny, the Town Hall, and the Brothers Grimm residences in Wendelgasse 4 and Barfüßerstraße 35, the University Church and Elizabeth's Church, which Jacob Grimm referred to as a *true masterpiece*. Visitors should also be aware of the following: manuscripts from the estate of the Brothers Grimm are stored in the library of Philipps University while pencil drawings by their brother, artist Ludwig Emil Grimm, are

Panoramic View: The picturesque castle of Marburg and the Old Town

House of Romanticism

Well-tended half-timbered houses

owned by the University Museum of Cultural Arts in the castle.

During their legal studies in Marburg, the Brothers Grimm received the necessary impetus to begin their activities collecting the *poetry of the people* – folk songs, fairy tales and sagas – from their teacher, Professor Friedrich Carl von Savigny (1779–1861). He established important contacts for them within the circle of key Romantic authors including Clemens Brentano (1778–1842), his wife Sophie Mereau (1770–1806) as well as to Achim (1781–1831) and Bettina von Arnim (1785–1859), Clemens Brentano's sister. Von Savigny's *Forsthof* (forest home) in the shadow of the castle, which Jacob and Wilhelm visited often, became the cradle of *Marburg Romanticism*. With special

Cannon in Marburg Castle

The Town Hall (16th century)

exhibits, lectures and concerts dedicated to the theme of Romanticism as well as fairy tale readings for children, the house at Markt 16, the *House of Marburg Romanticism*, serves as a memorial to this epoch.

After Clemens Brentano had alerted the Brothers Grimm to the existence of an old lady in Elizabeth's Hospital who had told him six to eight fairy tales, but had only written down single words of them, Wilhelm Grimm made an attempt to pull the fairy tales from the memory of this old woman in St. Elizabeth's Hospital, but the *oracle* wouldn't speak. Using other means, he was finally able to acquire a version of *Cinderella* and also *The Golden Bird.*

It is generally acknowledged that the majority of the 200 tales the brothers collected didn't come from single, older sources like the old woman but from acquaintances and friends. Jack Zipes writes that the *"primary method was to invite story-tellers to their home and then have them tell the tales aloud, which the Grimms either noted down on first hearing or after a couple of readings."* (Zipes, *The Brothers Grimm: From Enchanted Forests to the Modern World*, p. 280) That also meant that the typical story-teller was educated and from the middle class or aristocracy.

In their lifetimes, the Brothers Grimm never succeeded in publishing a volume of their domestic and foreign folk songs. It wasn't until Jacob Grimm's 200th birthday in 1985 that the first of a three volume scientific edition was published in Marburg under the title, *Brothers Grimm Folk Songs* (1985–89).

For truly serious students of folk culture, a visit to the *German Central Archive of German Folk Tales* with its 75,000 plus records is recommended. Its first Director, Gottfried Henssen, was the first one to systematize the study of narrative research. This is also where folklorist Charlotte Oberfeld (1915–1998) worked on her editions of *Hessian fairy tales.*

Another favorite son is the Marburg native and well-known Hessian painter, Otto Ubbelohde (1867–1922, see Lahntal) who used sites in the old town, at the castle, and around St. Elizabeth's Church as models for his illustrations of the *Grimm's Children's and Household Tales* and *German Sagas.*

Additionally, Marburg is the literary setting of Werner Bergengruen's *The Sisters from the Mohrenland* as well as in Ina Seidel's *Three Towns of My Youth.*

The ruins of St. Elizabeth's Hospital

The interior of St. Elizabeth's Church

History

The first thing the traveler sees in Marburg is Castle Hill. It is still being debated whether it was the Hessian noble family, the Gisons, or the lords of Gleiberg who built the first Marburg Castle to protect the Lahn ford next to the *Wine Street*, an important junction in trade and traffic routes between Frankfurt and northern Germany.

In 1122, the Landgrave of Thuringia inherited the Gison properties and they built the present-day *marcburg*, whose first documented mention is in 1138–39. In about 1140, a market settlement developed beneath the castle and by 1228 Marburg had received its municipal status.

Critical for the upturn of the town was the relocation of Elizabeth (1207–31), the widow of the Landgrave Ludwig of Thuringia, from Wartburg Castle after the unexpected death of her husband on a crusade. Like her spiritual model, St. Francis of Assisi, Elizabeth devoted herself completely to the care of the sick and poor in a hospital that she donated to the town. Just four years after her early death in 1231, Elizabeth was canonized and the Gothic St. Elizabeth's Church, constructed in 1235 over her grave, became an important pilgrimage destination.

Elizabeth's daughter, Sophie von Brabant, chose Marburg as her residence after the separation of Hesse from Thuringia following the War of Succession between the two states in 1247–64. Marburg became the residence town of the Hessian landgraves.

View into the Old Town

In 1526, Philipp the Magnanimous introduced the Reformation and founded the world's first Protestant university in Marburg one year later. That university still bears his name. In 1529, in an attempt to unify the Protestants, Landgrave Philipp hosted the two great reformers, Martin Luther and the Swiss Ulrich Zwingli, for a Marburg Colloquium that resulted instead in the fragmentation of the Protestant churches.

Ludwig IV died in 1604 as the last of the landgraves residing in Marburg.

What to See and Do

1. High above Marburg lies the picturesque **castle** of the Hessian Landgraves (13th–16th centuries though remains from the 10th–11th centuries are present). Note particularly the two-story **castle chapel** (dedicated in 1288), and the **Fürstensaal** erected around 1300, one of the largest non-religious internal rooms of the German Gothic. The chapel, built on the

Grimm Town Path: fairy tale figures and other highlights from the street Steinweg up to the castle of the Landgrave

model of the *Sainte Chapelle* in Paris, is known for its six meter tall painting of St. Christophorus, remnants of the wall murals and the original 14th century mosaic floor. The castle was fundamentally renovated in the 15th and 16th centuries. It now holds the fine *University Museum of Cultural Arts*, located in the Wilhelmsbau erected in 1492-98.

Below the castle is the Forsthof (Ritterstraße 15, today a student dormitory), the former home of Professor Savigny. The brothers spent their days here while at the college and got to know their fellow students. Savigny's library gave the Brothers Grimm access to the medieval literature and folklore.

2. The oldest purely Gothic church in Germany is **St. Elizabeth's Church**, for many centuries one of the most important pilgrimage destinations in Europe. Its décor includes the magnificent high **altar** consecrated in 1290, the mausoleum of St. Elizabeth with a stone canopy (in 1280), numerous tombs of the landgraves of Hesse-Thuringia and the **jeweled shrine of St. Elizabeth** in the sacristy, a masterpiece of German goldsmith's art of the 13th century. The stained glass windows depicting the life of Saint Elizabeth and the works of mercy are among the finest examples of Gothic art in Germany.

3. In the picturesque **old town** of Marburg there are numerous **half-timbered houses** from the 16th–19th centuries (Markt, Marktgasse, Wettergasse, Reitgasse, Barfüßerstraße, Steinweg) and some **stone houses** (Steinernes Haus 1319–23), Hochzeitshaus (Wedding House 1527–30). The often photographed Marburg **town hall** on the narrow southern side of the market, was built at the beginning of the 16th century and the striking gable of the stair tower was added in 1581–82. The Town Hall was a place where the Brothers Grimm viewed plays and comedies.

View onto the Old University

4. Visit **Philipps University** where the Brothers Grimm were awarded the honorary doctorate in 1819. It is the earliest Protestant university in the world and the place where the Grimms began their antiquarian studies. The **Old Auditorium** and the **University Church** (1291–1300), where the brothers went to services, give a more historical perspective.

5. Another good place to find reminders of the Grimms' Marburg years is in Marburg's **House of Romanticism** on the market square with its permanent and special exhibits on the theme of the German romanticism and the romantic circle of Marburg (1800–06). The Red Parlor (Roter Salon) with its portraits by Ludwig Emil Grimm provides insights into the social culture of this era.

6. Also recommended is a visit to the Marburg district of **Weidenhausen** with its half-timbered houses, some of which are decorated with rich wooden carvings. This part of town has a documented existence going back to 1235.

Saint Elizabeth in Marburg

(Paul Zaunert – English version: Thomas L. Johnson)

When the landgrave Ludwig IV of Thuringia died while on a crusade to the Holy Land in 1227, his nobles and advisors ignored the loyalty oaths that they had sworn to the pious sovereign and advised the landgrave Heinrich that he should take control of the land and banish his brother's wife and their children.

The prince was young and let himself be persuaded to do that so the nobles drove Elizabeth out of Wartburg Castle and from all her properties. As the remains of landgrave Ludwig were carried home and buried, the lords and knights who had carried them home attached themselves to the young landgrave Heinrich. In a harsh speech, however, Rudolph Schenk von Vargula so strongly condemned the injustice that had befallen Elizabeth that the landgrave Heinrich wept bitterly for the pain his behavior had created. He once again accepted Elizabeth in friendship and extended every imaginable goodness to her.

Elizabeth, however, renounced the world, parents, children, and friends. As the landgrave Heinrich saw that she had surrendered herself completely to God and didn't wish to remain with him, he gave her a dowry and a large sum of money. She then moved away from Thuringia to Hesse to follow Master Konrad of Marburg, whom the pope had commissioned to be her spiritual guide. When she arrived at Marburg, however, she failed to find a comfortable home because several of the nobles who had power there were resentful towards her.

The jeweled shrine of St. Elizabeth

Others, however, relate that so much honor was accorded to her in Marburg that she could no longer bear it. In any case, she moved into a nearby village named Wehrda. There she entered a ruined estate whose residence had a broken roof and walls. She was forced to make her bedstead under a staircase and Elizabeth suffered greatly from smoke, heat, rain, and wind. Meanwhile, a small house of plaster and wood was prepared for her in Marburg into which she and her servants moved with great humility and patience. There was a small church with a convent there in which three or four barefoot monks lived. Elizabeth built a hospital for poor, sick people near to this small cloister and received a gray dress from her confessor, Konrad. She diligently served the sick in the hospital, bathing and giving them beds while serving lepers and the impure with acts of mercy.

Once, as she washed and fed the sick, she exclaimed to her maidservants: "Oh, how well it is for us, that we wash, bathe, feed, and nourish our Lord Jesus!" One of them answered: "It is well for you but whether it is well for the other, I do not know."

One day a poor woman came into the infirmary to beg for alms bringing along her child, who was deaf and dumb. She set it down and left for a moment to take care of something. Meanwhile, Elizabeth came and saw the poor child sitting there all alone. She bent down to it and said: "Dear child, who brought you here?" When the child didn't answer her, she pressed it further to answer and said: "Good child, now answer me in the name of our Lord Jesus Christ!" God opened the mouth of the child at that point and it said: "My mother brought me here." The mother was called and Elizabeth left. When the mother entered and heard her child speak, she was astonished and asked: "Who gave you your speech?" The child answered her: "A good lady came and asked who had brought me here and begged me to answer in the name of Jesus." Then the lady took her child, returned home, and praised God the Lord.

The pious and charitable Elizabeth wished to give all the money that she possessed to God and let it be known within a radius of twelve miles around Marburg that anybody who wished to receive alms should come to Marburg on a specific day that she would fix for this purpose.

The lame, the blind, the invalids and the poor came then from all directions and many strong men were commissioned to keep the people orderly to ensure that each might receive alms. Those who stood up from their place or hindered others or who tried to receive alms twice out of greed would have their hair sheared off to show shame. When everything was completely organized, Elizabeth stood in the middle of them and let five hundred marks be distributed that day in the name of God. Once the alms were distributed, many lame and sick still remained in front of the barriers or wherever they would like to lie, and it was evening. As Elizabeth heard this, she assembled everyone and had a large fire built and gave bread to them. She washed and anointed the feet of many. Then the poor people started to get well and they began to sing. As Elizabeth heard that, she spoke: "I have certainly told you that we need to make people happy."

She donated the remaining money, which she had received as an annuity for life, to the sick in the hospital or distributed it further to poor people.

The Otto-Ubbelohde-Haus: the former art studio of the Painter O. Ubbelohde

Lahntal

Fairy Tale and Saga Matters

The pastor and educator Johann Heinrich Christian Bang (1774–1851) lived and worked in the parsonage and church of Goßfelden, one of the seven villages that form the community of Lahntal. He developed a close friendship with Professor Friedrich Carl von Savigny (see Marburg), who often visited the Bang home. Due to Savigny, the Marburg Romantic Circle with Achim von Arnim, the Brentanos, Jacob and Wilhelm Grimm among others found its way to Goßfelden. Even

Otto Ubbelohde: The True Bride, Rapunzel and Hansel and Gretel

after the Brothers Grimm had left Marburg, they remained in contact with Pastor Bang. He collected sagas from the Marburg area that found a place in the German Sagas.

Not far from the River Lahn, on which Goßfelden sits, one finds the Otto-Ubbelohde-Haus, the one-time art studio (built in 1900) of the painter Otto Ubbelohde (1867–1922). This is where his masterworks, namely hundreds of illustrations for the Children's and Household Tales and for the German Sagas of the Brothers Grimm, were created along with many paintings and drawings for songbooks and children's books.

History

Goßfelden was mentioned around 850 in a deed of gift to the Fulda Monastery. The place

The late Romanesque Parish Church

was a possession of the Teutonic Knights in Marburg for centuries.

The Cistercian monastery of Caldern was founded well before the middle of the 13th century and was named in 1250 in a gift deed to the Landgrave Sophie von Brabant. The late-Romanesque rectory church of Caldern is the former monastery church. Caldern, Goßfelden and Sterzhausen (below) are three of the seven villages that were knitted together to form the community of Lahntal after the Hessian regional reorganization.

The Devil with the three Golden Hairs

What to See and Do

1. In **Goßfelden** one should visit the **Otto-Ubbelohde-Haus** and subsequently wander on the Trail of Otto Ubbelohde across Goßfelden. One will recognize on this trail a series of motifs that Ubbelohde came back to in his paintings,

The Hare and the Hedgehog

drawings, and illustrations. His grave is situated upon the hill of Goßfelden cemetery offering a panaromaic view onto the village. You will also pass by the parish church built in 1749–52 based on the plans of master builder Giovanni Ghezzy as well as the old, historic bridge (1802) over the River Lahn.

2. The late Romanesque parish church (crucifix, 14th century, organ from 1703) with the former refectory (currently a barn) and parts of the monastery wall are preserved in **Caldern**.

3. The focal point of **Sterzhausen** is the church (murals in the choir from the 14th century) with its classic nave and its defense tower from 1836 that makes it visible from a distance.

Willingshausen

The oldest painters' colony in Europe

Fairy Tale and Artistic References

Willingshausen can thank Gerhardt von Reutern (1794–1865) and Ludwig Emil Grimm for its foundation as the oldest art colony in Europe (according to recent research, as early as 1824). The first ever drawings of the costumes of the Schwalm were made when the young Ludwig Emil Grimm drew Annels, a girl in festive Willingshausen costume with its "red riding hood," in 1824. Von Reutern, a Baltic German officer fighting in the Russian army, had lost his right arm in the Battle of Leipzig in 1813 and arrived in Willinghausen in 1814, where he lived in the castle of the Schwertzell family. He practiced drawing with his left hand and, inspired by the landscape of the Schwalm, its inhabitants and its costume, created important works of art. In 1820 Reutern got to know Ludwig Emil Grimm (professor at the Kassel Art Academy from 1832) from whom he received drawing lessons during his stays in Willinghausen.

Michael Henning: The Frog King (Sculpture)

Wilhelm Grimm's friendship with the Schwertzell family goes back to Fritz von Schwertzell, who attended the Fridericianum (secondary school) with him in Kassel and later studied at Marburg. The Grimms were joyfully welcomed as guests to Willingshausen castle. Wilhelmine Schwertzell, the sister of Fritz, also collected fairy tales and was in frequent correspondence with Wilhelm Grimm (75 letters are preserved).

A young couple wearing the historical costume of the Schwalm area

Spoiler alert: Little Red Riding Hood is not actually native to the Schwalm region. In fact, she is of French origin and her fairy tale was told to the Brothers Grimm by two sisters, Jeanette and Marie Hassenpflug (see Hanau and Kassel) who had French Huguenot ancestors on their maternal side. A version of Little Red Riding Hood, one in which Little Red Riding Hood is not rescued in the end, was already included in the collection of fairy tales by Charles Perrault (1628–1703). After visiting Willinghausen and through their brother Ludwig Emil Grimm, the Brothers Grimm became acquainted with the Schwalm costume. Because young girls of the Schwalm area wore the same red hood as part of their costume, there is a wonderful similarity to Little Red Riding Hood in the well-known fairy tale of the Brothers Grimm. So it is actually not that surprising that the inhabitants of the Schwalm area firmly believe that they live in the actual setting of the Little Red Riding Hood and the fairy tale of her name. And, of course, in the world of the imagination, they have every reason to believe it is so.

Gerhardt-von-Reutern-Haus: The little room (Malerstübchen) reminds us that Willingshausen was an important painters' colony in the 19th and early 20th centuries

History

The earliest documented mention of Willinghausen is in 1106 as *willichashuson*. It can be assumed that monks and representatives of the archbishop of Mainz built a chapel and settled in Willinghausen in the time of the conversion of the Chatti to Christianity because the wheel of Mainz is still found in a coat of arms above the entrance of the church of Willinghausen. There is documentary evidence of the lords of Schwertzell as early as the 13th century. In the middle of the 16th century they erected a castle of the manor which was added to in 1697 with a Renaissance style.

What to See and Do

1. The little room (Malerstübchen) in the **Gerhardt-von-Reutern-Haus** reminds us of the Willinghausen's golden times in the 19th and early 20th centuries when it was an important artistic colony (Gerhardt von Reutern, Carl Bantzer, Jakob Fürchtegott Dielmann, Hermann Kätelhön, Ludwig Knaus, Wilhelm Thielmann, Hans von Volkmann and others). Attached to

The old Shepherd's House (16th century)

the Gerhardt-von-Reutern-Haus is the new art museum (Kunsthalle). A scholarship existing since 1996 and creative courses maintain links to the artistic tradition. Within view is the **Renaissance castle** of the lords of Schwertzell (16th century), which is privately owned.

2. Scholarship winners each year are housed in the **old shepherd's house** (16th century).

3. The parish **church** of Willingshausen with its impressive classical patrons' boxes was built in 1511 and renovated in 1810.

4. The Grimm researcher and headmaster Wilhelm Schoof (1876–1975) lived in Willingshausen and has his final resting place in the cemetery.

Schwalmstadt

Treysa and Ziegenhain

Schwalmstadt came into existence when an administrative reform in 1971 combined two tradition-laden towns, Treysa and Ziegenhain, with eleven separate smaller communities in the Schwalm River valley. The history of today's Schwalmstadt is essentially that of Treysa and Ziegenhain.

Fairy Tale References:
The Capital of Little Red Riding Hood Territory

In the Schwalm valley, there has been special effort to maintain longstanding traditions in many areas: home construction, costumes, customs, fairy tales, and sagas. Friederike Mannel (1783-1833), the daughter of the Pastor Adam Mannel (1758-1834) from Allendorf on the Landsburg near Ziegenhain, sent some folk songs to the Romantic writer Clemens Brenta-

Treysa: The Church of the Dead

Little Red Riding Hood

Treysa: Elisabeth Wade: bronze sculpture, entitled fairy tale book

no, who included five of them in his influential collection *The Boy's Wonder Horn.*

Upon Brentano's invitation, Wilhelm Grimm came into the home of Pastor Mannel in Allendorf in September 1808 to recruit Friederike as a contributor for his collection. She procured among others the fairy tales *The Gold Children and Foundling Bird* and was able to convince the interim pastor, Ferdinand Siebert (1791-1847), to transcribe fairy tales like *The Poor and the Rich* or *The Clever Little Tailor* for the Brothers Grimm. It was also Siebert who submitted the first written version of *The Story of a Boy Who Went Forth to Learn Fear.* It is very possible that Friederike Mannel was in love with both Wilhelm Grimm and Ferdinand Siebert, neither of whom ever noted or returned her affections.

Treysa: Town Hall and figure of Roland

Well into the 20th century, scholars were still discovering fairy tales and sagas in the Schwalm region. In 1962, Charlotte Oberfeld published her *Folk Tales from Hesse* with its emphasis on the Schwalm. Erika Eckhardt followed this up in 1982 with her *Fountain of Schwalm Sagas.* Many of her sagas go back to the folk tale narrator and Ziegenhain school inspector, Johann Heinrich Schwalm (1864–1946), but she also added a number of sagas from the oral tradition.

View into the Burggasse

History

Documentary evidence shows that the counts of Ziegenhain ruled in the Schwalm area as early as 1107. At that time they were one of the strongest families in the Hessian region until their failure to produce a male heir resulted in rule reverting to the landgraves of Hesse in 1450.

Treysa and Ziegenhain received their municipal charters in the 13th century. The double-moated fortress of Ziegenhain was constructed after 1537 under Landgrave Philipp of Hesse. The heavily armored corner bastions became impregnable bulwarks and even today establish the outline of Ziegenhain. The builder and first fortress commandant, Heinz von Lüder, is known in sagas today for his unshakable loyalty to the Hessian landgraves.

What to See and Do

In Treysa:

1. Visit the ruins of the 13th century **Totenkirche** (Church of the Dead) with its storied buttermilk tower, the official emblem of Treysa. Its ruins serve as the backdrop for many programs during the year. It is called the Totenkirche because it was used exclusively for funeral services after 1610. The fact that it is a ruin reinforces that image.

2. Enjoy the town square that surrounds the Market Fountain (1683) with its figure of **Roland** and take in the town hall (15th and 17th centuries).

Ziegenhain: the Stone House (14th and 17th centuries) holds the museum of the Schwalm area

Ziegenhain: half-timbered house

3. Take a town walk to enjoy the beautiful half-timbered houses and the **Town Wall** with its Witches' Tower from the 15th century, the last surviving tower of the original fortification.

In Ziegenhain

1. View the **fortification** with its double moats that was the castle of the former landgraves. Notice how the modern prison in the fortification gives the whole historic center a different feel.

2. Visit the **Museum of Schwalm** in the Stone House (14th and 17th centuries) that contains traditional clothing, embroidery, and puts on periodic performances related to legends and sagas of the area. As part of their historical folk costume, unmarried young women in the Schwalm wear a red bonnet on their heads reminiscent of the Red Riding Hood of the Brothers Grimm fairy tale. (see Willingshausen).

3. Other worthy sites include the **Parade Grounds** and **Town Church** (1665–67), the

Evangelical **Deaconry** (ca. 1650), the **New Granary** (1577–79) and numerous well-kept half-timbered houses.

Why Roland?

Be forewarned: The Fairy Tale Route is remarkable for more than just the rich tradition of sagas and tales. Central and northern Germany is known for the number of places that feature a likeness of a medieval French hero Roland, usually over or near a fountain in the middle of the town square. Why would that be so?

As a hero, Roland's epic is the French Chanson de Roland from about 1100 and translated into German as Rolandslied in 1170. Roland, reputedly the nephew of Charlemagne, is a tragic figure who dies protecting the rear of Charlemagne's army during the campaign against the Basques (called the Saracens in the Chanson) in Spain in 778. The mythical aspect of the story revolves around Roland's sword, Durendart, which he uses mightily in the battle and the horn, Oliphant, which he refuses to sound to summon Charlemagne even though this refusal would eventually cost him and his small band their lives.

The question remains: Why Roland and what does he symbolize for Germans of the 14th and 15th centuries when most of the stone figures were erected? The quick answer can be read from the inscription around the shield of Bremen's Roland: freedom. Most who write on the Roland tradition, however, see the sculptural presence as a symbol of the adoption of Saxon law. The prominence of the sword, Durendart, promotes the idea of the divine origin of that law. In short, the Roland figure protects these towns the way he protected Charlemagne: fiercely and quietly.

Your task as you travel the Fairy Tale Route is to count the number of places that have either a sculpture or pillar depicting Roland.

Bad Hersfeld

Bad Hersfeld (*Bad* in German means spa) is one of several locations on the *Fairy Tale Route* whose combination of warm springs and good air make it a destination for people seeking a curative rest.

Fairy Tale and Saga References

The *Lullus Festival,* locally called *Lolls*, is a unique cultural-historical feature of Bad Hersfeld; first celebrated in 852, it qualifies as the ol-

The ruins of the Collegiate Church (Stiftskirche)

The Mosquito Stormers

dest folk festival in Germany. Another historical event, also mentioned in sagas, is that of the Hersfelder abbot who attempted on Vitalis Night of 1378 to violate the rights of the town.

A third saga of Bad Hersfeld is that of the *mosquito stormers*; this nickname applies to the citizens of Bad Hersfeld since a mix-up in the year 1674. "On a summer evening, the people of Hersfeld imagined that the town church was in flames when a thick cloud of smoke and fumes wafted around the church tower. As the fire bells rang and the concerned citizens streamed to the church, it became apparent that it was only a huge swarm of mosquitos that had collected around the peak of the church tower. Since then, the embarrassed Hersfelders wear the nickname *Mückenstürmer* (mosquito stormers) with humor." There is a wonderful bronze sculpture of five citizens rushing towards the church tower located in the town center.

Clothiers and tailors definitively characterized the life in Hersfeld until the end of the 19th century. So it is hardly surprising that people in Bad Hersfeld think that the Grimms'

Town Hall and Town Church

Brave Little Tailor has come back to *their* town from his adventure trip. A monument was erected in the Schilde Park to honor him.

History

The documented history of Bad Hersfeld begins in the year 736 when the Boniface follower Sturmius (around 710–79) erected a hermitage. Only three decades later Lullus (ca. 710–86), later abbot of Hersfeld and successor of St Boniface (see Fritzlar) as archbishop of Mainz, began the construction of a Benedictine monastery. This laid the cornerstone for the development of the town and of a religious territory, the imperial abbey of Hersfeld, which was promoted by Charlemagne. When Lullus died in 786, he was buried in the collegiate church he had built. The Lullus Festival has been celebrated annually to honor the founder of the town and of the abbey since the year 852.

A further prominent event in Bad Hersfeld's history is Vitalis Night of 1378. In the night of April 27th to 28th, Berthold II of Völkershausen (1367–87), the abbot of the monastery of Hersfeld, tried, with the assistance of the Stern knights' alliance, to gain control of the town. Due to a letter warning of vendetta, the attack was unsuccessful. The helmet of the robber baron Eberhard von Engern, which was pierced by the shot of a crossbow hung as a trophy on the gable of the Town Hall of Bad Hersfeld for many centuries. Even today a reproduction keeps the memory of Vitalis Night alive.

Monument to Lieutenant Colonel Lingg who cunningly rescued the town after Napoleon had ordered it to be burned down

The Reformation also had reverberations in Hersfeld; Martin Luther preached in the collegiate church in 1521 while returning from the Diet of Worms to Wartburg. Following the Peace after the Thirty Years War in 1648, the abbey of Hersfeld fell as a secular principality to Hesse-Kassel.

In 1807, the town narrowly escaped destruction by French troops. Lieutenant Colonel Lingg (1765–1842) cunningly rescued the town after Napoleon had ordered that it should be burned down by interpreting the command literally. Because the town was to be ignited on all four sides, Lingg had four standalone buildings, one on each side of the town, burned down, thereby saving the town. Bad Hersfeld created a monument in front of the collegiate church and named the place where he had entered with his hunters from Baden after him.

What to See and Do

1. Visit the ruins of the collegiate church **(Stiftskirche)**, the largest Romanesque church ruins in the world. In 1761 it was destroyed by fire during the Seven Years War by retreating French occupation troops who wished to annihilate supplies stored in the church. From July until August, the picturesque ruins of the collegiate church are the performance site of the renowned *Bad Hersfeld Festival* where famous dramas of world literature are played.

Catherine's Tower (ca. 1120)

2. Places of interest in the abbey quarter are the **Catherine's Tower** (Katharinenturm, ca. 1120) with the **Lullus Bell** (the oldest dated bell in Germany), *the Gallery* in the **Collegiate Museum** in the east wing of the former abbey: history of the imperial abbey and of the town, ceiling paintings (11th century), original Vitalis Cross etc.; at Burggasse 11 the former *abbot's castle* (stone construction, dating from the 16th century) as well as stately *half-timbered houses.*

View into the Gothic Town Church

3. The symbol of Bad Hersfeld is the church tower of the storied Gothic **Town Church** (14th through 16th centuries). Murals have been uncovered in the choir of the triple-naved church. Further objects of interests in the town center are the *Hospital Chapel*, a narrow high rectangular building (second half of the 14th century), and the stately **Town Hall** (on the spot where a smaller town hall from the year 1371 previously stood). Renovated in 1612, the construction style was fully integrated; there are five imposing dormer gables from this epoch displaying aspects of the Weser Renaissance style.

4. Notice the multitude of well-preserved beautiful **half-timbered houses** and of some **stone structures** in the Wein-, Klaus-, Obere Frauenstraße, Hanfsack, New Market and Church Place (with the sexton's house, the oldest half-timbered building in the town). There are Gothic *patrician houses* with Renaissance gables on the **Market Place** and well-kept half-timbered houses on the opposite side.

Kurhaus

5. While in a spa-town, it makes sense to visit the **Kurbad Therme** (thermal brine baths) with its landscaped pool area, relaxation world, and sauna landscape as well as the **Kurpark** (spa gardens) that includes four smaller parks dedicated to the four seasons. This park belongs to the *European Garden Heritage Network* and that was singled out in 2008 as the second most beautiful park in Germany.

Monument
left: Konrad Zuse: Inventor of the Computer; right: Konrad Duden: Father of German orthography

6. A special destination for young and old is the **Experiential Museum** *wortreich.* This singular experiential exhibit deals with the themes of language and communication that honors two famous Hersfelders, Konrad Duden (1829–1911), father of German orthography, as well as Konrad Zuse (1910–1995), inventor of the computer. In over 90 interactive stations visitors take an exciting journey and awaken a history full of adventure for life; they can speak, listen, laugh, act, sing, write poetry, solve puzzles, and discover new things.

7. Some three kilometers from the inner-town area is the former summer residence of the Hersfeld abbot, **Eichhof Castle**, that was built in the 14th century as a moated castle and renovated in 1572 in the style of the Weser Renaissance. Its inner court serves in the summertime as an artistic setting for theatrical productions in the program of the Bad Hersfeld Festival.

Knüllwald

Hesse's municipal reforms in 1971 created communities composed of multiple smaller villages and, in the case of Knüllwald, there are exactly sixteen components. Rengshausen in the Beise Valley, Wallenstein in the Efze Valley und Schellbach on Allmuthsberg are the places preferred by tourists in the municipality of Knüllwald, whose administrative center is Remsfeld. There you will find the Tourist Information with a *Little Red Riding Hood* bronze figure nearby.

The legendary ruins of Wallenstein Castle

Saga References

The sagas of Knüllwald deal with a number of interesting characters. There's the *imp* who prevented the church of Remsfeld from being torn down, a *little gray man* who did mischief in the church of Renghausen as well as the *Preacher's Chair of Wallenstein*, which got its name as the result of the devout prayer and sermon delivered on this site by an orphaned young man who had been rescued as a boy while lost in the impenetrable forest.

Little Red Riding Hood

History

Wallenstein Castle was probably built in the 12th century. Around 1220, the castle was owned by the Count Albert I of Schauenburg, who called himself *waldinsteyn* (Wallenstein). His son, Albert II, sold half of the land belong-

Church in Remsfeld (ca. 1500)

ing to the castle Wallenstein to Abbot Werner von Hersfeld and built the castle Neuwallenstein for himself; it later received the name Neuenstein. In 1637, during the Thirty Years War, the castle Wallenstein was destroyed and never rebuilt.

Military cemeteries that were created in the Middle Ages for the purpose of self-defense exist in Berndshausen, Niederbeisheim, Oberbeisheim and Remsfeld.

What to See and Do

1. Visitors can wander on one of two award-winning pathways through the extremely attractive **highland landscape**. The deep creek gorges between Wallenstein and Hülsa are especially impressive as is the pastoral forest (Hutewald) near Rengshausen with its gnarled old stand of trees.

2. The castle ruins of **Wallenstein** serve today as a romantic background for camping. Still preserved from the castle are the late Gothic round tower and large pieces of the internal ring wall.

3. Visitors who enjoy **village churches** will be attracted to those in Berndshausen (1729), Niederbeisheim (1775), Oberbeisheim (1720–25), Reddingshausen (1600) and Remsfeld (ca. 1500) with murals from the 16th century. The small church of Schellbach with its half-timbered raised square choir was erected around 1500. The stonework of the storied church of Rengshausen derives from the 13th century.

Church in Reddingshausen (1600)

4. Once upon a time there were twenty-six mills along the Beise rivulet of which twelve still exist. Some of the mill-wheels exist and are still in usage, as, for example, the 450 year old **Knotten Mill** in Rengshausen.

Homberg (Efze)

Fairy Tale, Saga and Literary References

Homberg's most famous legend is that of the *Woman in White* who risked her life to save the town from an enemy assault and reappears every seven years since then on the Schlossberg. The saga-collector Karl Lyncker (see Kassel) tells of a giant who lived in the Homberg

Homberg by night

Castle while Jacob Grimm writes in his *German Mythology* of a giantess who hurled a stone from the Homberg Castle in the direction of the village of Gombeth.

The author Hans Staden, writer of the first travel accounts about Brazil with their comprehensive account of the lives of the Brazilian Indians during the early colonization era (see Wolfhagen) was born in Homberg around 1525. The well-known Hessian native writer

Pförtchen (Little Gate), an ancient Walkway along the Wall

and storyteller Heinrich Ruppel (1886-1974) lived in Homberg writing *Fairy Tale Hours of the Brothers Grimm* and *The Rogue among the People* among other things. The Brothers Grimm researcher Wilhelm Schoof came from the Angel Pharmacy.

History

Homberg was first mentioned in documents in 1162 as the representative of the *Hohenberg* Castle that was built high above the valley of the Efze to secure the trade route through the long Hesse (Frankfurt-Leipzig). In the 12th century Homberg was a possession of Thuringia and has been in the hands of the Hessian landgraves since the 13th century. Notarized documents of 1231 granted town rights to Homberg. In 1356, the lower-town, *Freedom*, came into existence, making this a twin town, each with its own town wall and defensive towers. On the occasion of the union of the two towns in 1536, a passage called the New Gate was created through the town wall.

Landgrave Philip the Magnanimous convened a synod in the Town Church of Homberg

Dörnberg Temple, a garden house where conspirators met

in 1526 to decide on the introduction of the Protestant Reformation in Hesse. During the Thirty Years War, Homberg was destroyed in 1636 and again in 1640 down to a few houses; the castle was a ruin.

Colonel William Caspar Ferdinand Freiherr von Dörnberg led an ultimately unsuccessful revolt against Jerome Bonaparte (see Baunatal) in 1809 from Homberg. The conspirators met to make preparations in a garden house, today the Dörnberg Temple, which stands on the remains of the former Bächten tower of the town wall.

What to See and Do

1. Homberg depicts the *Little Brother and Little Sister* fairy tale (Brüderchen und Schwesterchen) of the Brothers Grimm in a dramatic fairy

The magnificent Town Church St. Mary and Market Square

tale fountain in the market square and also offers nightly town tours with several legendary figures including the *White Woman* and the *Night Watchman.*

2. The town of Homberg is known far beyond the borders of North Hesse for its **half-timbered gems.** Of particular attraction is the **market place** with its many historic buildings (15th-19th centuries, including White Farm, Lion House, Angel Pharmacy) and the town hall. The **inn** *Zur Krone*, built in 1480, is, next to the *Riesen* in Miltenberg, one of the oldest inns in Germany and at the same time also one of the most important timber-framed buildings in Hesse.

3. Visible from afar, the high Gothic **St. Mary's Basilica** (begun in the early 14th century) towers over the rooftops of the town. The three-naved church is one of the largest Gothic hall churches in the Hesse region (contains seven passion reliefs of sandstone, richly decorated organ pipes of the 18th century, grave stones

Fabled Castle Hill

from the 16th to 18th centuries). Below the church level there are the medieval Schirnen (previous sales vaults).

4. Visitors should not miss a climb up the **fabled Castle Hill** to the castle ruins Hohenburg, from where they can enjoy a more panoramic view of the North Hessian landscape.

5. Of further interest are the **Wedding House** (16th century) that today houses the *Homeland Museum* (Heimatmuseum: exhibition on the history of the town and its crafts), the former *convent endowment Wallenstein* (16th century), large parts of the town wall with little gates and a powder tower, the fairy tale *Little Brother and Little Sister Fountain*, the *town park Old Cemetery* (Alter Friedhof: historical park with grave monuments) and the Hohlebach mill (15th century).

6. The mighty choir tower of the parish church in the **Cassdorf** district was built in the 14th century; the simple nave was built in 1767. The half-timbered houses in the village were built in the 18th century.

7. The small church in **Allmuthshausen** in the Knüll district is of Romanesque origin; in 1781 it was renovated and expanded to the east with half-timber construction. In *Nature Center Wildlife Knüll* with about 350 animals (40 species, including mountain sheep, red deer, fallow deer, wild horses and lynx), the bear and wolf exhibits are a special attraction for visitors.

The Reformation and the German Fairy Tale Landscape

Although the first edition of the *Children's and Household Tales* of the Brothers Grimm appears almost three hundred years after Martin Luther pinned his 95 theses to the door of the Castle Church in Wittenberg in 1517, it is impossible to ignore the impact of the Protestant Reformation on the Romantic Period and, more specifically, on the collection and publication of the world's most beloved book of fairy tales and on the various locales of the German fairy tale landscape. The year 2017 marks the 500th birthday of the Reformation that changed the religious landscape of Europe and the world.

First, it is important to note that the family Grimm itself finds its religious home in the Reformed tradition, not in the Lutheran one, largely due to the accident of geography as the county of Hanau and the landgraviate of Hesse-Kassel were largely Reformed. Known also as Calvinists, the Reformed tradition stereotypically focuses on human sinfulness, total depravity, and the requirement of a sovereign act, God's election, to lead the sinner to salvation. Jack Zipes sees the following impact of their Reformed faith on the Grimm Brothers: *"They eliminated erotic and sexual elements that might be offensive to middle-class morality, added numerous Christian expressions and references, emphasized specific role models for male and female protagonists according to the dominant patriarchal code of that time ..."* (Zipes, The Brothers Grimm ... 2002, p. 46). This tradition will emphasize the serious moral judgments and lessons to be extracted from the tales they assemble from a largely oral tradition.

The French Reformed tradition, represented by the persecuted French Huguenots, was brought to the Fairy Tale Landscape when settlers were welcomed in Hesse and the Weser area by the German Protestants. More importantly, they carried with them the French oral fairy tale tradition. Several sources of the collected tales, most notably the Hassenpflug sisters and Dorothea Viehmann, were directly descended from these Huguenot roots. This explains, for instance, the structural similarities between several tales of *Perrault* and those of the *Grimms.* Their revisions of those tales, however, demonstrate the sanitizing influence the Brothers Grimm bring from their austere Reformed value system.

Beyond the tales themselves, the various locales of the Fairy Tale Route played significant roles in the Protestant Reformation. Marburg, home of the first Protestant university, figured importantly when Martin Luther and the Swiss Reformer, Zwingli, met and chose to disagree over doctrinal issues at the Marburg Castle. A majority decision at the Synod of Homberg in 1526 supported the initiative of the Landgrave Philip of Hesse for the introduction of the Reformation in Hesse.

Luther also preached in the Collegiate Church in Bad Hersfeld while returning to Wartburg Castle from the Diet of Worms. In fact, Martin Luther at Wartburg Castle is the subject of a famous legend (no 562) collected by the Brothers Grimm for their second volume, *German Sagas*:

Doktor Luther zu Wartburg

He sat at the Wartburg and translated the Bible. The devil found that unpleasant and wanted to disturb the sacred work, but when he tried to tempt him, Luther picked up the ink pot from which he was writing and hurled it at the head of the Evil One. Even today, when they show you the room and the chair where Luther sat, you see the stains on the wall from the flying ink.

Finally, almost all areas of the German Fairy Tale Landscape were subject to the massive decimation of the population and destruction of the Thirty Years War, 1618 through 1648, that raged through the region for decades as a direct result of the Protestant Reformation, but that is an even more complicated story.

Fritzlar

Fairy Tale and Saga References

Bettina von Arnim (1785–1859), sister of the German Romantic Clemens Brentano, was a student at the Ursuline convent in Fritzlar. She fictionalized her experience in her novelistic tale *The life of the Imperial Countess Gritta von Ratsinourhouse*. When Jacob and Wilhelm Grimm published their *Children's and Household Tales* in 1812, one of the first copies was

Ursuline Convent

especially dedicated to Bettina and her small son, Johannes Freimund.

There are many legends about St. Boniface, the most famous being the felling of the huge Donar's Oak near Fritzlar. Venerated by the pagan Saxons as a holy tree, this event had

View of Four Towers

Cathedral treasury: Cross of Henry (1010)

symbolic implications and eventually led the Saxons of this area to become Christians.

History

Although the name Fritzlar derives from *frides-lar* – place of peace –, this town finds its origin in a legendary act of defiance. St. Boniface, who had received the German apostleship from Pope Gregor II, arrived in Lower Hesse and promptly cut down the holy Donar's Oak of the pagan Saxons. From its wood he built a small chapel dedicated to St. Peter and founded a Benedictine Abbey in 724. In 774, the pagan Saxons reacted by devastating Fritzlar, whose citizens took refuge in the nearby fortress of Büraberg.

Charlemagne (768–814) took Fritzlar into his royal properties as he did with all of the abbeys founded by St. Boniface and created a royal territory. It was in Fritzlar that Henry I became King of the Holy Roman Empire in 919; to his Saxon successors the town became an important site of the German Empire, a fact demonstrated by the numerous visits of German kings and large church conferences. The brilliance dimmed after the Salian line of German kings died out in 1125.

Under Henry IV (1056–1106), however, Fritzlar passed from royal possession into that of the archbishops of Mainz. The town was a bone of contention between the archbishops of Mainz and the landgraves of Hesse, who didn't succeed in bringing Fritzlar into their possession until 1803.

What to See and Do

1. Explore the **medieval townscape**, distinguished by its almost completely intact town wall (12th through 14th centuries) with fourteen towers and around 450 half-timbered houses and some significant stone houses. Enjoy the **town square** with its picturesque half-timbered houses (Markt 4, 20, 22 etc.) and the Renaissance fountain with the **Roland Statue** (1564). Another impressive site is the modern bronze **sculpture of St. Boniface** with his axe atop the stump of the legendary Donar's Oak.

Fritzlar's Town Square with Roland Fountain

2. The **Graue Turm** (Gray Tower) is considered the highest remaining urban watchtower in Germany. It has three levels that offer exhibits detailing the history of Fritzlar as well as a marvellous view of the old town itself.

3. Visit the 11th–14th centuries **Peter's Cathedral**, a triple-naved Romanesque-Gothic basilica with its golden altar, cloister walk and original stained-glass windows. It has a valuable cathedral treasury and museum that includes the Heinrichkreuz (Cross of Henry, 1020) as well as goldsmith objects (12th–14th centuries) among its many relics. Also worth visiting is the cathedral library with its collection of manuscripts from the 9th through the 19th centuries.

Peter's Cathedral

Garvensburg castle

Züschen: Stone Chamber Grave (3rd century), one of the most important prehistoric archeological monuments in Central Europe

4. Visit Fritzlar's **Town Hall** (Rathaus), documented as early as 1109, the oldest town office in Germany. The Regional Museum (pre- and early history, fossils, minerals, collections of folklore and town history) is housed in the historical **Hochzeitshaus** (1580–90) and in the adjacent **Patrizierhaus** (patrician house, 1520).

5. The romantic **Garvensburg** castle (1894–98) in the Züschen district of Fritzlar is known nowadays as a hotel and wedding place. Also located in Züschen is a stone chamber grave from the 3rd century that is considered one of the most important prehistoric archeological monuments in Central Europe.

6. The Ungedanken district of Fritzlar lies southwest of Fritzlar on an steep hilltop of **Büraberg**. In the Merovigian-Carolingian period there was a weir installation (mentioned in 714 as *buriaburg*). For its protection, Boniface founded the short-lived diocese of Büraburg of which the bishop's church St. Brigida (now pilgrimage and chapel of the dead) remains.

Saint Boniface and Donar's Oak at Fritzlar

(Franz Flaskamp/Johann J. Winkelmann – English version: E. Michael Iba/Thomas L. Johnson)

Boniface entered the land of the Chatti, near the border of Saxony, converting and baptising many thousands. As he reported this in a letter to the pope, the Holy Father invited him to visit Rome, made him a bishop and placed him also under the protection of the Duke Charles Martel. With the permission of Charles, who ruled at that time over the Franks, he returned to the land of the Chatti, the predecessor of the land of Hesse.

For a long time, only a minority of Chatti converted; many of them secretly made offerings to trees and springs, others did it very publicly. Still others practiced prophecy and fortune-telling and looked for signs and bird flights or made offerings to the gods.

At Geismar, there was a holy spring near which a large oak tree called Donar's Oak stood that had been honored from ancient times by the pagans. Boniface arrived on a stormy autumn day in the year 723 under the protection of armed guards from neighboring Büraberg with the intention of cutting down the oak. A large crowd of people had assembled: the heathen Chatti around the tree in order to honor its holiness; the Christians in the hope that God might reveal himself. The unbaptised counted on the power of their god, Donar, to come down in lightning to smite Boniface, the evildoer; thereof they were completely convinced. A moment of highest tension came when Boniface walked up to the powerful tree,

whose crown was being constantly shaken by a stormy wind. Mighty axe blows delivered from one side and then from the other side caused the mighty giant oak to fall down with a huge crash and break apart into four mighty parts.

As the heathens saw this, their sentiments changed completely because they had witnessed together how powerless Donar had been. They immediately opened their ears and hearts, praised God, and let themselves be baptised. The Christians, on the other hand, viewed the act as a confirmation of their beliefs.

Boniface had a chapel dedicated to Saint Peter built out of the wood of the Donar's Oak. The legend of the fall of Donar's Oak spread quickly and it came to pass that soon the whole land of Hesse was converted.

Bad Wildungen

The Hessian spa *Bad Wildungen*, crossed by the river Wilde, lies in the foothills of the Kellerwald-Edersee Natural Park. Along with other beech forests in Germany, the beech forest in the Kellerwald was declared a UNESCO World Heritage Site in 2011.

Fairy Tale and Saga References

Of the handful of places in Germany that claim to be the true home of *Snow White (Oberweser* – see there, *Alfeld* near *Hildesheim, Lohr am Main)* the *Bergfreiheit* district of Bad Wildungen makes its claim with some forceful arguments.

In Bergfreiheit one can visit the old Bertsch copper mine where the Brothers Grimm fairy

Bad Wildungen: Panoramic View

Margarethe von Waldeck, upon whom Snow White is allegedly modeled

tale *Snow White and the Seven Dwarfs* is held to have originated. Margarethe von Waldeck (1533–54), the beautiful sister of the founder of the mine, Count Samuel, was sent to live at the Spanish court in Brussels with the widowed Queen Mary of Hungary and Bohemia where she supposedly fell in love with the future king of Spain, Philipp II. She travelled to Brussels by way of the *Seven Mountains* near Bonn. As a result of an intrigue in court, she is alleged to have been poisoned at the age of 20 years. The teacher Eckhard Sander has promoted the connection between the fictional *Snow White* and the historic Margarete von Waldeck in several monographs, most famously *Snow White: Fairy Tale or Truth* (1994). This idea seems to underlie the plot of the 2012 movie *Snow White and the Huntsman.*

Louis Curtze (see Waldeck) recorded four tales and a series of sagas from Wildungen (among them *Aquarius* and *From Sweet Mush*) in his collection published in 1860 as *Folk traditions from the Principality of Waldeck.*

History

A village called *villa wildungun* at the foot of Castle Hill in the Wilde Valley is mentioned around 800, but does not seem to have really developed. Around 1200, the castle settlement Altwildungen was founded by Count Frederick of Ziegenhain; it belonged until 1247 to the landgrave of Thuringia and since 1263 to the count of Waldeck. On a hill across from Altwildungen sprouted a place called Niederwildungen, which was granted town rights in 1242. Since 1263 the castle, Altwildungen and Niederwildungen were owned by the counts who later became the princes of Waldeck.

The springs of Niederwildungen have been known since the 14th century and already had their first guests in the 15th century but were not developed as a spa until the end of the 19th century. The town of Niederwildungen was renamed Bad Wildungen in 1906, and only

Market Square and Town Hall

in 1940 merged with Altwildungen, Reinhardshausen and Reitzenhagen.

Fürstenhof (Art Nouveau Building, 1911)

What to See and Do

1. Fairy tale enthusiasts will be interested in the **Snow White's village**, *Bergfreiheit*, in the Kellerwald. Bergfreiheit was founded in 1561 for the planned mining of ore; upon registration you can visit the exhibition mine and the small museum in the historic mining office. If you want to know more about the relationship of Snow White and Bergfreiheit, the *Snow White House* (Schneewittchenhaus) is the right place. In a period house of surprisingly small dimensions, the house recreates the milieu of the small copper mining septet known as the *seven dwarfs*.

Snow White House in the district of Bergfreiheit (Snow White's Village)

2. Towering above Bad Wildungen, instead of the medieval castle, is the newly built castle of

Friedrichstein (largely from 1708–14, round tower from 1550): it accommodates a hunting and arms museum and a rock collection.

3. The high steeple of the late Gothic **town church** (around 1300 until the end of 15th century) dominates the skyline of Bad Wildungen and is one of Hesse's most beautiful hall churches. Inside the church one sees a crucifix of 1518 above the ornate altar, a twelve-sided baptismal font from the 14th century and three remarkable grave monuments of the counts and princes of Waldeck (17th–18th centuries), but especially the art-historically significant late Gothic **Wildungen Altar** of Conrad von Soest, an artwork of Westphalian panel painting of **European status** (completed in 1403).

Town Church

Conrad von Soest: Wildungen Altar: Fine Example of European Gothic Painting

Friedrichstein Castle

4. Numerous stately **half-timbered houses** from the 16th–18th centuries lend the picturesque town its character, for example in the Brunnenstraße 11–13 (about 1619) and 42 (1601), Lindenstraße 2 (1511) and 9 (1682, the seat of the *Regional Museum*) and Münzstraße 7 (Hainaer yard of 1564).

5. Take a tour through the **historic spa district.** A magnificent spa building (1928–30, neoclassical foyer "Wandelhalle", renovated 2005–09) and Art Nouveau villas (clinic Fürstenhof, a castle-like Art Nouveau building 1911) were built around the more than twenty mineral springs. In the foyer is the Spa (Quellen) Museum that gives an excellent insight into the history of the spa.

6. The **Bad Wildungen** and the **Kurpark Reinhardshausen** were joined together at the end of the 20th century, creating at 50 hectars (ca. 124 acres) the largest Kurpark in Europe. It

Bad Wildungen Kurpark

belongs to the *European Garden Heritage Network*. As a modern spa center, Bad Wildungen and the district of Reinhardshausen with more than 20 large clinics, belong to the top group of the German spas. Ask at the spa and tourist information for the diverse treatment options.

Frankenberg (Eder)

Saga References

With Karl Lyncker, there are a number of sagas about Frankenberg such as *The Battle of the Spirits on the Hill of the Dead, The Swedish General, The Little Elves of Frankenberg* and *The Woman among the Elves:* "Without knowing it, a nanny is called one dark night to an elfin, whom she helps give birth. In gratitude, she gets all the dirt lying behind the door. She gathers it into her apron and, upon arriving home, dumps it onto the table and wonder of

The Town Hall, an architectural jewel

wonders! Suddenly there is a pile of shimmering gold."

History

Frankenberg owes its existence to its location at the intersection of two ancient trade and military routes as well as to the construction of

The former monastery St. Georgenberg (13th/14th and 16th centuries) now houses the County Museum

a fortified Frankish site (hence the name Frankenberg) on the castle hill during the time of the battles between the Franks and the Saxons. At the beginning of the 8th century, Charles Martel (around 688–741), the grandfather of Charlemagne, built fortifications and secured them with a permanent garrison. In 1122, the castle hill became the property of the landgraves of Thuringia, who in 1234 planned and erected a castle and a townsite to its east on land of the county of Battenberg (Mountbatten) belonging to Mainz. First mentioned in 1244 as a town, Frankenberg developed – the chronicler Wigand Gerstenberg (1457–1522) reports – despite the resistance of the archbishopric of Mainz into a thriving trade center with drapers, woolen weavers and tanners' guilds.

Founded in 1335 by Henry II Landgrave of Hesse, the New Town of Frankenberg stretches in an elliptical shape from the northern slope of castle hill to the Eder River. They were twin towns (each with its own town hall and wall) until they were finally consolidated in 1556. Wigand Gerstenberg gives an impressive description of the large fire that destroyed almost the entire old town in 1476. Later, in 1507, half of the New Town also burned down. Frankenberg, which had been one of the most important towns of Hesse, never fully recovered from these two fires and the subsequent Thirty Years War.

Master Tyle von Frankenberg: Stone Sculptures (14th century) in the Gothic Church of Our Lady

What to See and Do

1. The place in Frankenberg to begin with, rising impressively above the town on Castle Hill, is the Gothic **Church of Our Lady** (1286–1360). It was modeled largely on the Elizabeth Church in Marburg and reconfigured around the middle of the 14th century by Tyle von Frankenberg. Inside the three-aisled cruciform church hall are the original 14th century Gothic stained glass windows, pillars festooned with vines and foliage on the capitals, masks and animal heads, and a sacramental booth. The octagonal **St. Mary's Chapel** (around 1370–80) is attached to the Church of Our Lady and accessible only from the outside. Noteworthy is its 6.5 meter high stone altar wall, the main work of the architect and stone sculptor, Tyle von Frankenberg.

Philipp Soldan: carved piggyback figures (16th century) at the Town Hall

2. Take a town walk starting at the ten-towered **Town Hall**, an architectural jewel, located between the upper and lower markets (Ober- and Untermarkt). This picturesque building, similar to the famous half-timbered Hessian town halls of Alsfeld, Melsungen and Michelstadt, was restored as two stories in 1509–13, incorporating the old town hall of 1421 and the previous building that burned in the fires of 1476. Admire the silhouette of its roof, the large full-length hall (Schirn) and portals with magnificently carved supporting beams (cleats: Christopher and piggyback figures) created by the famous Frankenberg wood carver and sculptor Philipp Soldan (c. 1500–70).

3. Don't forget to have a look at the half-timbered houses which surround the Town Hall before you walk to the **Stone House** (1240) the oldest house in Frankenberg at the corner of Obermarkt/Pferdemarkt with its distinctive stepped gables. Carry on with your tour of the old and the new towns and view the attractive half-timbered houses (16th–19th centuries) at Pferdemarkt, Obermarkt (note **Hotel Die SONNE Frankenberg** – a fairy-tale like, luxurious first class hotel of eight historical buildings: old brewery, old wine house etc.), Steingasse, Ritterstraße and Neustädter Straße.

4. Down the hill (Bahnhofstraße) lies the former monastery of St. Georgenberg, built from 1249

as a Cistercian convent. The oldest parts of the impressive horseshoe-shaped building (chapel of St. Maurice with arched portal) are still Romanesque, while the north wing was altered in the 14th and 16th centuries. The **County History Museum** contains among others valuable historically important collection pieces, such as the beam ends, the sculptures and the beautiful stone pulpit (1554) of the Frankenberg sculptor and carver Philipp Soldan (1500–70), works by Tyle of Frankenberg (14th century) as well as the oldest blueprint in Hesse.

Hotel Die SONNE Frankenberg: historic half-timbered house with spa and bridal suite

5. Another worthwhile museum is the **Museum Thonet** (Michael-Thonet-Straße). It informs about the pioneer of furniture design, Michael Thonet (1796–1871), and his unique

Museum Thonet

method of bentwood processing, Art Nouveau furniture, the production of tubular steel furniture (Bauhaus), etc.

6. Open every day in Frankenberg is the **Wild Game Park** (Wildpark), where, other than the wild goats and wild boars, all of the animals move freely without cages. Passing through Frankenberg is the 63 km long Ederhöhenpfad from Hatzfeld to Vöhl, considered one of the ten most beautiful hiking trails in Germany as it runs past woodland, juniper heaths and through beech forests.

Waldeck

Fairy Tale and Saga References

The fact that Waldeck is also a town with a significant fairy tale tradition was long forgotten. The teacher and historian Louis F. C. Curtze (1807–70), born in Korbach, published his volume *Folk Tradition from the Principality of Waldeck* in Arolsen in 1860. In this comprehensive 518 page work, one finds 274 pages devoted, to thirty-seven fairy tales and one hundred and forty sagas from Korbach, Twiste, Bad Wildungen, Waldeck and other places. Thirteen of Curtze's fairy tales (about 100 pages) have their origin in the current Waldeck subdivisions of Alraft and Dehringhausen.

Fairy Tale Village Dehringhausen: The Chapel

Waldeck Castle (13th–16th centuries)

Other important collectors of fairy tales from the Waldeck area are the teacher and folk-

lorist Rudolf Nord (1904–44, *Folk Tales from Waldeck, Low German Folk Tales*), the teacher and professor Gustav Grüner (1924–88, *Waldeck Folk Tales*) and the Marburg folklorist Charlotte Oberfeld (1915–98, *Tales of the Waldecker Land*).

History

Sachsenhausen is the administrative seat of Waldeck and received its town charter from Count Adolph of Waldeck as early as 1246. The township of Freienhagen (now belonging to Waldeck) is about the same age; it is first referred to as a town in 1253.

The name of the town of Waldeck and of a whole region comes from the picturesque Waldeck Castle mentioned in documents as early as 1120. In 1180, it passed by marriage to

Waldeck Castle

the Count of Schwalenberg, who was known as the Count of Waldeck after 1189. A settlement that was first called *rhode* but later became known as Waldeck was built adjacent to

View from Waldeck Castle onto the Eder Lake

the castle in the early 13th century. The Cistercian monastery Marienthal had already been established by the Schwalenberger counts in the current district of Netze in 1128.

Over the centuries, the counts of Waldeck slowly increased the size of their territory. In 1625, they acquired the county of Pyrmont; Count Friedrich Anton Ulrich of Waldeck (1676–1728) was elevated by the emperor to imperial princely status in 1711. Burg Waldeck was originally a residential and administrative headquarters; Arolsen assumed this role in 1655.

In 1807, the Principality of Waldeck-Pyrmont joined the *Confederation of the Rhine* and in 1815 the *German Confederation*. It became part of the *German Empire* and the *Weimar Republic*. After the First World War, Waldeck-Pyrmont became a free state in November 1918. In 1922, Pyrmont became part of *Prussia* (Hanover Province), and in 1929, after a referendum, the core part of Waldeck joined the

Netze: The former Monastery Church with its magnificient altar and Chapel of St. Nicholas: Burial Place of the Waldeck Counts

Prussian Province of *Hesse-Nassau*. Since the end of the Second World War, Waldeck belongs to *Hesse*.

What to See and Do

Waldeck and its ancient castle is one of the highlights of the German Fairy Tale Route.

1. **Waldeck's landmark** is the picturesque **castle high above the Eder Lake** (with outer bailey, keep, bastions, large courtyard, north wing, stair tower, 120 m deep well). A magnificient panorama is offered from the terrace and also from the 13th century castle keep. The majority of the other parts of the building were erected in the 15th and 16th centuries.

2. The small town center of Waldeck is dominated by the elevated **Town Church** (built in 1300 and the 16th century); it holds a valuable three-piece, late Gothic Marienaltar, the oldest carved altar in the Waldecker land. The well-preserved **half-timbered houses** in the core town of Waldeck originated in the 17th through 19th centuries.

3. The neighboring village of **Netze** has the former **monastery church** (Romanesque west tower of the 12th century and double-spanned nave of the 13th–14th centuries) and holds not only one of the oldest bronze bells in Germany (12th century) but also the historically significant **Netze Altar** (around 1370), a monumental Gothic winged-altar that depicts the life of Christ in thirteen images. The chapel of St. Nicholas on the southern wall of the church is the

burial place for the members of families of the Waldeck counts (1267–1690).

4. Deserving attention in **Sachsenhausen** is the Church of St. Nicholas of 1296 with early Gothic murals (13th century), the fine Town Hall (built 1817), a large number of half-timbered houses (18th–19th centuries) and, just outside of town, the ruins of the Romanesque Klinger Church and the Warte, a late Gothic round tower.

Waldeck-Sachsenhausen: Town Hall (1817)

5. At **Ober-Werbe** are the ruins of the one-time Benedictine monastery of St. Mary built in the 16th century and the hunting lodge Friedrichsthal of 1701 (private property).

6. Places of interest in **Freienhagen** are the former fortified church (13th century), the well-maintained, half-timbered houses that are under monument protection and two water mills north of the town. The **Watter Mill** received the Hessian monument preservation prize in 2008.

The Dwarfs of Waldeck Castle and the Stone of Allegiance

(Oswald Koenig – English version: E. Michael Iba/ Thomas L. Johnson)

On the path up to Waldeck Castle, the old family seat of the counts of Waldeck, one sees a mighty stone called Treustein (Stone of Allegiance), directly on the way to the castle. Probably a thousand years may have passed since their builders completed a contract with the Hollen, those dwarfs who live deep in the interior of the castle rock and the Eder Mountains.

The count of Waldeck promised Eck, the mighty ruler of the Eder dwarfs, that the mountain depths beneath his castle would be safe for dwarfs for all times. In return, the ruler of the dwarfs pledged to permit the foundation walls of the castle to be built and joined so rock-solid that it could never sink and fall. At the same time, Eck vowed to protect all the forces of good and to avenge all wrongs in his kingdom.

The entrance to the underground dwarf kingdom lies behind the big rock, the Treustein, about which the saga says that the final lord of the castle of Waldeck would be buried under its weight and mass. The dwarfs often assemble at midnight on the Treustein.

Whenever a count of Waldeck passes away, Eck strikes with his sparkling hammer made of Eder gold against the rocks. Then all the hills and slopes of the Eder come alive in the dark night. The dwarfs light countless little lights that sparkle as the torches swarm and buzz through the summer night like fireflies. Then the shining little lights brighten the dark far into the Eder Valley. The memorial service in honor of the deceased begins, a wondrous hour in the dark silence of the night. Only waves of faint sounds well up from the valley. Eck talks for a long time to the crowd listening in silence. When he finishes, the dwarfs swear allegiance to their new lord on the Treustein, and, turning towards Arolsen castle, they call in unison:

Strive always in the noble quest
As the ancestors of old
Thus, O lord, the very best
Of joy and love unfold.

And once again Eck's golden hammer rings down three times on the rocks. The little lights of the dwarfs scurry away. They hurriedly search the depths of the mountain for their homes.

The dwarfs treasure and cherish even a flower, the one with a black stem, red flowers, and golden leaves. The flower grows in the deep solitude of the forest and becomes invisible as soon as a human hand stretches out to it. Few have seen it, but anyone who has breathed its fragrance in passing will be driven by a longing for home his whole life.

Wolfhagen

Fairy Tale and Saga References

In the third volume of their German Sagas, published posthumously by Barbara Kindermann-Bieri in 1993, the Brothers Grimm include two smaller sagas, namely *The Wolf in the Woods*, which clarifies the name of Wolfhagen, as well as *The Glockenborn*. The linking of wolf and woods makes it no surprise that the town of Wolfhagen is represented on the German Fairy Tale Route by the Grimms' fairy tale, *The Wolf and the Seven Little Goats*. Further

The Wolf and the Seven Little Goats (Fairy Tale Fountain), the Old Watch and St. Anne's Church

The Regional Museum, note the permanent exhibition about the early renowned Brazil researcher Hans Staden

known sagas from Wolfhagen and its region such as *The Town Forest of Wolfhagen, Agnes of Bürgel* or the *White Maiden of Weidelsberg* are to be found in Karl Lynker's Hessian saga collection.

The Brothers Grimm collected a vast number of folk and children's songs in addition to sagas and fairy tales. Jacob Grimm transcribed more than a half dozen folk songs from the Wolfhagen district of Ippinghausen (often with erotically off-colored content) as well as two riddles. The youngest Brother Grimm, the artist and painter Ludwig Emil Grimm, was quartered as a lieutenant in Teichstraße 6 in Wolfhagen. In addition to other motifs from Wolfhagen, L. E. Grimm also drew the legendary Weidelsburg (Weidels Castle) not far from Ippinghausen.

One can view a permanent exhibit on the renowned researcher of Brazil, Hans Staden (ca. 1526 in Homberg – died 1576 in Wolfhagen or Korbach), in the Regional Museum of Wolfhagen. Staden reports about both of his voyages (1547 und 1554) and his captivity by the cannibalistic Tupinamba Indians in his *True History and Description of a Landscape of Wild, Naked, Ferocious Man-eating People ... (Warhaftig His-*

toria und beschreibung eyner Landtschafft der Wilden/Nacketen/Grimmigen Menschenfressen Leuthen ...). This is a comprehensive presentation of the Brazilian indigenous life during the early colonization of Brazil that has appeared so far in 85 editions.

History

The Landgrave Ludwig IV of Thuringia built the castle and town of Wolfhagen (town charter 1264) on the Hagen Mountain (Hagenberg) and surrounded them with strong walls and defensive towers to defend against the castles Weidelsburg and Naumburg around 1226. The completely fortified Wolfhagen resisted attacks in the years 1318, 1336 and 1349 but was almost completely destroyed in the Thirty Years War (1618–48) and suffered great damage in the Seven Years War (1756–63).

The deserted landgraves' dairy farm Leckringhausen near Wolfhagen was settled after 1701 by fourteen Huguenot families who earned their living working mostly as hosiery knitters. The Huguenot church was built in 1768–74. The Landgrave Friedrich II of Hesse-Kassel founded the three settlements in 1778 for French Protestants from the region of Darmstadt naming them after his wife Philippine of Brandenburg, Philippinenburg, Philippinendorf and Philippinenthal.

Leckringhausen: Huguenot Church

What to See and Do

1. Wolfhagen is the westernmost point of the **Fairy Tale Route Trail,** a fabulous, long hiking

The Old Watch (1667) and the Old Town Hall (1657–59)

path about 400 km long that passes through more than 30 locations in and around Kassel and through the fairy tale landscape of the Brothers Grimm. Local legends, stories and fairy tales as well as legends of Jacob and Wilhelm Grimm are brought closer to visitors in a variety of ways: by living panels, sculptures, plays, storytelling fairy tales, fairy food, etc.

2. Surrounded by picturesque **half-timbered houses** of the 17th and 18th centuries, the early Gothic **St. Anne's Church** (13th century) with its tall looming west tower is central to the town silhouette. The inside of the three-naved hall church makes an impression as a result of its felicitious frescos (restored 1958) in their original shades of bright gray and red as well as by its beautiful Baroque organ (1725).

Somewhat outside of the church one finds the **Old Watch** (Alte Wache), a two-storied half-timbered house from 1667, the Fairy Tale Foun-

The Grimms' Fairy Tale Cellar

tain *The Wolf and the Seven Little Goats* as well as the old town hall, an elongated structure (1657–59) with a massive ground floor and two half-timbered upper levels; in *Grimm's Fairy Tale Cellar,* the historical domed cellar of the town hall, (1611, with reproduced Wolfhagen themes of L.E. Grimm), weddings and fairy tale reading take place.

Cemetery Chapel

3. The so-called Landgrave Building built in 1513 as a tithe barn is preserved from the castle that was destroyed in the Thirty Years War. **The Regional Museum** with its collections, for example the geology and history of the region of Wolfhagen as well as the life and work of the Brazil researcher Hans Staden, is lodged in the renovated stables of the 17th century. If you go in the opposite direction through the Schützenberger Street, you arrive at the *Friedhofskapelle* (cemetery chapel), a beautiful Gothic structure dedicated in 1337.

Limited remains of the town wall of Wolfhagen as well as of the tower of the Chatti (Chattenturm) are still preserved.

4. The moated castle **Elmarshausen** (privately owned) lies north of the old town of Wolfha-

The legendary Weidelsburg

gen; it was erected in 1442 by the lords of Gudensberg and rebuilt in 1534 in the form of the Weser Renaissance.

5. The district **Viesebeck** pleases with its countless well-maintained half-timbered houses from the 18th century – in part with barn and stall – as well as through its church.

6. From the town district of **Ippinghausen** (church 1772–73, stone bridge 1782) one reaches the largest castle ruin in North Hesse, the legendary **Weidelsburg**. Set on the 492 meter Weidels Mountain, the castle ruin is surrounded by a weir system; both of its residential towers and the two portal towers of the ring wall raise themselves majestically, widely visible over the land of Wolfhagen. It counts as one of the most impressive castle ruins of north Hesse and is a beloved hiking destination.

Schauenburg

The Community of Schauenburg, created in 1972 through the merger of five localities, receives its name from the castle ruins of Schauenburg lying on the pass heights between the Habichtswald and the Langenberge.

Fairy Tale and Saga References

Schauenburg is a community with a fairy tale and saga tradition and a successful example of how one can nurture this tradition in appropriate fashion in today's world. The obviously impoverished retired Dragoon sergeant Johann Friedrich Krause (1747–1828) begged for hand-me-down clothing from the Brothers Grimm in exchange for some fairy tales

Panoramic View towards Castle Hill (Burgberg)

that he had collected and written down. His fairy tales *Old Sultan* and *The Three Snake Leaves* among others found entrance into the Children's and Household Tales. The Märchenwache (Fairy Tale Watch) in Breitenbach commemorates Krause and the Grimm folk tale teller Marie Hassenpflug (see Kassel) who was married in 1814 to Captain Friedrich von Dalwigk, who lived in Hoof at the time. A descendant of Krause, the draftsman and graphic artist Albert Schindehütte (*1939), was in charge of turning the former fire hall into a site for cultural programs. He designed it skillfully incorporating woodcuts and drawings

Breitenbach: Fairy Tale Watch

Breitenbach: Fairy Tale Watch: interior - calligraphies by graphic artist Albert Schindehütte

from the Grimms fairy tales into a Fairytale Watch.

History

Schauenburg arose as a (residential) dwelling place and asylum sanctuary probably between 600 and 800. The castle *scouwenburg* was first mentioned in documents in 1089. The counts of Schauenburg ruled the territory around the Habichtswald and the Bauna Valley in the Middle Ages. They were the lords of the court of law in Ditmold (Kassel) and owned a piece of the castle acreage of the estate of the present community of Hoof. The counts of Schauenburg, who suffered mightily in the battles between the landgraves of Thuringia-Hesse and the archbishopric of Mainz, acquired Wallenstein Castle (see Knüllwald) from the Hersfeld Abbey and soon named themselves after it.

Breitenbach: Fairy Tale Watch

Schauenburg was sold to the archbishopric of Mainz. The family von Dalwigk received Schauenburg in 1332 as a fiefdom.

The barons of Dalwigk, whose major line resides in Dalwigksthal in Waldeck, belongs to the Hessian ancient nobility. The Schauenburg line left the castle as early as the 14th century and occupied an estate at the foot of the castle mountain from then on. The village of Hoof developed around it. The most renowned Dalwigk was Reinhard V (ca. 1400–61), the Unborn, who came into the world through a Caesarian section and who made his name as a feud-loving knight. The barons of Dalwigk were lords of the Schauenburg court of law

The castle ruin Schauenburg

with the villages of Breitenbach, Elmshagen, Großenhof and Hoof until into the 19th century.

What to See and Do

1. The church of Schauenburg-Breitenbach with its late Gothic choir tower derives from the Middle Ages.

The **Märchenwache** in Breitenbach is open Sunday afternoons. Memorials to the young Marie Hassenpflug (married von Dalwigk) and the retired Dragoon sergeant Johann Friedrich Krause are displayed there. The graphic artist Albert Schindehütte, who grew up in Breitenbach, honors as do the Grimm researchers Heinz Rölleke und Heinz Vonjahr, those Grimms fairy tales and the folk tale contributors from Schauenburg and has created calligraphy and drawings for many first edition books (among others *Krause's Fairy Tales, Once Upon a Time: The True Fairy Tales of the Brothers Grimm* and *Who told them …*).

2. The castle ruin Schauenburg is located on the castle mountain close to Hoof, the administrative center of the community of Schauenburg. In **Hoof**, a row of well-maintained half-timbered houses from the 17th and 18th centuries has been preserved as well as the one-time courtyard of the Dalwigk family.

The church is a recent construction from the 19th century with marginal remains of the earlier structure. The former synagogue, a half-timbered structure, stands nearby.

3. In **Elmshagen**, there is a preserved half-timbered chapel. Worth seeing in **Elgershausen** are the erstwhile village justice place (already mentioned in 1123) with its ancient stone table

Elmshagen: Chapel

Martinhagen: Church and Martin Stone (a massive basalt crag)

under a linden grove; not far from here is the late Gothic church with its early Gothic west tower. The charming half-timbered parsonage was erected in 1767.

4. A special attraction in **Martinhagen** with its parish church from 1767 (Gothic steeple) is the Martinstein (Martin stone), a massive basalt crag.

Kirchberg: Mountain Gate of the old Estate with Manor House (18th century), an amazing place famous for the birth of septuplets, called the Dogs

Niedenstein

Fairy Tale and Saga References

Of the sagas and legends that are native to Niedenstein, one saga that is particularly influential tells about a noblewoman who brings septuplets into the world and wants to kill six of them in a basket like young dogs. The nobleman, her husband, comes upon the secret by chance and brings up six young *dogs*, his sons. The proud noblewoman speaks her own mind when she is asked about it by her husband, saying: *"The person who did this deserves to be put into a barrel with nails and rolled down a mountain."* Thus the noblewoman pronounced her own death.

Niedenstein has enthusiastically accepted its godparentage of *King Drosselbart* as symbol of its association with the *German Fairy Tale Route.*

Kirchberg: A fine example of a half-timbered house

Niedenstein: Linden, called Tanz-Linde, which is said to be 1000 years old and where people danced high in the tree

History

Nydensteyne was founded in the first half of the 13th century by the landgrave of Thuringia and came over to the landgrave of Hesse in 1247. Niedenstein was designated as a town in 1529 whose customs and rights were regularly confirmed by the ruler in his inauguration. In the years 1553 and 1579 by-law allowed that only the landgrave of Hesse would have the right to introduce statutes, regulations and ordinances to the town of Niedenstein. Two fires during the Thirty Years War, 1636 and again in 1647, devastated large parts of the town.

Panoramic View of Niedenstein

What to See and Do

1. On a hill in the middle of the town lies the **church** of Niedenstein, built in 1777 as a hall structure. A very special natural monument is the thousand-year-old **dance lime tree** under which, as the name suggests, dances were held on the dance floor high in the branches and where it is also likely that courts were convened.

2. A special attraction in Niedenstein is the 475 m high Niedensteiner Kopf (Head), where the Niedenstein Castle once towered. The **Hessenturm** (Hesse Tower) stands on the same site today with a platform that offers a magnificent panoramic view over the wooded heights of the landscape of the Chatti. The Chatti lived from around 10 BC until 200 AD and fought against the Romans during their campaign to conquer Germania.

Niedenstein by night

3. Distinctive hiking destinations in the area include the **Altenburg**, the largest prehistoric circular wall installation in north Hesse in the manner of a fortified mountain town (destroyed 15 AD), the *Lautarius Grave*, a prehistoric stone chamber grave, and the nature reserve *Wartberg*.

Gudensberg

Saga References

The area around Gudensberg is ancient saga country. Jacob Grimm's *German Mythology* includes three legends of the Odenberg, namely the legend of the *Thirsty Army* and the legend of *Charlemagne*, who fought a big battle at the foot of Odenberg and rests in Odenberg after his exploits, as well as the legend of a *Blacksmith*, who enters the wonderful world of Odenberg. The saga of a *Sharp Stone* that a giant had thrown in his anger also goes back to Jacob Grimm.

Fountain: The Blue Flower and the Shepherd at Töpfermarkt (Potters Market)

In Karl Lyncker's German *Sagas and Manners in Hessian Districts*, you discover the saga of a *Shepherd in Odenberg* who found a beautiful flower, and of a *Young Miller*, who had to

spend seven years in Odenberg, and of a *Child in Odenberg*.

History

The region around Gudensberg is an area of prehistorical settlement. The predecessors of the Hessians, the tribe of the Chatti, already had their meeting place on the Wotan's Mountain (Wodansberg) in the gray prehistory. Wotan, the Teutonic storm and war god and father of the gods and people, was worshipped here. *Wodansberg,* from which the town of Gudensberg derives its name, was the religious and political center-point of the Chatti.

Remains of the walls of the Obernburg

The Drummer in the streets of Gudensberg

The first documented mention of Gudensberg, a possession of the Gisons that later fell to the Thuringian and Hessian landgraves, comes from the year 1121. In the early Middle Ages, the site was the official seat of the district counts who managed the land of Lower Hesse and dispensed justice as administrators of the German kings.

The Fairy Tale Stage: Meeting of Fairy Tale Characters

When the political center of Gudensberg was relocated to Kassel in the middle of the 13th century, Gudensberg retained the Hessian judgeship and was designated in documents as the capital of Lower Hesse as late as 1324. The Archbishop Adolph of Mainz stormed the town in 1387 and burned it completely down. The Wenigenburg was reduced to rubble and ashes as a result of this attack though the defenders of Obernburg held off all of the attacks and defied the besiegers. The Thirty Years War brought bitter times; in 1640, the Croatians occupied Gudensberg for ten days and ravaged the town.

What to See and Do

1. On top of the legendary **Odenberg**, located about two kilometers from the town center, is an observation tower offering a wide panora-

ma view. The ARS NATURA, a hiking and panorama trail, provides wonderful views onto the basaltic hill landscape of the Chatti.

Well-tended half-timbered houses at the Old Market

The former synagogue, today a cultural house

2. The **remains of the walls** of the Obernburg and the foundations of the Romanesque castle keep are preserved on the castle mountain. The Wenigenburg is privately owned.

3. An excursion through the Gudensberg old town reveals countless **half-timbered structures** from the 17th and 18th centuries. Worth particular attention are the well-tended half-timbered houses on the old market. The **parish church** of Gudensberg with its mighty abutments raises itself high over the town at the foot of the castle mountain. The choir of the church originates from the 13th century, the attractive eight-sided, domed sacristy chapel St. Crucis, was erected in the year 1500. The former synagogue testifies to the bygone Jewish life in Gudensburg; it is used today as a culture house. A highlight of the town is the Fairy Tale Stage in the middle of the town park. Its fairy tale-like architecture delights both visitors and performers alike.

The former hospital was founded around the end of the 13th century

4. The **former hospital** on the west-side of the town was founded around the end of the 13th century. The two-storied stone hospital building (ca. 1400) and two adjacent half-timbered houses from the 17th and 18th centuries are preserved.

5. The church in the **Maden** subdivision derives from the 18th century. On the road leading to Obervorschütz lies a prehistoric, storied Menhir, Wotan's Stone (Wodanstein) in the vernacular.

Baunatal

Birthplace of the Fairy Tale Woman Dorothea Viehmann

The entire landscape of the town of Baunatal, which came into existence in 1964–72 through the merger of seven communities, is dominated today by two Volkswagen component parts plants.

Fairy Tale References

Catharina Dorothea Pierson was born on November 8, 1755, near Rengershausen, a village just south of Kassel, in the Gasthaus *Zum Birkenbaum*, which later took on the name *Knall-*

Dorothea-Viehmann-Fountain in the inner courtyard of the historic Hütt Brewery

The Knallhütte Brewery

hütte. She was the firstborn of a Huguenot family from Hofgeismar-Schöneberg descended from the innkeeper, Johann Friedrich Isaac Pierson. The *Knallhütte*, just outside the gate of Kassel, was one of the most beloved inns on the road to Frankfurt. In the family restaurant, where she lived until she was thirty-two, Dorothea listened in on the tales related by wagoners, craftsmen, soldiers and farmers stopping by for a bite to eat.

Ludwig Emil Grimm: Dorothea Viehmann

In her married name, Viehmann, she later became famous as the *Fairy Tale Woman* (Märchenfrau) of the Brothers Grimm. Among the fairy tales attributed to her are such beautiful stories as *The Devil with the Three Golden*

Hairs, The Goose Girl, The Devil and His Grandmother, a version of Cinderella, *Doctor Know-it-all and The Smart Farmer's Daughter.* Because as a Huguenot child she understood both French and German, many of the stories are of either German or French heritage.

The 250-year old *Knallhütte* still stands where it did when Dorothea Pierson-Viehmann lived there, right next to the current Autobahn 49 Exit Baunatal-Nord. The ancestors of the fairy tale woman still own the restaurant and adjoining Hütt Brewery and have added special touches like the *Fairy Tale Room* and the *Dorothea Viehmann Stube* (parlor) to create a fairy tale-like ambiance in a historical context.

The Fairy Tale Fountain in the town center of Baunatal

History

Prehistoric and early historical finds point to an old settlement; as early as 775 there was mention of a *rittahe* when Archbishop Lullus, the founder of the abbey at Hersfeld, turned over the possession of the abbey to Charlemagne. In 1123, Archbishop Adalbert I of Mainz approved endowments to the cloister Hasungen in *altdenbune* and *kilechbune.* In the year

1303, Landgrave Heinrich I rewarded the knight Riedesel with estates in Altenritte and Großenritte. Later, during the Thirty Years War, Croatians ravaged the villages in the Bauna Valley. Thirty-two men from the villages of the Bauna valley (Baunatal) took part in the American Revolutionary War in 1776.

What to See and Do

1. Visit and perhaps have lunch and a home-brewed German beer at the **Knallhütte**, still owned nine generations later by the heirs of the family of Dorothea Pierson-Viehmann, the source of so many fairy tales. Attached is the Hütt brewery that offers sight-seeing tours. On Saturdays after 5:30 p.m., an actress playing the part of Dorothea Viehmann takes guests of the restaurant into the world of the fairy tale world of D. Viehmann and the Grimms.

2. In Baunatal itself there are various fairy tale sculptures including the Fairy Tale Fountain (Dorothea Viehmann and the Brothers Grimm) in the town center. After that, spend some time wandering on the **Fairy Tale Country Path.** The church of Rengershausen is on your way.

The legendary Hünstein

3. Of culture-historical interest in Baunatal are the ringwalls from prehistorical and early historical era on the **Baunsberg** and on the **Burgberg** (Castle Mountain) and the legendary **Hünstein**, a prehistoric menhir in Großenritte. Additional attractions in Großenritte are the late Gothic church with weir system and the former rectory (1164).

The Town Museum and the Local History Museum are worth a visit

4. In **Altenritte**, a row of half-timbered houses have been preserved and the Town Museum and the Local History Museum, with old forge, are both worth a visit.

5. Stop at the **Volkswagen plant** to take a tour of this sprawling facility. It is necessary to arrange this beforehand. The numerous, colorful Volkswagen Beetle sculptures found throughout the town provide an excellent photo opportunity.

Kassel

Capital of the German Fairy Tale Route and World Heritage Site

Geographically, Kassel lies almost in the middle of the *German Fairy Tale Route* and, with the surrounding region of north Hesse, the city is virtually its heart. The overwhelming majority of the Grimms' *Children's and Household Tales* are native to or written down in and around Kassel. No wonder that the *Association German Fairy Tale Route* has its central headquarters in downtown Kassel and that it is regarded as the capital city of the German Fairy Tale Route. What is even more important, Kassel was selected twice as **UNESCO World Heritage.**

UNESCO WORLD HERITAGE SITE: Mountain Park Wilhelmshöhe

First, there are the Brothers Grimm *Children and Household Tales* inclusion into the *UNES-*

UNESCO WORLD HERITAGE SITE: The grandiose Statue of Hercules

CO World Document Heritage; second is the unique *mountain park of Wilhelmshöhe* with its grandiose statue of *Hercules* and its impressive *cascades, fountains and aqueducts*, a UNESCO World Heritage Site.

Fairy Tale, Saga and Literary References

The charming old cityscape of Kassel was almost completely destroyed in the Second World War by forty air raids and today very little still evokes the former architectural brilliance of the Hessian landgraves and the subsequent electors. With the destruction of the old city, the first residence of the Grimms (1805–14), the *fairy tale house* in the Marktgasse, was lost forever. Despite its destruction during the war, at least the façade of their residence in *the northern Guard Gate* (Torwache) remains today as a part of the Hessian Higher Administrative Court. From 1814–22, the Brothers Grimm lived here with their sister Lotte in the roomy lodgings on the second floor during the time when they were working on the second edition of the *Children's and Household Tales* and on the *German Sagas*. A further residence of the

Grimms was the house reconstructed after the war at *Schöne Aussicht 9*. The *Fridericianum*, at the time of the Brothers Grimm the electors' library, was their work site; Jacob Grimm worked in the *Castle Wilhelmshöhe* in the private library of King Jerome during the Napoleonic Occupation.

Wilhelmshöhe Palace

The city of Kassel, where the Brothers Grimm spent around thirty years, was the center of the life and work of Jacob and Wilhelm as well as of their brother Ludwig Emil Grimm, who received his professorate at the Art Academy of Kassel in 1832. The *Children's and Household Tales*, the *German Sagas*, the periodical *Old German Forests* (Altdeutsche Wälder) as well as Jacob Grimm's *German Grammar* (I + II) all came into existence in Kassel. Although lauded for their groundbreaking philological works

The Ballhouse near Wilhelmshöhe Palace

such as the *German Dictionary* or the grammars, the *Children's and Household Tales*, appearing in its first edition in 1812, is the most widely read and translated German-language book in the world. Hand-annotated reference copies of the *Children's and Household Tales*, a total of fourteen fairy tale volumes that appeared between 1812 and 1857 in a number of editions. The first one of 1812/15 is now *UNESCO World Document Heritage*. All this is displayed in GRIMMWORLD Kassel (GRIMMWELT Kassel), a recent exhibition center with historical, media and participative exhibits for children and adults that not only feature the fairy tale and saga collections of the Brothers Grimm but also their extensive language research. It includes hand-written manuscripts of the brothers, portraits and landscapes by Ludwig Emil Grimm as well as furniture, personal items and other memorabilia from both the Grimm and the Hassenpflug families (the later Hessian Minister of State Hassenpflug was married to Lotte Grimm). Furthermore, you will find contemporary art by documenta-artists and other internationally renowned artists.

Over a third of the fairy tales in the first edition of *Children's and Household Tales* derive

City district Kassel-Niederzwehren: The authors of The Fairy Tale Landscape in front of the half-timbered house at Märchenweg 11 where Dorothea Viehmann and her family lived from 1787–98

Niederzwehren churchyard: Gravestone in her memory

from the Hassenpflug (Amalie, Jeanette, Marie) and Wild families (Mrs. Wild, Dortchen, Gretchen, Lisette and Marie Elisabeth). Dortchen married Wilhelm Grimm in 1825. The marriage produced three children. Their eldest son, Herman (1828–1901) contributed *The Pea Test* and a parallel version of *The Poor Miller's Boy and the Cat* while still a child for the *Children's and Household Tales.* He was later also a professor in Berlin (Art History: *The Life of Michelangelo*), published the Weimar edition of Goethe's works and supervised new editions of the Grimms' *Children's and Household Tales* and the *German Sagas* after the death of his father and uncle. One can only wonder how many additional tales we might have today had not Jacob remained a bachelor for his full life. The Hassenpflugs (see Hanau) were of Huguenot ancestry, a commonality they share with Dorothea Viehmann (1755–1815). This village tailor's wife from Niederzwehren (see Baunatal) contributed over thirty tales to the second edition of the *Children's and Household Tales*. Between April 1813 and September 1814, less than a year before her untimely death, the *Märchenfrau* spent hours reciting her tales while either Jacob or Wilhelm carefully transcribed them. Given this French connection, it is hardly surprising that a substantial number of the tales the Grimms collected have French origins including *Puss in Boots, Little Red Riding Hood, Blue Beard, Sleeping Beauty* and others.

On the way to the city section Niederzwehren, there is little castle *Schönfeld*, once a meeting place for young Romantics around the electress Auguste, including the Brentano family as well as the Brothers Grimm. It's in the city of Kassel that Clemens Brentano and Achim von Arnim, supported by the Brothers Grimm, finished volumes 2 and 3 of their significant work, the *Boys Wonder Horn*. In the city section Niederzwehren near the church in southwest Kassel around the *Grunnelbach* (a brook) there are some well-tended half-timbered houses from the 18th and 19th centuries including the half-timbered house at *Märchenweg 11* where Dorothea Viehmann and her family lived from 1787–98.

Schönfeld Castle, once a meeting place for young Romantics around the electress Auguste, including the Brentano family and the Brothers Grimm

An important collector of Hessian sagas was the writer and folklorist Philipp Hoffmeister (1804–74) who got to know the Brothers Grimm in the home of an aunt. Among his contributions are *Hessian Folk Poetry in Sagas and Fairy Tales, Droll Stories and Funny Tales.* Karl Lyncker (1823–55), born in Kassel, worked in the same spirit with his 1854 work *German*

Sagas and Manners in Hessian Districts, a collection of sagas and folklore gathered largely from oral sources. The collection *Sagenkranz* from *Hesse-Nassau* (1889) by rector Carl Heßler (1859–1930) from Kassel went through several editions. Paul Heidelbach (1870–1954) worked in Kassel collaborating on the book series *Folk Tales in the World Literature* and writing Kassel: *A Millenium of Hessian Urban Culture.* Others connected to Kassel include the folklorist and fairy tale saga researcher, Paul Zaunert (1879–1959, *German Fairy Tales since Grimm*).

Between 1928–32, the young Samuel Beckett (1906–89) spent many months in Kassel where his first great love, cousin Peggy Sinclair,

Fridericianum, formerly the Elector's Library – the work site of the Brothers' Grimm, today a central hub for contemporary art exhibitions and the heart of the documenta

lived. During his time in Kassel, he worked on his novel *Dream of Fair to Middling Women.*

History

Kassel itself arose quite naturally on the Fulda River at a spot likely first settled by Franconian royalty at the intersection of two important

The Orange Palace (1702–17) in the spacious Karlsaue State Park

trade routes, one connecting the Main River to the Weser and the other leading from the Rhine towards Thuringia. Mentioned for the first time in 913 as *chassella*, the castle passed in 1008 as a gift from Emperor Henry II to his spouse Kunigunde and then back again to the Empire upon her death. In the 12th century, Kassel received municipal rights. Its size and economic significance grew once it was chosen to be the official residence city of Landgrave Henry I of Hesse in the year 1277.

In the 16th century, Kassel eventually became one of the political centers in the west of Germany under Philipp the Magnanimous. He introduced the Reformation into Hesse and was, alongside the Prince Elector of Saxony, leader of the Protestant Schmalkaldian Bund (League). After the French King Louis XIV lifted the Edict of Nantes in 1685, Landgrave Karl (1670–1730) was one of the first in Germany to accept countless French believers (Huguenots) into his province, leading to the founding of

Jacob and Wilhelm Grimm sitting on a garden bench

the Upper New Town (Oberneustadt) of Kassel for the Huguenots.

In 1803, Landgrave William IX (1785–1860) was elevated to elector when Kassel became the capital of a new electorate. In the Napoleonic era, Kassel became capital of the short-lived Kingdom of Westphalia under the control of Jerome Bonaparte (1784–1860), the youngest brother of Napoleon. In siding with Austria against Prussia in 1866 during the Seven Weeks War, the electorate of Hesse lost its independence to Prussia after the defeat of Austria in the Battle of Königgrätz.

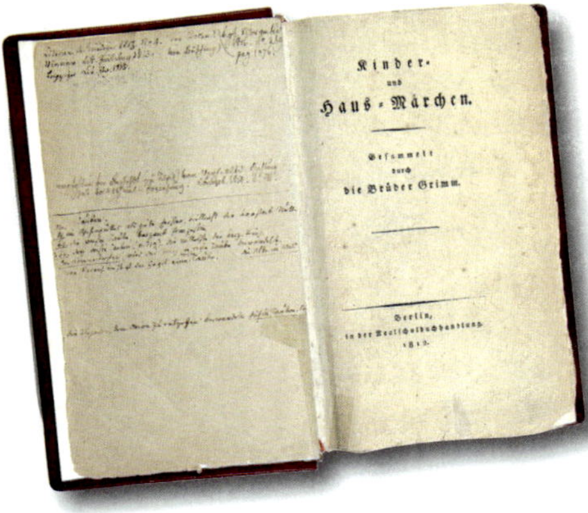

GRIMMWORLD Kassel: UNESCO WORLD DOCUMENT HERITAGE: Brothers Grimm: Proof Copy of the Children's and Household Tales with their annotations; Berlin 1812

What to See and Do:

1. Fairy Tale Kassel:

– The exhibition center **GRIMMWORLD Kassel** features historical as well as *multi-media dis-*

Brothers Grimm: The Children's and Household Tales, Second Edition, Part I, illustrated by their brother L .E. Grimm, Berlin 1819

plays, contemporary art and participative attractions for children and adults. It hosts numerous exhibits that document the fascinating career and works of the Brothers Grimm. The showpiece is the proof copy of the first edition of the *Children's and Household Tales*, part of the UNESCO World Document Heritage. There is a great collection of fairy tale illustrations of both of the last centuries until today as well as fairy tale films. Additionally, there is a significant display of drawings from Ludwig Emil Grimm and of personal items, furniture and other memorabilia of the Grimm and Hassenpflug families.

– Other Grimm locations include Brüder-Grimm-Platz with **Brothers Grimm Monument,** several meters away the former *Guards Building* (their residence from 1814–1822) and, at No. 4, you will find the *Brothers Grimm Society*. Another residence is *Schöne Aussicht 9* as well as their workplace at the **Fridericianum.**

– *The Old cemetery* at the Luther Church holds graves of the Grimms' mother and sister Lotte.

– Little *Schönfeld Castle* is on the way to the city district of Niederzwehren: At the church, there is a stone in memory of *Dorothea Viehmann*; her former residence (1787–1798) is on *Märchenweg 11.*

Ludwig Emil Grimm, self-portrait 1813

Mountain Park Wilhelmshöhe: Waterfall

2. UNESCO World Heritage Site: Mountain Park Wilhelmshöhe

The symbol of Kassel and the region, the grandiose statue of **Hercules** (1713–17), is located above Kassel in the **mountain park of Wilhelmshöhe** with its impressive cascades, fountains, aqueduct, and the **Wilhelmshöhe Palace** (1786–1803) with its renowned gallery of old masters including Rembrandts, Jordaens, van Dycks and its collections of antiquities and graphics as well as the *Palace Museum*. Among those who resided in the palace in addition to the electors of Hesse-Kassel are Jerome Bonaparte and Kaiser Wilhelm II, who spent summers there. Nearby are the *Ball House* and the *greenhouse* while the neo-Gothic castle ruin **Löwenburg** (1793–1801) is some 500 meters away.

3. **Wilhelmshöhe** is not only a World Heritage Site, but also a **spa** with thermal hot springs and hydrotherapy facilities (natural method of

wellness therapy from Sebastian Kneipp). In the North Hessian spa of Bad Wilhelmshöhe, one can manage stress wonderfully and relax.

4. Though smaller than Wilhelmshöhe, the spacious **Karlsaue** State Park offers the *Orange Palace* (1702–17) with its Marble Bath (1722–28) and the Kitchen Pavillion. Nearby are statues and the flower island *Siebenbergen.*

The Ottoneum, the first theater in Germany (1603–06); nowadays it's the location of the Museum of Natural History

5. Though 78% destroyed during the allied bombings, a hike through the **historical inner city** offers remains of Kassel prewar opulence including *Martin's Church* (14th and 15th centuries), *Karl's Church* (1689–1706, built for the Huguenot parish), the *Brother Church* (1292–1376) and the Weser Renaissance style *Market Hall* built originally as a stable in 1591–93.

6. The **Ottoneum**, once the first theater in Germany, serves now as a natural history museum. Other museums worth visiting are the *Museum of Sepulchral Culture* and the **Spohr Museum** dedicated to the Romantic composer (1784–1859) and Paganini contemporary.

Jonathan Borofsky: Man walking to the Sky

7. Modern Kassel is most famous for its **documenta**, a display of worldwide contemporary art that is held every five years in *documenta-halle* (1992), around the *Fridercianum* (1769–76) and in other diverse locations.

Nieste

Fairy Tale and Saga References

In Nieste, the most celebrated saga is that of the *Giants of Nieste*: "In order to destroy the Hessian castle Sensenstein, Duke Otto of Brunswick Quade (Evil) once called the most dangerous and malevolent giants of the area to help. The giants hurled huge boulders at the castle and its inhabitants, but a forest spirit protected the castle and residents and turned the giants into tall trees." To commemorate the legendary figures of the Niester giants, a four-meter-high metal sculpture, *The Giant*, was installed in 2004 in front of the gate to Sensenstein by the sculptor Robert Colnago.

Additionally, there is a fairy tale story of the scrawny, white and black Nieste, the river flowing through Nieste.

Well-tended half-timbered houses

The Königs-Alm (King's Pasture) in Nieste is a prominent tourist attraction in northern Hesse

History

In the 13th century, the name was first mentioned when Hermann Nyste donated the altar of Gimte in 1289; his brother Conrad was councilor of Münden in 1323. It can be assumed that their name evokes their place of origin, Nieste. The village was located on the border between Hesse and Brunswick, and there was no clear boundary between the two territories for a very long time. Hesse and Brunswick agreed in a contract to manage Nieste together in 1536. Nieste finally went over completely to Hesse after an exchange for the Hessian enclave of Laubach in 1831.

In about 1372, Landgrave Hermann of Hesse built the Sensenstein Castle, close to the neighboring Castle Sichelnstein, as a defense against the predations of the Brunswickers. In the 15th century, Sensenstein served as a hunting lodge in the Kaufunger Forest for the landgraves of Hesse, but the castle lost more and more importance from the 16th century onwards and fell into disrepair. Today only high walls remind us of Sensenstein. The name was transferred to the youth castle Sensenstein (sports training center) whose administration is

Robert Colnago: The legendary Giant of Nieste

housed in the former mansion of Sensenstein, a handsome half-timbered building.

What to See and Do

1. A prominent tourist attraction in northern Hesse is the king's pasture **(Königs-Alm)** located above Nieste. It can serve as the starting point for over one hundred kilometers of hiking and biking trails. A special natural experience presents itself on the *GrimmSteig* (hill climb) or on the *Premium hiking* around the natural monument of the Niester Giant near the Sensenstein.

2. Particularly decisive for the character of the small village is its pleasant location, its preserved half-timbered houses and the beautiful and peaceful **landscape** directly adjacent to the *Münden Nature Park* and *Meißner-Kaufunger Forest.*

Fairy Tale Characters at the Lake

3. The *Eco-Path Archeology* offers a wealth of information about the historical ore mining and the castle **Sensenstein**.

4. Glass production in the 16th century is featured on the ecological path to *Gläsnertal* with the largest glass slag heap in Europe.

Kaufungen

Saga References

There are a number of myths and legends from diverse authors about the German Empress Kunigunde, who was canonized after her death. The most famous legend is the miracle of ploughshare with the apology of her husband, the Holy Roman Emperor, Henry II. It is also found in the *German Sagas* of the Brothers Grimm. This quite plausible version (p. 167) was recorded by their younger brother Ferdinand Grimm.

Half-timbered Houses and Kaufungen Collegiate Church

Choir of the Collegiate Church

Saint Kunigunde

History

In the year 1008, the German king and eventual Emperor Henry II (1014–24) made a gift to his wife Kunigunde of the fortified royal court (curtis) Kassel as a replacement for Bamberg. He moved the royal court not long afterwards to Kaufungen, first mentioned in documents as *coufunga* in 1011. The empress Kunigunde donated a Benedictine abbey to the area of the royal court in 1017. The abbey church of the Holy Cross, today Kaufungen's collegiate church (Stiftskirche), was dedicated on July 13, 1025, one year after the death of Henry II. Kunigunde entered the Benedictine Abbey on the same day; she remained there until her death in 1033 and was buried next to her husband in Bamberg Cathedral. Childless, Henry II and Kunigunde marked the end of their royal line.

What to See and Do

1. The rich legacy of Kaufungen can still be traced in its historical buildings. The collegiate

Left: View from the Cloister Garden towards the Collegiate Church

Right: Cloister Garden

church **(Stiftskirche),** which received countless changes in the late Romanesque and Gothic eras, is well preserved. Concerts with national and international orchestras, choirs, and soloists are regularly presented in the church. Deserving special attention in the interior of the impressive **Romanesque** hall church are the wall paintings from the 15th and 16th centuries, the baptismal font from the 14th century, the organ (1799) and countless grave markers from the 16th through 18th centuries. Only the foundations of the south and west wings of the cross-coat still remain of the former abbey.

The *Rebental* building is the former sleeping quarters (dormitorium) of the nuns and is adjacent to the early Romanesque *St. George's Chapel.* In the former collegiate courtyard

are located the **Stiftsrenterei** (collegiate bursary), a superb half-timbered building from 1606 and the Gothic manor house, rebuilt in 1714.

Collegiate Church: Historic Ensemble

2. On a tour through Kaufungen, one can enjoy countless well maintained decorated **half-timbered houses** (for example at Mühlenplatz 4, Leipzigerstraße 74 + 125) from the 17th and 18th centuries and gardens.

3. In the museum *Alte Schule* (Old School) there is, among others, a display relating the history of everyday life and the world of work in the area of Kaufungen from the Middle Ages to the present including a room featuring life in Kaufungen during the Nazi Era (1933–1945). The unusual monument to technology, the mining museum **Rossgang**, shows how brown coal was once removed from the earth.

Regional Museum Alte Schule: Classroom of 1925

Kaufungen: archway

4. The **Hessian Brickwork Museum** is in the former brickworks of Oberkaufungen. A guided tour explains the various production steps required to manufacture bricks.

Empress Kunigunde

(Ferdinand Grimm – English version: Thomas L. Johnson)

Henry II heard whispers that his wife, to whom he was deeply devoted, was secretly consorting with one of the senior knights of the court. The emperor was shocked. He went to his wife and spoke to her about these rumors, even adding some bitter words. Kunigunde, deeply disturbed by his speech and proud of her virtue, designated an hour of the day when she could prove her innocence.

She took seven glowing iron ploughs with her bare hands from the fiery furnace, laid them before the Emperor, walked atop them with her feet and said: "If I have violated our marital fidelity, may this glowing iron injure me." *

* Kunigunde shows her innocence here
That she is still a virgin pure,
Bearing this glowing ploughshare
Without a single care;
And all saw the great wonder,
To her lasting fame and honor.

The Emperor joyfully embraced Kunigunde and asked her a thousand times for forgiveness. He then punished her detractors. It was said that the devil had appeared in the form of a young man in front of her bedroom and had thereby deceived the court.

Helsa

Fairy Tale and Saga References

According to the *Chronicle of Helsa*, three of the professors, Dahlmann, Gervinius, and Jacob Grimm (see Göttingen Seven), who had been expelled from the Kingdom of Hanover, turned up on December 17th, 1837, with a large number of students at the restaurant *The White*

The Parish Church of Helsa

Horse, at that time the leading inn of place, while on their way to Kassel.

Of merit for regional history was the work of local historian, teacher Carl Löwer (1891–1968)

Rumpelstiltskin Fountain in Helsa

of Wickenrode and Pastor Ernst Werner Magdanz (1912–84) of Eschenstruth, both of whom collected legends and stories. Löwer contributed the Wickenröder saga *Honighof and Mother Holle.* Karl Paetow, author of *The Most Beautiful Weser Sagas* (Die schönsten Wesersagen – see Bad Oeynhausen) published the two fairy tales *Frau Holle and the Glassblower* and *Heilwurz.*

The Merten-Jäger Fountain, which commemorates the legend telling how Merten Jäger allegedly robbed the church bell of Helsa from the Croatians during the Thirty Years War, stands in the center of the village.

A second fountain, this one honoring the Brothers Grimm fairy tale character, *Rumpelstiltskin*, is also in the heart of Helsa.

History

The earliest mention of Helsa was in 1353. Close connections were maintained with the Kaufungen Abbey, which held jurisdiction over it and appointed community leaders. Out of necessity, the church in Helsa was built as a fortified church to protect it against approaching enemies. The district of Wickenrode was first mentioned in 1293 as glass manufacturing took hold in Germany. The basic materials needed to produce glass are found in abundance in the Wickenröder Valley, which subsequently developed numerous glassworks. The district of St. Ottilien, located on the slopes of Mount Ottilia (Ottilienberg), was founded in 1699 for twelve Huguenot families.

What to See and Do

1. Stately timber-frame houses from the 17th–19th centuries that are protected as historical monuments complete the pretty picture of the community of Helsa. The **parish church** of

Stately half-timbered houses in Helsa

St. Ottilien: The Huguenot Church

Helsa with its separately-standing tower is impressive in the middle of a former military churchyard. The tower, which was protected by a ring wall and encircled the cemetery, was massively built in its foundation (13th century), and provided with bay windows and openings for military action.

2. The tower of the parish church of **Eschenstruth** dates from the 12th century; the half-timbered house with the exquisite portal in Mühlweg was built in 1680. Also of interest is the historic **Most Mill**, where the working conditions of a miller in the first half of the 20th century are demonstrated, as well as the handloom room.

3. The small half-timbered church for the Huguenot community in **St. Ottilien** was, as the French inscription testifies, dedicated in 1727 (enlarged with an addition in 1932). Its special feature is the combination of church hall, school and teacher's house under one roof.

Hessisch Lichtenau

The Fairy Tale Land of Frau Holle

On the southwest exit of Hessisch Lichtenau-Hollstein stand the Hollsteine, two powerful dolomite rocks whose name essentially means *Stones of Frau Holle*. The *Hollsteine* offer a wonderful view of the High Meißner, the *king* of Hessian mountains. A number of fairy tales and sagas arose in the High Meißner area to be acquired by the Brothers Grimm and others. Foremost among them is the Frau Holle story.

The Old Town Hall of Hessisch Lichtenau: Frau Holle is shaking out her featherbed

View into the Holleum, a museum dedicated completely to Frau Holle

When winter snowflakes fill the sky, people living in the Meißner Mountains say: *"Frau Holle is shaking out her beds."* On the bottom of the *Frau Holle Pond*, whose bells are still perceptible in very quiet evening hours as they ring from the depths, rests the sunken castle of Frau Holle. Ancient folk belief holds that newborn children enter the world from the water of the Frau Holle Pond.

The Brothers Grimm have extensively studied the mythological figure of Frau Holle (variously named Mother Hulda or Holda) and memorialized her in both the *German Sagas* and in the *Children's and Household Tales.* Jacob Grimm, who devoted several pages to Holda (Frau Holle) in his *German Mythology*, visited the High Meißner in 1819 to inquire in the villages, unfortunately in vain, for existing folk tales. Wilhelm Grimm writes in his diary on July 22, 1821: *"Afternoon amidst magnificent beech trees on the Frau Holle Pond."*

History

Hessisch Lichtenau *(lichtenowe)* can thank Landgrave Henry I of Hesse whose directive

The Upper Tower (Oberturm)

established the town and gave it its name *(on these bright meadows I will build a town ...)* as he consolidated a series of villages and made them the town of Lichtenau. Landgrave Hermann of Hesse built a castle in the years 1385-87 but it had already been razed by 1413. Nearby, the castle Reichenbach (today a ruin) served as a hunting castle of the Hessian landgraves and was the residence of the district magistrate of the landgraves.

The death of Landgrave Ludwig II in 1471 and the eventual decline of the castle led in 1490 to the relocation of the administrative seat to Lichtenau. From then on, the seat to which the town of Lichtenau, the town of Waldkappel and eighteen other villages belonged has been called *Lichtenau.* Since 1889, the town bears the official designation as *Hes-*

sisch Lichtenau to distinguish it from eleven other *Lichtenaus.*

The town has been visited often by both war and fire, sometimes simultaneously. In the Thirty Years War, the community was destroyed by the Croatians on April 11, 1637. It also was visited by misfortune in the Seven Years War as well as during the Napoleonic occupation. Fires through the centuries have claimed many of the original buildings. Further, it has the misfortune to have been the locale of a forced labor camp making munitions during Hitler's Third Reich. Judith Magyar Isaacson's *Seed of Sarah* (1991) tells the author's story of her time in Hessisch Lichtenau Labor Camp, a satellite location of the Buchenwald Concentration Camp, during the Second World War.

View into Burgstraße

What to See and Do

1. Walk the old town with its picturesque half-timbered houses of the 17th–19th centuries, stopping to see the **Old Town Hall** (1651–54), now a restaurant and meeting-place. Walk the medieval town wall with its two remaining watchtowers, stopping off to see the *Kanzler Feige Fountain*, an example of early 20th century Art Nouveau.

2. Since opening in 2006, the **Frau Holle-Park** has depicted the Frau Holle character with other aspects of the famous Grimm tale. The **Holleum** is a museum dedicated completely to Frau Holle. All can be taken in while enjoying a bicycle tour or hike on the fairy tale country path.

Frau Holle

3. In nearby Hessisch Lichtenau-**Reichenbach,** visit the castle ruins, the 12th century *Cloister Church* and the *Great Stones*, the largest dolomite outcropping in North Hesse.

4. In the area of the fairy tale and saga surrounded **High Meißner,** visit the many natural monuments including the basalt *Kitzkammer*, the *Sea Stones* and the *Holle Stone* and the mysterious *Frau Holle Pond.*

Happy Endings/Sad Endings: Which are Better?

Like many of the fairy tales, *Frau Holle* places two characters in the same stressful situation and then hands out rewards based on how the characters perform. The difference between the reward of gold given to the less-favored daughter and the bath of pitch to her stepsister is so profound that one recent English version of the tale, John Warren Stewig's *Mother Holly* features the good daughter, Rose, teaching the less good daughter the meaning of hard work. In Stewig's version of the tale, then, both daughters survive with their self-esteem intact. The author is very clear about his intentions in changing the tale, stating in the foreword that it *reinforces the belief, useful to children, that with help we can all change the way we behave.*

Stewig's redemptive approach is full of the sort of second-chance optimism that has been a characteristic of enlightened modernity while the Grimm's story reminds the reader of a stern reformed theology where grace is less important than punishment.

Which is the better message for children? The reader might want to discuss this issue with children: is it better to see a bully (often a wolf) or a deceiver get their *just rewards* or is it better to rewrite each story to show how even bad people can change their behavior given a second chance? How one answers this question has implications for everything from educational philosophy to prison programs.

Melsungen

Saga References

The citizens of Melsungen are known in Hesse as the "axe sharpeners." How might such a legend have arisen? Well, as early as the 19th century, Philipp Hoffmeister had included a legend from the oral tradition about the axe sharpeners in his collection, *Hessian Folk Poetry in Sagas and Fairy Tales, Droll Stories and Funny Tales*: "Once upon a time the youth of Melsungen were more interested in idleness than in working in the forest chopping down wood. They claimed that the Barten (axes) were not sharp enough and that they needed to sharpen them first. In order to kill time, ten or twelve of them sat down on the Fulda Bridge and conversed with one another. When a passer-by came and asked what they were doing there, the boys replied: 'We are sharpening our axes.'" Ever since then, people from Melsungen have been referred to as "axe sharpeners."

The legends set in and around Melsungen bear such titles as *The Night Watchman in Melsungen, An Oak Forest Attests to Innocence, Charlemagne and Melsungen, The Treasure of the Schwarzenberger Knights' Castle* or *The Mermaid in the Milky Well near Kirchhof.*

Modern day Axe Sharpener (Bartenwetzer) and the Goose Girl

History

Mentioned as early as 802 in Latin as *pagus milisunge*, Melsungen was clearly laid out by the Thuringian landgraves as a town-like settle-

The picturesque Melsungen Town Hall (1562–68)

ment at the old river crossing on the left bank of the Fulda River in 1189. Three important trade routes, the Sälzerweg (west-east), Nuremberg Road (north-south) and "through the long Hesse" (Frankfurt-Leipzig) sustained the economic development of Melsungen.

The place passed over to the landgrave of Hesse in the middle of the 13th century. Long a bone of contention between the archbishops of Mainz and the landgraves of Hesse, things finally came to a head in 1427 with a battle that was decided in favor of Louis I, Landgrave of Hesse.

A fire in 1554 destroyed parts of the town, including the Old Town Hall that was rebuilt in the years 1562–68. From 1627–32, the Melsungen Castle served as the residence of the Landgrave Moritz of Hesse after he had abdicated his office in favor of his son. The town suffered heavy looting by passing troops during the Thirty Years War and the Seven Years War.

Well-tended half-timbered houses in Brückenstraße and Kasseler Straße

What to See and Do

The Old Town of Melsungen is characterized by the closed facades of its ornate, medieval half-timbered houses. The wide main street intersection connects the three significant squares of the town: market, church and castle.

1. The symbolic figure of Melsungen, the **Bartenwetzer** ("axe sharpener"), shows up at 12.00 and 18.00 o'clock in the tower of the town hall. Situated in the middle of the market square, the stand-alone Melsungen **Town Hall** is one of the most important in Hesse. The picturesque three-story (29 m high) timber-framed building with its distinctive corner tower was built between 1562 and 1568.

The Bartenwetzer shows up at 6 pm (Tower of the Town Hall)

A number of **half-timbered houses** have been preserved in the neighboring streets, Burgstr. 5 (1622 – commonly referred to as *Adam and Eve* after the corner posts) as well as the magnificent patrician houses Fritzlarer Str. 3 (1600), the corner house Market Square/Brückenstr. (late 16th century), Brückenstr. 5 (late 17th century) deserve special attention. The houses Brückenstr. 7 (1423) and 9 (1426) are the oldest half-timbered houses in town.

2. At the end of Brückenstraße is the historic **Bartenwetzer Bridge** (1595–96) with two life-sized *Axe Sharpener* figures and the local museum (including the development of the town, framework and descriptive models for this purpose, ancient crafts and local industrial history, such as B. Braun Melsungen AG).

3. The triple-nave Gothic **town church** was built in several sections between 1352 and 1425. The Tower (1232) and the main entrance to the nave (1200) were taken over from an earlier Romanesque structure. In the town church, several key stones attract one's attention including a head of Christ (above the altar) and figures of saints (Archangel Michael).

4. A Renaissance style **small palace** complex (now administrative buildings) was built between 1550 and 1577 under the Landgraves Philip the Magnanimous and William IV. It consists of a three-story main building (1550–57) with oriel windows and stair towers, the inland revenue, the stables and the former residence of the landgraves.

Castle Grounds with view towards the former Residence of the Hessian Landgraves

5. Sections of the **old town wall** are preserved at several locations including the Castle Garden (old stand of trees) and the Eulenturm (Owl's Tower, late 14th century).

6. The **Hospital Chapel** of St. George (first documented mention in 1332) dates from the Middle Ages and the Stone House (Kemenaty bower) from the mid-14th century.

7. The **classical Casino**, built in 1837–38 and rebuilt and extended in 1976–77 into a convention center is noteworthy for its two-story central block and distinctive arched windows.

8. In the **old cemetery** we find the unique memorial to the Russian Colonel Bedriaga who was killed in the battle of Kassel in the Napoleonic Wars.

Bad Sooden-Allendorf

Fairy Tale and Saga References

In the High Meißner region, there is still a rich, vibrant narrative tradition having to do with Frau Holle. In addition to the Brothers Grimm, the well-known Thuringian saga and fairy-tale collector Ludwig Bechstein (1801–60, *German Saga Book, German Fairy Tale Book*) has an especially decisive influence on the image of Frau Holle due to his successful and still very popular fairy tale version called *Die Goldmaria und die Pechmaria* (Gold Mary and Pitch Mary). This fairy tale also plays a special role in Bad Sooden-Allendorf, particularly at Eastertime during the annual eight day Fairy Tale Week with its extensive program that includes, among others, a fairy tale pageant, fairy tale theater, and appearances by storytellers.

Goldmaria, Pechmaria and Frau Holle

In the Bad Sooden-Allendorf town district of Hilgershausen in the Meißner region, a world full of sagas and fairy tales, there is the so called *Hohlstein* (hollow stone), once a pagan place of worship. In his collection *Legends from Hesse and Nassau*, Karl Wehrhan comes to the conclusion that the Hohlstein must be the place in Meißner where the fairy tale of *Goldmaria and Pechmaria* is set.

History

The salt court *westera* was created and developed on the right bank of the Werra River

Pfennigstube (ancient Penny Parlor)

under Frankish rule in order to protect salt springs lying on the left bank of the Werra. Charlemagne gave the royal court and the salt springs to the monastery of Fulda between 776–79.

At the beginning of the 13th century, the Thuringian landgrave received the estates of the monastery of Fulda as a fief and founded the town of Allendorf at the *alden dorf* (old village) near Westera in 1219.

The settlement *in den sothen* developed at the foot of a medieval castle near the salt springs on the left bank of the Werra River. *Sothen* and the town of *Allendorf* came over to the landgraves of Hesse in 1264. Lucrative salt production was carried out by the Association of Pan-owners (Pfännerschaft = owners of the salt springs), which leased the salt springs to the landgraves of Hesse in 1535. In 1929, Soo-

Graduation House, a salt brine structure

Kirchstraße: Fine half-timbered houses

den and Allendorf, now Prussian, were united, becoming Bad Sooden-Allendorf.

What to See and Do

1. The town of **Allendorf** is a gem of Hessian-Thuringian half-timbered construction. The consistent appearance of the town of Allendorf is largely due to its almost complete destruction by the Croatians in 1637. The **half-timbered façades** in the Schusterstraße, Ackerstraße, Weberstraße and in the Kirchstraße are nearly perfectly preserved. The *Bürger-Haus*, a three-storey timber-framed building from 1639, the *Eschstruth-Haus*, which originated in the years 1640–42, and the *Kraus-Haus* from the second half of the 17th century are great examples of medieval timber-framed houses.

Inside the **Town Church St. Crucis** (Holy Cross), with its high bell tower from the year 1424 and multi-leveled roof there is a Baroque altar and the splendidly decorated pulpit by H. Edinger (1684).

2. North of the town lies **Heiliggeisthospital** (Holy Spirit Hospital), first mentioned in 1363,

whose Gothic chapel has valuable murals that have been preserved from the 14th–15th centuries.

3. Well worth seeing in **Sooden** district are parish *church St. Mary*, renovated in the 17th–18th centuries, with its Baroque furnishings, the former Salt Office from 1782, the *Pfennigstube* (penny parlor, the former customs and tax office) of 1631, the picturesque Söder Gate (1704–05), in which the *Salt Museum* is housed, as well as numerous half-timbered houses from the 17th–19th centuries.

4. A walk through the landscaped **Kurpark** of Bad Sooden should include the *Fountain Square*, the picturesque *Weinreihe Street* and

Thieves' Tower (Diebesturm)

Church St. Mary: Baroque Organ

Söder Gate (Salt Museum)

Söder Gate with the Salt Museum, the *Gradierwerk* (graduation house), which serves as open air inhalation site, dates originally from 1638. It is a great place to relax with a good book and breathe in the salty air. Adjacent to it is the **Werratal Therme** (thermal brine baths), where you can get healthy in body, mind and soul.

5. In a scenic location high above the Werra River southeast of the twin towns is **Rothestein** Castle. The Baron of Gilsa had the pretty castle built in 1891 in neo-Gothic building style (extension in 1911). From the terrace of the castle there is a wonderful panoramic view of the Werra and the saga and fairy tale filled **High Meißner**.

Witzenhausen

Fairy Tale and Literary References

Jacob Grimm, along with fellow Göttingen professors Dahlmann and Gervinius, who had been relieved of their positions and expelled from Göttingen because of their protests against the constitutional violations of the new Hanoverian king, Ernest August, arrived in the

Cherry Blossom

Hessian town of Witzenhausen on December 17th, 1837 and spent the night in the Gasthaus *Zur Krone*. They were greeted on an icy day by almost 300 students from Göttingen on the Werra Bridge who led them in a triumphal parade to the town hall, where an impressive rally took place.

In saga matters, a legend about the construction of Ludwigstein was included in the third volume of the Brothers Grimm *German Sagas*; their brother Ferdinand Grimm transcribed the short saga, the *String of Pearls of*

Frau Holle. Another, more rustic, saga by Philipp Hoffmeister is the one about *The Exodus of the Gnomes* from the castle mountain near Ermschwerd.

The writer Ernest Koch (1808–58) lived in a house next to the old Werra Bridge between the ages of eight and fourteen and described his school days in the fictional Lenzbach (Witzenhausen) in his novel *Prince Rosa-Stramin*.

History

A Frankish estate was the origin for the development of Witzenhausen, which was a legal fiefdom in possession of the landgraves of Thuringia after 1180. The town of *witczenhusin* received its market rights under Ludwig IV of Thuringia and became a town in in 1225. As a result of a war of succession between Hesse and Thuringia, Witzenhausen fell to Henry I of Hesse in 1264. The town came into possession of a family branch of the landgraves of Hesse-Rotenburg and remained there until they died out in the year 1834.

The Ludwigstein was erected on a steep mountain ridge by the Landgrave Ludwig I of

The historic old Werra Bridge

Hesse in 1415 to protect the Hessian border against the neighboring Hanstein Castle belonging to the archbishop of Mainz on the other side of the Werra. It was the permanent seat of an administrator.

The Berlepsch Castle on the border of Hesse and Lower Saxony has been the property of the lords of Berlepsch since the Middle Ages. It was built as a castle in 1368–69 by Arnold von Berlepsch after the destruction of their family seat, Barlissen. Castle Berlepsch attained its present design after some considerable late 19th century historical renovation projects.

Berlepsch Castle, according to a broadcast survey the most beautiful castle in Hesse

What to See and Do

The town of Witzenhausen lies in the middle of one of the oldest and largest cherry orchard areas in Germany. The mild climate of this location directly on the Werra River allows the approximately 150,000 cherry trees around the town to blossom spectacularly.

1. For lovers of fairy tales and sagas, the most fascinating attraction in the Witzenhausen region may well be the picturesque castle site **Berlepsch Castle** (14th–19th centuries) located about eight miles north of the town. In a 2012 Hessian broadcast survey, Berlepsch Castle was elected by viewers as the most beautiful castle in Hesse. This gem has everything that is expected of a fairy castle: a **castle lord** in its 20th generation, **fortifications** with towers, battlements, fortified walls, castle, dungeon. It is hardly surprising that even Goethe visited the castle in 1801. The castle has an annual calendar of events to entertain both children and adults.

2. In the **old town** of Witzenhausen there are excellent examples of half-timbered buildings from the Gothic period and the Renaissance: German House (1480), Stone House (1584), Gasthaus *Zur Krone* (around 1605), the houses Ermschwerder Str. 4 (1579) and 17 (1511), and

Town Hall Square

Knight Isenbard on a torch-light patrol (Fackelrundgang) through the historic old town of Witzenhausen

on the market square the houses No. 4 (1606), and 5 (around 1600).

Other notable buildings are the picturesque **Liebfrauenkirche** (Church of Our Lady – 14th–16th centuries), *St. Michael's Chapel* (1392), the Renaissance *town hall, the Wilhelmiten Abbey* (site of the Department of Organic Agricultural Sciences, University of Kassel), remnants of the double fortification of 13th–14th centuries with *Diebesturm* (Thief's tower) and *Eulenturm* (Owl's Tower) and the historic *Werra Bridge*.

3. Worthwhile destinations in the town are also the **Ethnographic Museum**, the tropical **greenhouse** and the tobacco factory with **tobacco museum.**

4. Of value in the legendary district of **Ermschwerd** (Exodus of the Gnomes) is the *domain* with its manor house dating from the 16th century.

Just a few miles away in the Ziegenhagen District lies the *theme park Ziegenhagen* with its car and motorcycle museum.

Ludwigstein Castle, erected in 1415 to protect the Hessian border (see Heilbad Heiligenstadt)

5. Very popular with visitors is the picturesque **Ludwigstein**, just some miles northwest of Witzenhausen, with its high, round castle keep; three residential wings group around a narrow rectangular inner courtyard. Not only beautiful to look at Ludwigstein Castle keeps also alive the memory of the very interesting history of the youth movement (the castle houses the archives of the *German Youth Movement*). Shortly before World War I, on the 11th–12th October 1913, about two thousand students, health educators, scouts, poets, naturalists and hikers of the First Free German Youth, met on the Meißner Mountain. The participants of this legendary meeting objected to any German jingoism and stood for peace and living in harmony with nature.

Mackenrode

Fairy Tale and Saga References

Located on the German Fairy Tale Route in Thuringia, the community of Mackenrode has a real gem in her Fairy Tale Park where young and old can dive into the world of fairy tales of the Brothers Grimm.

For friends of sagas there is a legendary place in Mackenrode – the Crown Mill. As recorded by the Eichsfeld teacher Schneppe, the story holds that *the owner of the Crown mill had plowed a neighboring wooded valley. Suddenly he was being followed by a large snake that wore a shining crown on its head. The man fled to his home and locked the door. The snake, however, put the crown down in front of the threshold and disappeared into the forest. The miller stored the crown in his house.*

Another version relates how *the Crown Miller was plowing near his mill. Suddenly he*

View of Mackenrode

Fairy Tale Park

came upon a hard object. He stooped down and all at once a brilliant crown came to light. No sooner had he picked it up than an ugly snake wriggled out of the hole he had made in the ground. The hissing snake chased the miller. Reaching his yard gate, he closed it rapidly behind him smashing the snake's head. He retained the crown in high honor.

History

The first mention of Mackenrode occurred in 1236, when the Archbishop Siegfried of Mainz granted it to the lords of Hanstein as a tithe. In the Middle Ages, Mackenrode was one of the villages in the territory of the Hanstein where court was held.

When feuds erupted into serious warfare in 1424 between the Lords of Hanstein and the Free Imperial Town of Mühlhausen, Mackenrode burned down. In secular terms, Mackenrode belonged until 1848 to the High Court of Hanstein, religiously, however, to the realm of Kirchgandern.

In the 20th century, Mackenrode and its surroundings experienced the end of Second World War and the division of Germany into occupation zones in dramatic fashion. Mackenrode found itself directly on the demarcation line between the Soviet and American occupation zones. The major north-south railroad between Göttingen to Bad Hersfeld (American zone) crossed into the Soviet Zone, where trains were repeatedly stopped and checked. As a result of the *Wanfried Agreement* of September 15, 1945, which was negotiated, according to a rumor, with whiskey and vodka, there was an exchange of territory. The trains traveling on the "Whiskey-Vodka-line" now passed exclusively through the American zone. The previously Thuringian villages of Neuseesen and Werleshausen were added to the American zone, while the Hessian villages Asbach, Hennigerode, Sickenberg, Vatterode and Weidenbach all became part of the Soviet zone.

The two villages of Hennigerode and Weidenbach now belonged to Mackenrode. Because of their proximity to the border near the restricted area, visits to either were permitted only after the granting of a request led to police authorization. For Mackenrode and its two districts, the Iron Curtain lifted only after the peaceful East German revolution in November of 1989.

Fairy Tale Park

What to See and Do

1. Winding past the fabled **Crown Mill**, which is still in operation today, the road passes through the valley landscape of the so-called Eichsfeld Switzerland, uphill towards Mackenrode. Due to its well-maintained local image, Mackenrode is one of the most beautiful villages in the Eichsfeld area (see Heilbad Heiligenstadt).

2. The free **Fairy Tale Park** contains fairy tale characters and fairy tales houses from tales of the Brothers Grimm: Hansel and Gretel, the Wolf and the Seven Little Kids, Rapunzel, the Frog King, among others. There is also a fairy tale hill, an entrance to a small mine, a fairy tale tunnel and a bakery with a huge oven.

The neo-Gothic St. Martin's Church

3. The neo-Gothic **St. Martin's Church** with its tower surrounded by half-timbered gables and verdant ivy provides a popular photo location. The remarkable high altar inside the Catholic church dates from the Baroque period. The neat half-timbered houses of Mackenrode were built in the 19th and 20th centuries.

4. The Protestant church of St. Martin in the district Weidenbach was built in 1883.

5. The **Border Museum Schifflersgrund** is located on the death strip at the former German-German border in the neighboring village of Asbach-Sickenberg, about seven kilometers from Mackenrode. This is on the border between Thuringia and Hesse and, before 1990, formed the inpenetrable border between NATO and the Warsaw Pact alliance. It emphasizes the effects of the Cold War division of Germany. In addition to the original boundary line facilities, there are military vehicles from East and West, helicopters and an exhibit describing the living conditions during the Cold War era.

Heilbad Heiligenstadt

When the German Fairy Tale Route was established in 1975, Heilbad Heiligenstadt was not in the original roster of towns for a very simple reason: it was then part of the German Democratic Republic (East Germany), just kilometers behind the fences and guard towers of that Warsaw Pact nation. Due to the sensitive nature of the Cold War border, the citizens of Heilbad Heiligenstadt could visit neither Göttingen, less than 30 kilometers to the northwest, nor the nearby ruins of Hanstein Castle, though also in East Germany. Under the instigation of the former leader of the Tourist Information, Marie-Theres Nolte, after the reunification of Germany in 1990, however, Heilbad Heiligen-

St. Martin's Church and Baroque Gardens

stadt took its place on the German Fairy Tale Route on February 22, 1993.

Fairy Tale and Cultural-Literary References

On April 20, 1838, just months after their removal from their academic positions as part of the Göttingen Seven expulsion (see Göttingen) Jacob and Wilhelm Grimm met with family members in Heiligenstadt, where the publisher Karl Reimer and Solomon Hirzel from Leipzig negotiated with them about the publication of a *German Dictionary.* Jacob Grimm later described this meeting to Friedrich Christoph Dahlmann, his co-conspirator of the Göttingen Seven, as a *sweet time together in Heiligenstadt.*

The fairy tale *The Drummer,* said to have been told to the Brothers Grimm by an Eichsfelder rag picker, has appeared as number 193 since the 5th edition of the *Children's and Household Tales* came out in 1843. The rich treasure of sagas of the Eichsfeld area that belongs partly today to Thuringia and partly to Lower Saxony was collected and published by the teacher and local colorist, Karl Wüstefeld (1857–1937).

Heinrich Heine Park: Waterfall

In Eichsfeld the citizens of Heiligenstadt are nicknamed *carrot kings,* and here is how it came to pass: *"Once upon a time the town of Heiligenstadt was under siege. A sudden alert from the sentinels on the Old Church Tower did not give all the gatekeepers enough time to bolt the town gates. One of them could not locate his wooden bolt and, in desperation, used a large carrot, which was later eaten by a hungry goat. When the assailants attacked the*

The Carrot King

town a short time later, they were surprised to find the gate unbolted and easily penetrated into Heiligenstadt."

The carver and sculptor Tilman Riemenschneider (ca. 1460–1531) was born in Heiligenstadt in the *Claus Mill.* Anyone who has traveled the *Romantic Road* has seen his famous wooden altarpieces in Rothenburg ob der Tauber or Creglingen.

Heinrich (born Harry) Heine (1797–1856), one of Germany's most famous writers, *Germany: a Winter Fairy Tale* and *Harz Journey,* converted from Judaism to Lutheranism and was baptized in Heiligenstadt in June 1825 while still an unknown legal student at Göttingen university.

In the *Theodor Storm Literature Museum* in the Mainz House just below St. Martin's Church, the life and work of the writer and poet Theodor Storm (1817–88) is honored. From 1856–64 he worked as county judge in Heiligenstadt and wrote eight novellas there (among them *Veronika*), three fairy tales, and countless poems. In 1870, he wrote a remembrance of the jail across from his residence in Heiligenstadt, the novella *Pole Poppenspäler.*

Theodor Storm Monument

History

The town Heilbad Heiligenstadt, literally *Healing Bath-Holy Town*, has its earliest documented reference in 973. Around 1000, the village of Heiligenstadt, now promoted to town status, was acquired by the archbishop of Mainz, a fact that strongly impacted the town and its county, Eichsfeld. Eichsfeld County, a Teutonic district mentioned under the description *land of oaks* as early as 897, was governed from Heiligenstadt, where an emissary from the archbishopric of Mainz lived.

The effects of the Lutheran Reformation (Luther spent time at the Wartburg in nearby

Castle of the Elector of Mainz (1736-38), Kurmainzer Schloss

Eisenach) were later reversed in Heiligenstadt after the Peace of Augsburg (Sept 25, 1555) established the principle *cuius regio, eius religio* (Loosely: Whoever owns the region determines the religion) that put the decision of state confession into the hands of the ruling prince or town council. In 1575, a Jesuit college was established that remained until 1773. In 1802, Heiligenstadt and all of Eichsfeld fell to the Prussians and five years later became capital of the Harz Region of the newly created Napoleonic Kingdom of Westphalia.

After the Congress of Vienna (1815), the Upper Eichsfeld area became part of the Prussian province of Saxony where it remained until the division of Germany after the end of the Second World War. Following German reunification on October 3, 1990, it was placed in the State of Thuringia and the former counties of Heiligenstadt and Worbis were merged into the new Eichsfeld adminstrative district. Heiligenstadt was selected as its capital.

Fairy Tale Park

What to See and Do

1. Friends of fairy tales, whether young or old, will enjoy the small Fairy Tale Park of Heiligenstadt (near the Vitalpark) with its focus on the fairy tale world of the Brothers Grimm.

Take a trip around the **town**, viewing the old and new town halls and walking past numerous old half-timbered buildings including the **Claus Mill** where Tilman Riemenschneider was born.

2. Tour the **three Gothic churches** of St. Martin, St. Mary, and St. Aegidien to determine which of the three is Protestant in confession. Then refresh yourself at the seven-meter high waterfall near the town center.

3. Visit the **Theodor Storm Literary Museum** in the Mainz House to learn more about this very important German literary figure. Finally, have a look at the *Eichsfeld County Museum* inside the former Jesuit college.

The ruins of Hanstein Castle

4. If you want some rest and relaxation, visit the Vitalpark (Wellness and Beauty) with its **Eichsfeld Therme** (thermal brine baths).

5. Take an excursion to the ruins of **Hanstein Castle**. These heralded castle ruins have been around since 862 and rise attractively above the nearby village of Bornhagen on a volcanic cone near the border of Thuringia and Hesse. The romantic structure, often destroyed and established in its current form after the year 1308, attracted students and professors alike from the University of Göttingen, including the Brothers Grimm, Heinrich Heine, Alexander von Humboldt and Carl Friedrich Gauss.

The Brothers Grimm as well as Johann Wolfgang von Goethe are said to have spent nights in the historical Klausenhof beneath the castle, still a functioning Gasthof.

King Dagobert Founds Heiligenstadt

(Ferdinand Grimm – English version: Thomas L. Johnson)

Not far from Heiligenstadt in Eichsfeld lies the steep Rusteberg peak upon which the knights of Rusteberg, who were often at war with their neighboring castles Hanstein and Ludwigstein, are said to have lived centuries ago.

Once upon a time a pilgrim from a foreign land took refuge atop Rusteberg. That pilgrim was Dagobert, the King of the Franks. Suffering from leprosy, he had been instructed by an angel in a dream to go to Germany in order to find a cure for his dreaded disease. After doing many good works, including endowing a cloister in the name of the holy Dionysius, laying him in a gold and jewel encrusted casket, and then spending time at the mountain castle of Isenberg in Alsatia as well as in the cloister Hülfensberg between Geismar in Eichsfeld and Wanfried in Hesse, he reached Rusteberg. The residents of this castle, however, saw through the camouflage of the riches that he brought with him and robbed him, forcing him to flee for his life.

The king came into the region of Heiligenstadt, rested on a beautiful plateau, then built a solid castle there and inhabited it.

One day Dagobert rode off into the valley on a hunt. Overcome by fatigue, he got down from his horse, laid himself down in the tall grass and fell asleep. As he awoke, he felt incredibly refreshed from the dew of the flowers that bathed him and felt that his pains had been greatly diminished. He returned again to this place and the disease disappeared.

The king gave thanksgiving to heaven and named the site where he had received such wonderful healing, *heilige stätte*, the holy site. He had a cloister built there and gave it the name *Heiligenstätte* (Heiligenstadt) and around it the town was built.

Dagobert's castle near the town was called the Old Castle. The Rusteburg fell later in battle with Hanstein and Ludwigstein.

Ebergötzen

Ebergötzen in the Aue Valley is the adminstrative center of the joint community of Radolfshausen.

Humorist Wilhelm Busch

A reminder of the close historical linkages between Radolfshausen and Ebergötzen is the Herrenmühle (mill of the lords), widely known as the Wilhelm-Busch-Mill. Wilhelm Busch (1832–1908), renowned author of the *Max and Moritz* series, came to the village of Ebergötzen as a nine-year-old, where he lived in the rectory with his uncle, Pastor Kleine, from 1841–46, receiving private lessons in writing, arithmetic and drawing. A close, lifelong friendship linked the painter, illustrator, humorist and poet Wil-

European Bread Museum: Post Mill (1812)

Wilhelm-Busch Mill: Where Max and Moritz concocted their pranks

helm Busch with Erich Bachmann (1832–1907), the son of the miller of the Herrenmühle that Busch visited every year and *where he always quickly fell asleep to the rumbling of the mill-work and the rushing of water.* In his *Max and Moritz* tales, Tailor Böck fell into the water behind the mill in Ebergötzen as Max and Moritz concocted their pranks in the village. No German humorist has captured the affection of smaller and larger readers so enduringly as Wilhelm Busch (see also Wiedensahl).

History

The bailiwick of Radolfshausen with the villages of Ebergötzen, Landolfshausen and Falkenhagen was an old Guelph fiefdom in the hands of the dukes of Grubenhagen, from whom the nobles of Plesse acquired the district in the 14th century. To secure the fiefdom, the noblemen of the fief built a moated castle in 1508, of which the three-story residential tower still stands today. After the noble line of Plesse died out in the 16th century, the landgraves of Hesse wanted to claim the bailiwick of

The entrance of the European Bread Museum

Radolfshausen for themselves, but they failed due to opposition from the Guelph dukes.

What to See and Do

1. Awaken or create childhood memories in the **Wilhelm-Busch-Mill**. In the last escapade of the rapscallion story *Max and Moritz* one hears, *"Give me that! – Up, into the funnel."* And the miller shakes the villains (Max and Moritz) and they are ground up in the mill. The Wilhelm-Busch-Mill is not just the same as it was in the days of Max and Moritz, but it is also the same as it was when grain was ground and flour was milled.

2. The former bailiwick of Radolfshausen in Ebergötzen, with its triple residential tower (1508), a water mill, built in the Tyrol (in 1600), and a trestle windmill from Hotteln (1812), houses the **European Bread Museum** where the 5000-year history of bread is shown in a cultural-historical exhibit that traces the history, arts, culture and customs of this *staff of life.*

Third Trick – Tailer Böck falls into the stream

(Wilhelm Busch – English version: E. Michael Iba /Thomas L. Johnson)

For miles around his little town
Was Tailor Böck of some renown.
For week-day coats, and Sunday skirts,
Bob-tails, swallow-tails, finest shirts,
Gaiters, breeches, hunting jackets;
Waistcoats, with big, roomy pockets, –
So many things to really mention,
Claimed completely Böck's attention.
For, if clothing needed mending
Darning, shortening or extending,
Piecing, patching, – if a button
Needed to be fixed or put on, –
Anything of any kind,
Anywhere, before, behind, –
Master Böck could make it whole,
That seemed to warm his very soul.

Therefore all those in the township
Formed with him the closest friendship.
But Max and Moritz began to plan
Ways to annoy this kindly man.
Right before the tailor's dwelling
Ran a swift stream, roaring, swelling.
This swift stream a bridge did span.
And the road across it ran.

Max and Moritz not awed at all
Were rather busy with a saw:
Ritze-ratze! So it ran!
Sawed a gap across the span.
When this evil deed was done
The village heard them making fun

"Hallo, there! Come out, you buck
Tailor, Tailor, muck! muck! muck!"
Böck could bear all sorts of jeers,
And let them fall around his ears;
But this insult roused such anger,
That he could not take it longer.
Yard-stick grasping, out he darted,
Becoming deeply brokenhearted;
With each and every frightful jeer,
"Muck! muck! muck!" rang loud and clear.
Onto the bridge he quickly bounded;
Crash! beneath his weight it sounded.
Once more round of cries: "Muck! muck!"
In, head over heels, plumps poor Böck!
While the scared boys ran skedaddling,
Up the stream came two geese paddling.
With a death-grip, does Böck grasp
The legs of both as they swim past,
And, with both geese well in hand,
Flutters out onto dry land.
Once he found himself ashore
He truly wished for something more
For it seemed poor tailor Böck
Ached from his belly to his neck
Noble Mrs. Böck! She quickly rises
Fully equal to this crisis;
Hot iron pressed against his chest
The icy cold did she arrest.
Soon 'twas out the mouths of men,
All through town: "Böck's back again!"

Bovenden

Fairy Tale and Saga References

The many legends of Plesse Castle and its inhabitants, such as *The Incredible Depth of Plesse Well* or *How the Beautiful Adelaide of Plesse was Kidnapped by the Lords of Hardenberg* establish Bovenden's linkage to the German Fairy Tale Route.

Two publications address the sagas of Bovenden, namely a doctoral dissertation by Gudrun Keindorf, *Wege der Überlieferung. Zu Funktions- und Bedeutungswandel der "Sagen" von der Burg Plesse (Methods of Transmission. Concerning the Functions and Changes of Meanings in the "Sagas" on the Plesse Castle)* as well as a small collection of Carl Heinz Kurz, *Bovender Sagen.*

Plesse Castle: Aerial View

With *The Swanrings of Plesse* and *The Silent People of Plesse,* the Brothers Grimm published two Plesse sagas in their *German Sagas.*

Panoramic View

History

The market town of Bovenden and its associated districts of Harste and Lenglern can look back over a thousand years of history. Reyershausen, Oberbillingshausen and Spanbeck lay in the dominion of the lords of Plesse, which came into Hessian feudal relationship in 1447. After the extinction of the family in 1571, the control of Plesse and its territory fell to the landgraves of Hesse. Only in 1816 did an exchange transfer rule to the kingdom of Hanover.

The locales of Emmenhausen, Harste and Lenglern however, were always integral parts of the Guelph domain. The old villages of Plesse still belong to the Reformed confession, in contrast to the Lutheranism of the neighboring villages. By 1600, the landgraves of Hesse-Kassel bestowed market and brewing rights upon Bovenden. That exceeded the normal framework justified for village rights and elevated Bovenden to the status of a market town.

What to See and Do

1. Mentioned in documents for the first time in 1015, **Plesse Castle** rises over Bovenden on a

Plesse: Castle Keep

Former secondary residence (1777) of the landgraves of Hesse-Rotenburg

highly visible mountain spur. With its protected front court, courtyard, knight's building and seventy-five foot high castle keep, the ruins make it one of the most important hill-forts in southern Lower Saxony. In 1801, Goethe was inspired by his visit there to compose a poem.

2. A recommended hike from Plesse is to **Hünstollen** (423 m – with look-out tower), three consecutive ridges as well as to *Hainburg*, where one finds is the largest contiguous yew forest in Germany.

3. An impressive historical monument from Hessian times is the **Bovenden building** of the former Lower Saxon forest district office (privately owned) that was erected as a secondary residence of the landgraves of Hesse-Rotenburg in 1777.

4. Located in the center of Harste is the former domain (18th century) with office house and four outbuildings as well as a church from the 18th century.

Hann. Münden

Fairy Tale and Literary References

The town is best known for its connection to the infamous Doktor Johann Andreas Eisenbart (1663–1727). This traveling physician of the late 17th and early 18th centuries has actually seen

his reputation improve over time. During his lifetime, he was regarded as a quack whose cures were always permanent; now he is seen as a gifted physician-surgeon.

For the Brothers Grimm, Hann. Münden was distance-wise halfway between Kassel and Göttingen, two of their most important locales. The three-river town was a stopover for them where they occasionally ate lunch and met up with friends, such as the professors Hugo Müller or

The researcher and geographer Alexander von Humboldt (1769–1859) is said to have described Hann. Münden as one of the seven most beautifully situated towns in the world

Well-tended half-timbered houses

Benecke. The steep Mündener Mountain, which the painter-brother Ludwig Emil Grimm drew, was a transportation challenge on the way.

Hann. Münden was for a long time the residence of the renowned Grimm researcher, Ludwig Denecke (1905–96), author of *Jacob Grimm and His Brother Wilhelm* and director of the *Murhard Library of the City of Kassel and* the *Provincial Library* as well as Director of the *Brothers Grimm Museum* in Kassel. Denecke was the publisher of the research series *Remembering the Brothers Grimm* that has appeared regularly since 1963.

Born in Hann. Münden was the antiquities researcher, Georg Friedrich Grotefend (1775–1853) who first decoded the old-Persian alphabet in 1802. Also hailing from Hann. Münden is the field researcher and publisher of countless fairy tale collections, Alfred Cammann (1909–2008), *Folk Tale World of Prussian Country; German Folk Tales from Russia and Romania.*

History

Hann. Münden was probably founded around 1170 by Henry the Lion or the Hessian-Thurin-

The Old Town Hall (Weser Renaissance Style) and its magnificent entrance portal

gian dynasty of Ludowinger. Conveniently located on the confluence of the Fulda, Werra, and Weser Rivers, the town received its town charter at the end of the 12th century. The early wealth of the town derived from what is called the *Staple Right*, which existed between 1247– 1823. It allowed the locals to unload and purchase the goods that were heading upstream at cost. This explains the Weser Renaissance features of the town including its wealth of half-timbered houses and the old Town Hall. From 1488–1585 the town was the permanent residence of the Duchy of Calenberg-Göttingen that became, with the addition of other territories, the Electorate of Hanover and, following the Congress of Vienna in 1814, the Kingdom of Hanover.

Hann. Münden was planned with a grid pattern; it is largely intact despite the ravages of the Thirty Years War (1626, conquest and plunder by Tilly and his troups), the Seven Years War as well as in the Napoleonic Era.

On the Weser, north of Hann. Münden, lies the picturesque Cloister Bursfelde, a Benedictine Abbey founded in the year 1093. In the 15th century, the abbey was the center of an important cloistral reform movement, *the Bursfelde Congregation* that brought over 100 clois-

Doktor Eisenbart at his practice

ters of middle Europe (among others Maria Laach, Alpirsbach) into association. Since the Reformation, the cloister is Protestant; preserved are the Romanesque basilica and the west wing that was transformed into a farm house in 1722, later restored and now serves as a religious conference center.

What to See and Do

In Hann. Münden with its 700 half-timbered houses and remarkable river setting, we encounter a town which the scientific researcher and geographer Alexander von Humboldt is said to have described as *one of the seven most beautifully situated towns in the world.* Originally called simply *Münden* (mouth) in reference to its location at the point where the Werra and Fulda Rivers flow together and become the Weser River, it now uses the abbreviated form of Hannoversch Münden, a legacy of the time it spent as part of the Kingdom of Hanover.

1. Wander in the footsteps of **Doktor Eisenbart** through Hann. Münden. Lead and go to his little office hours small consultations at the Town Hall (Rathaus Lower Hall) (Saturdays 1:30 pm, 15 minutes, free entrance). The middle part of this **magnificent town hall**, significantly redesigned into a significant example of **Weser Renaissance** architecture from the 1603–18, was originally Gothic.

Listen to the Doktor Eisenbart *carillon* located on the colorful north side of the town hall (played daily at noon, 3:00 and 5:00 pm), pass the house at *Lange Straße 79* where

Guelf Castle

Doktor Eisenbart died and walk to *St. Aegidienkirche* to see his grave marker on the north side of the church. Visit the new theatrical spectacle about Doktor Eisenbart in Hann. Münden, "WHAT A MAN – Doktor Eisenbart," a modern staging in the impressive ambiance of the historic Packhof warehouse. Additionally, there are daily costumed tours by "Doktor Eisenbart" and his crew through the historic old town of Hann. Münden during the summer months.

2. The **historic town center** of Hann. Münden is a gem: visit the church of *St. Blaise* (13th–16th centuries) and the numerous **half-timbered houses** including the Ochsenkopf (1528), the Deanery (1570–80) and the oldest *sexton's house* (Küsterhaus) in Lower Saxony built in 1457, with its well-preserved carved wood reliefs.

3. The superb **Guelph Castle**, reconstructed in the *Weser Renaissance* Style after a fire in 1560, was previously the residence of the dukes of Brunswick-Lüneburg. Today it is headquarters of the community administrators and the **municipal museum.** Highlights inside the mu-

The former Cloister Bursfelde (12th century)

seum, which contains a valuable collection Mündener faience, are the *Roman Chamber* (1574), and the *Chamber of the White Horse* (1562).

4. Follow the *Traces of Water* in three central squares where water was brought into the town in an artistic form. The *Hanover World Exhibition Expo 2000* recognized this project.

5. The **river setting** is perfect for a canoe, boat or rafting trip on one of the three rivers (Werra, Fulda, Weser) that Hann. Münden claims.

6. Take a walk into the abundant forests of Reinhardswald, Bramwald and Kaufunger Wald that surround Hann. Münden or cycle along the Weser River to the former **Cloister Bursfelde** (12th century). There are late Gothic murals in the main room of the abbot's church.

Doctor Ironbeard

(Traditional – English version: Thomas L. Johnson)

I am the Doctor Ironbeard
Applying cures you may have heard
That help the blind to walk again,
The lame to see like other men.

While in Wimpfen for a birth
Brought a child out to this earth
The neck of whom I gently broke
The mother died to her great luck.

In Potsdam I was called to treat
The cook of Frederick the Great
With a maul I hit his head
He chose to die in his own bed.

In Ulm I cured a bleeding man
Whose leg was red with blood that ran.
He wished a shot to help him heal,
I pierc'd him with a shaft of steel.

To the sextant's son in Dideldum
I gave ten pounds of opium.
Day and night he lay at rest
And snoozes still I must confess.

From Langensalz there came a man
Whose goiter weighed almost a ton;
I wrapped it with a hay cord tight
Probatum est, he sleeps just right.

To Prague, I took an ailing crone,
from her body took ten tons of stone;
a tombstone was the final word,
you see she was completely cured.

In Vienna town I cured forsooth
A man who had a hollow tooth.
I shot it out with my own gun
Dear God, the pain was quickly done.

My all-time-favorite masterwork
Was made one time in Osnabrück
Gout ridden were the feet of an old guy
I simply cut his legs away.

This is the way I dispense my cure
I give my word, you can be sure,

That every treatment has its effect –
I swear that by my doctor's hat.

Refrain

I am the Doctor Ironbeard,
Viddeviddevitt bumm bumm!
Applying cures you may have heard,
Viddeviddevitt bumm bumm!
That help the blind to walk again,
The lame to see like other men.
Viddeviddevitt yuch hairassa,
Viddeviddevitt bumm bumm.

Grebenstein

Fairy Tale and Saga References

The sagas of Grebenstein tell of the construction of the *maiden's tower* (Jungfernturm), of the *Crossstone*, of the *cress well* (Kressenbrunnen) out of which the babies of Grebenstein allegedly arrive and of castle hill (Burgberg). There are two sagas about castle hill, the first one about an *enchanted virgin* and the second one about a *white virgin*, whose appearances are said to signal that something very good or very bad is about to occur in Grebenstein.

The character representing Grebenstein on the German Fairy Tale Route is the *Goose Girl* from the *Children's and Household Tales* of the Brothers Grimm.

Burgberg: the ruins of the legendary castle

Panoramic View of Grebenstein

History

Grebenstein owes its 13th century origin to a conflict between the archbishopric of Mainz and the landgraves of Hesse. The nucleus of Grebenstein was the castle built on a steep mountain in 1266 by Count Ludolf of Dassel V, the castle was later sold to the Landgrave Henry I of Hesse in 1297. Plans were made about this time for an urban settlement; a mayor and council were first documented in 1322. The so-called Freedom (New Town) was built between this settlement (Old Town) and the castle in the Esse Valley in 1356 and the Old Town and New Town were unified in 1370. With assistance of the landgraves, an exceptionally strong town wall with thirteen towers was erected. The construction of the major Gothic town church took place during this time.

The Maiden's Tower

With nearly 2,000 inhabitants, Grebenstein was a prosperous town in the 16th century. The Thirty Years War brought death and destruction when Croatians looted, pillaged and plundered the town in 1637, burning 242 town houses, the church, the town hall and the school. Few more than 600 inhabitants remained in Grebenstein at the end of the war. The Seven Years War opened new wounds and the town was slow to recover.

What to See and Do

1. The most prominent building in Grebenstein, the **town church** (around 1355), has a rich décor (14th–17th centuries). Next to it is the stately **town hall** (14th–18th centuries) a free standing building with a half-timbered upper level.

2. Rambling through the streets and byways of Grebenstein, one will discover four Gothic stone chambers and numerous 15th through 18th centuries **half-timbered houses** of Diemel-Saxon design (among them the oldest in North Hesse from 1428). The Leck House (1431), one of the earliest examples of a Low German farming community house and currently the local museum (Heimatmuseum), has a place in architectural history.

The Town Hall

3. The **town wall** from the 14th century, in places over 19 feet tall, remains mostly intact and surrounds historic Grebenstein.

Just outside the town wall is the *Hagemühle*, an old mill, mentioned in documents for the first time in 1429. This mill is still working and worth a visit.

4. Though highly visible, only the four-story palace walls remain of the **castle hill** whose

Aerial View of Burguffeln (Church, Manor House etc.)

location outside the town walls allowed it to be destroyed by Bavarian troops in 1626; abandoned since 1641, it is supposed to be a storied place.

5. The ancestral residence of the von Uffeln family in today's *Burguffeln* district is now state domain: 16th century manor house, 1752 Tenants' House, mid-13th century church.

Hofgeismar

Town of the Sleeping Beauty

Fairy Tale and Saga References

If you are looking for *Sleeping Beauty's Castle*, you need look no further than Sababurg Castle. Completed in 1334 in the green oak forest Reinhardswald, it has served both as a hunting palace of the Hessian landgraves and was the site of a 500-acre animal park as early as the 16th century. The thick thorny hedge that once surrounded it and the ancient still existing stone wall convinced people, as the Grimm's fairy tales became known and beloved in the 19th century, that Sababurg Castle was the actual castle of Sleeping Beauty.

Sababurg Castle, home of the Sleeping Beauty

Monument:
The Dice Tower Saga

Located between Kassel and Göttingen, Sababurg is closest to Hofgeismar, a town that has made its own rich contributions to the world of the fairy tale and saga. First is Dorothea Viehmann, née Pierson (see Baunatal), the storyteller who contributed so many of the eventual Grimms' tales, who was a direct descendant of the Huguenot colony of Hofgeismar-Schöneberg through her father Johann Friedrich Isaac Pierson (1734–98) and her namesake and godmother, Catharina Dorothea Graff.

Born in Hofgeismar were the historian and saga collector Carl B.N. Falckenheiner (1798–1842), the pastor and later lecturer at the University of Marburg Ludwig F. W. Boette (1862–1932), considered the founder of scientific folklore in Hesse who also assembled a number of Hessian fairy tales, legends and farces *(Folk Poetry in Hesse according to Fairy Tales, Legends and Songs),* as well as the fairy tale author Walter Iba (1915–85, *New Children's Fairy Tales*).

Others include cantor and regional writer Heinrich Rohde (1863–1946, *Weserwaves. His-*

Marketplace: Half-timbered Houses

tories and Sagas from the Area of the Upper Weser and Diemel), the headmaster and writer Adolf Häger (1892–1959, *The Rogue amidst the People)* and the teacher und museum director Helmut Burmeister (*1940, *Encounters in the Fairy Tale Forest. The Painter Theodor Rocholl and Reinhardswald*).

Of the numerous traditional Hofgeismar sagas (among them *The Goblins in Kelzer Mountain, the Wippe Pond*) there are two historical legends collected by Falckheiner almost 180 years ago of great importance in Hesse, namely *The Dice Tower* and *The Triple Roll* (Stutewecke). Since 1428 there is this tradition: On the Wednesday before Easter, the Stutewecken (white bread shaped into little figures) are distributed to the kindergarten and primary school children of Hofgeismar in the Old Town Church after a procession.

Little Schönburg Castle (1787-89), an important example of early German classicism

History

Hofgeismar lies just west of Reinhardswald (Reinhard's Forest). Likely founded as a Frankish royal residence, Hofgeismar belonged fairly early to the Archbishopric of Mainz and received its status as a municipality in 1223. Mortgaged in the 15th century to the Hessian landgrave, the town ultimately joined Hesse and became a Protestant center following the Reformation. After France exiled the Huguenots and Waldensians over their Protestant faith at the end of the 17th century, many of them moved to Hofgeismar to resettle in the colonies of Carlsdorf, Schöneberg, Kelze and later Friedrichsdorf.

It was the discovery of two mineral springs in the lower valley of the Lempe in 1639 that drew the frail and ill from all over in Germany to the miraculous therapeutic fountains in the hopes that these might heal their ailments. In the 18th century, the landgraves of Hesse-Kassel erected a cure and bath structure and the fountains turned into a regional bath.

Very old tree in the Primeval Forest of Sababurg

Sleeping Beauty and her Prince in the Primeval Forest of Sababurg

What to See and Do

One of the **highlights** of the German Fairy Tale Route is the saga-rich **Reinhardswald** with its natural **primeval forest preserve**. It includes the elector's hunting palace from 1829 in the Beberbeck division (today home for senior citizens), the **Sababurg Animal Park** designed in 1571 by Landgrave William IV (bred originals: bison, wild horses, tarpon) and, of course, the magical **Sababurg Castle**.

1. Visit **Sababurg Castle**, widely known as *Sleeping Beauty's* castle and grounds. Enjoy afternoon coffee in the castle and make a fairy tale circuit meeting Briar Rose (Sleeping Beauty) and her prince. Visit the rose garden with its 45 different types of roses.

It also ranks as one of the top three sites to hold a wedding in all of Germany according to *GEO magazine Saison*. Finally, wander down to the **animal park** or a bit further on to the **primeval forest** with its 600-year or more old oaks.

2. Worth visiting on an walk through the old town of **Hofgeismar** are the Old Town Church, a triple nave Romanesque-Gothic hall-church with its **altar** (1310), the Dean's Building and the **marketplace** with its half-timbered houses (16th–19th centuries), noting the flower shop with French, German, and Latin inscriptions, the New Town Church, the almost completely preserved town wall ring, the **Regional Museum** with its rich collections of Judaica, Huguenot bibles and paintings of the historical painter Theodor Rocholl (1854–1933), including landscapes and animal portraits from the region of Reinhardswald and the remarkable Apothecary Museum in a building from about 1200.

The Old Town Church, a Romanesque-Gothic Hall Church

Schöneberg: historic Huguenot House with French Inscription above the door

3. Gesundbrunnen: Ancient bathing facilities: Fountain House, adjacent baths (18th century) and inside the historic park little **Schönburg castle** (1787–89, today Evangelical Academy) which is regarded as one of the most important examples of early classicism in Germany.

4. Worthwhile destinations in the vicinity are the French **Huguenot half-timbered churches** in Carlsdorf, Schöneberg and Kelze.

5. In the town district of Hümme there are half-timbered houses from the 17th and 18th centuries and an 18th century church with a defensive tower from the Middle Ages.

The Disneyfication of Sleeping Beauty

Disneyfication is a pejorative term often used to describe the way Disney adapts real things into imaginary Disney objects. The castle of Sleeping Beauty is, as most know, the symbol of Disneyland and becomes the castle where Princess Aurora sleeps her less-than-100-year-Disney-sleep before being kissed awake by Prince Philip in the classic animation, Sleeping Beauty. Students of Disney tell us that their model for Sleeping Beauty's Castle is actually Neuschwanstein, the Bavarian castle built by mad King Ludwig II from 1869–86, not Sababurg Castle. Ludwig's castle, however, is a Wagnerian-inspired version of Wartburg Castle in Eisenach, Germany. So perhaps Jean Baudrillard is onto something when he writes: "Disneyland is presented as imaginary in order to make us believe that the rest is real, when in fact all of Los Angeles and the America surrounding it are no longer real, but of the order of the hyperreal and of simulation. It is no longer a question of a false representation of reality (ideology), but of concealing the fact that the real is no longer real, and thus saving the reality principle" (Baudrillard, p. 25).

And, of course, simulation wins, at least if one compares annual Disneyland visits (60 million) to those to Neuschwanstein (1.3 million) or Wartburg (500,000). Having visited all three, the American author can say that each has its fascination, not the least of which is the room in Wartburg where Martin Luther is reputed to have thrown an actual inkpot at the real devil.

All of which brings us to this dilemma: If Disney disneyfied Sleeping Beauty – and he certainly did – what do the Grimms do with the Sleeping Beauty Tale that Charles Perrault published in Paris in 1697? They rename it Dornröschen (Briar Rose) and actually create two versions, 1812–57, between which, according to Jack Zipes: "They eliminated erotic and sexual elements that might be offensive to middle-class morality, added numerous Christian expressions and references ..." (Zipes, The Brothers Grimm. From Enchanted Forests ..., p. 46). In fact, Perrault's tales emerge grimmified just as Perrault's and Grimm's are both eventually disneyfied. So when Sababurg Castle stakes its claim as the castle of the Grimms' Dornröschen (Briar Rose), that is precisely what it is, just as the Château d'Ussé in France is the castle of the Belle au Bois Dormant of Charles Perrault and Disney's dramatic remaking of Neuschwanstein is that of the animated heroine of Sleeping Beauty in 1959.

Trendelburg

Fairy Tale and Saga References

The castle of Trendelburg along with the Grimm fairy tale of *Rapunzel* makes the town of Trendelburg an intriguing location on the German Fairy Tale Route. Two Trendelburger Sagas *(The Water Sprite of the Diemel, The Sinkhole at Gottsbüren)* are included in the third volume of

Picturesque Trendelburg Castle

German Sagas of the Brothers Grimm. The giantess Trendula, who figures in five different sagas, is the source of the name of the castle and is featured in a huge statue located at the bridge over the Diemel River. Other well-known legends are *The Body of the Saviour in Gottsbüren* and *The Greening of the Pilgrim's Staff.*

History

Constructed in the 13th century by the counts of Schöneberg as a town with a castle, Trendelburg was managed since 1305 by an administrator employed equally by the bishop of Paderborn and the landgrave of Hesse. Due to its strategic importance as a ford on the old road of the Carolingians from Kassel to Bremen, the castle was a bone of contention between the bishop of Paderborn and Mainz and the landgrave of Hesse for decades. After a long war and protracted negotiations, it passed into Hessian possession in 1471. Trendelburg was awarded town rights by the landgrave one year later.

Gottsbüren was already mentioned as *buria* at the beginning of the 9th century. In 1329, word spread of a miracle, originating with drops of blood on the consecrated host, as well as the discovery of a dead man with the physical characteristics of Christ. Numerous pilgrims flocked to the sanctuary (built in 1331), which was under the patronage of the monastery Lippoldsberg (see Wahlsburg). The nearby castle of Sababurg (see Hofgeismar) was built with money donated for the protection of pilgrims.

Trendelburg: Rapunzel Tower

What to See and Do

Worth seeing in **Trendelburg** are the medieval castle with its Castle Keep and the over 40m fairy tale Rapunzel Tower, situated picturesquely on a sandstone rock. You can enter the Rapunzel Tower with its up to 7m thick walls, keeping fit by climbing the more than 130 steps to the top. There you will find Rapunzel's golden braid attracting fairy tale princes. After that climb, you may want to visit the torture museum (Foltermuseum) in the lower level of the tower and the Grimm floor with silhouettes by the artist Albert Völkl.

1. The Lantern Way (Laternenweg) begins in the courtyard of the castle with cut-outs that lead into the adjacent old town with a **Gothic church** (murals of the Magi, Saint Christopher and grave slabs of knights, 16th century).

2. Next to the church, the façade of the historic **town hall** with sundial and cubit measurements is interesting. The Tourist Office is at Brunnen 6, where there is also a rare **mikvah**, a 17th century Jewish ritual bath.

The former moated manor of Wülmersen

3. Of note in the Trendelburg district:
– The former moated manor of **Wülmersen** is located on the Diemel River, a nine hundred year old knight's manor with an associated museum and historical archive for tools.

One of the legendary cloudbursts (sinkholes)

– A classical palace in **Stammen** (von Pappenheim), behind which the recreation center of the Stammen estate lies.
– The thousand year old village **Deisel** with its old half-timbered farmhouses and a church from the 16th century painted with apple tendrils.

4. In Reinhardswald is Gottsbüren. On the way there from Trendelburg, one passes two large legendary sinkholes, the Cloudbursts (Wolkenbrüche).

The triple-naved **hall church of Gottsbüren** is decorated with late Gothic wall paintings and especially interesting sculptural detail and a valuable organ. Grouped around the church are many half-timbered farmsteads.

Late-Gothic Wall Painting in the Church of Gottsbüren

5. The ramparts of the **Eberschützer cliffs,** locale of the Christian legend of the greening pilgrim's staff, are worth an excursion.

Oberweser

Oberweser came into existence in 1971–72 as a result of the merging of six villages on the upper reaches of the Weser River. The administrative seat is in Gieselwerder.

Fairy Tale and Saga References

For Oberweser, the Grimm's fairy tale *Snow White and the Seven Dwarves* is the German Fairy Tale Route's promotional focus for Gieselwerder while *Puss in Boots* is specified for Oedelsheim. In a 2011 opinion poll of the Second German Television Network (ZDF) asking which was the most popular fairy tale of Germans, *Snow White* came in first place, followed by Harry Potter. There is some supporting evi-

Panoramic View of Gieselwerder

Oedelsheim: Puss in Boots

Gieselwerder: Open-Air Museum Mill Place

dence to consider Gieselwerder as Snow White's village. During renovation work in the old half-timbered house *Kleiner Schneider* (Little Tailor), home of the *weaving museum Kircher*, a clay wall was discovered in which seven small, very old pointed caps and broken glass from small broken plates were discovered. Two kilometers from Gieselwerder, there was at one time an *iron mine* on the upper slope of St. George's ground in the forest Reinhardswald. Not that far away on the opposite bank of the Weser is the site of Polier, where mirrors were manufactured earlier and only where the evil stepmother Queen could have bought her magic mirror. Across the mountains is the castle of *Sababurg* and not so far away, in Kassel, the Island of the *Seven Mountains*.

History

Gieselwerder, whose moated castle was probably built around 1100 to secure the Weser crossing to the monastery of Lippoldsberg, was originally on an island (Werder means island). The castle was initially owned by the counts of

The Weser River and the Town Hall of Oberweser

Northeim and passed over through inheritance to the dukes of Brunswick. Often a bone of contention between Mainz and Brunswick, Gieselwerder was pledged to Hesse in 1462 and was under full Hessian ownership after 1583. The two villages, Gewissenruh and Gottstreu, whose histories were closely linked to each other, were founded on the left bank of the Weser River in 1722 at the behest of Landgrave Karl for the once-persecuted Waldensians from Piedmont. The French family names and French inscriptions on houses in the two Waldensian communities bear witness to this day of the origin of their inhabitants.

What to See and Do

Of note in the various districts are pretty, **half-timbered houses**, some including inscriptions from the 17th–19th centuries, often built in Lower Saxon design.

1. The only remaining evidence of the lost castle Gieselwerder are remnants of the outside walls with a gate close to the Weser and the semicircle of an earlier tower. The Snow White sculpture near the Town Hall reinforces Gieselwerder's claim as Snow White's Village. The cross-shaped half-timbered **church of Gieselwerder**, with its characteristic ridge turrets, derives from the year 1813.

2. The **weaving museum Kircher** is housed in the nearly 300-year-old Lower-Saxon, half-timbered house Kleiner Schneider (Little Tailor), where objects of the dwarfs have been uncovered. It has extensive holdings over the topics of weaving and textile history. Special weaving and handwork classes are held in the weaving parlor.

The Weaving Museum Kircher and Snow White

3. In Lumbachtal, on the outskirts of Gieselwerder, one finds the **open-air museum** Mill Place (Mühlenplatz), a miniature exhibit of about 60 faithfully reproduced water mills, castles, palaces, churches and town halls. If you walk from there through the Reinhardswald to Gottsbüren, you will encounter a truly unique phenom-

left: Gottstreu – right: Gewissenruh: Waldensian Churches

enon: **water that flows uphill**. Of course, it is all due to an optical illusion.

4. The neo-classical parish **church of Oedelsheim** was built in 1829–30. At the parking lot of the village museum of Oedelsheim, the visitor encounters a greater than man-sized wooden figure of the Grimm's fairy tale character, *Puss in Boots*. The village museum is housed in a half-timbered house from 1656. In the immediate area, there is a half-timbered barn displaying various objects of agrarian history.

Rich in tradition, the Weser Ferry from Oedelsheim to Gottstreu was mentioned in documents as early as 1288. Today it bears the fairytale name *Puss in Boots Ferry*.

5. In **Gewissenruh** (with French inscriptions from 1779) and **Gottstreu** (1730) are simple Waldensian churches. In addition, there is a small Waldensian museum in Gottstreu.

Wahlsburg

The community of Wahlsburg, which takes its name from the relatively well preserved circular fort of Wahlsburg, came into existence in 1971 through the merger of the two locales of Lippoldsberg and Vernawahlshausen.

Saga References

Wahlsburg legends are *The Haunted Nun of Lippoldsberg, The Ferry Building*, and *The Magic Flower.*

Another intriguing aspect of Wahlsburg is the case of the writer Hans Grimm (1875–1959). Despite his surname, the controversial ultra-na-

Handsome old half-timbered houses

Tombstones

tionalist journalist and writer was not a descendant of the Brothers Grimm. After WWI he purchased the manor house of a dissolved abbey in Lippoldsberg on the Weser and established himself there as a writer. His 1926 colonial novel *People without Space* found a large audience during the Nazi rule and became the slogan of the German National Socialistic expansionist policy. The reputation of Hans Grimm continues to be debated in Lippoldsberg.

History

In the years 1051–59, Archbishop Luitpold of Mainz built a wooden church on a swath of land on the right bank of the Weser traded to him by the monastery of Corvey and had a village constructed next to it that was named after him. At the end of the 11th century, Archbishop Ruthard of Mainz founded a Benedictine monastery that adopted the Hirsauer reforms. The construction of the monastery church by the Provost Gunter followed in 1142–53. Lippoldsberg passed into the control of the landgraves of Hesse in 1462, and, after the introduction of the Reformation in Hesse, no more novices were accepted into the monastery, so that the Lippoldsberg monastery became extinct with the death of the last abbess.

What to See and Do

1. The former monastery church St. Georg and Maria, in its measurement and shape clearly constructed as a cruciform basilica, counts as **one of the most important Romanesque**

The former monastery Church St. Georg and Maria, one of the most important Romanesque buildings of the 12th century in Germany

buildings of the 12th century in Germany. A special feature is a nuns' gallery included in the nave, which has an impressive portico as its base. Inside the Romanesque church is an important late Romanesque baptismal font (1220). Exhibits about monastic life and Romanesque architecture can be seen in the **information center Klosterpforte** (convent gate).

The Church of Vernawahlshausen

2. A row of handsome old **half-timbered houses** in Lower Saxon style presses around the monastery church, the landmark of the village. The museum in the Schäferhaus (Shepherd's House) depicts the everyday life of the people of the village in earlier times.

3. Noteworthy in Wahlsburg-Vernawahlshausen are significant remains of Romanesque and Gothic frescoes in the choir of the **parish church** as well a Renaissance pulpit (17th century) in the nave.

Bad Karlshafen

Saga References

In volume three of the *German Sagas* of the Brothers Grimm, there are three small historical sagas of Bad Karlshafen as well as a more famous one of Helmarshausen about a *Wizard on the Krukenberg*, which also appears in other saga collections.

Ludwig Emil Grimm was quartered in *Carlshafen* with his guard regiment in the autumn of 1814 and drew a view of the Huguenot town with its brine graduation house.

History

The earliest documented mention of the royal court *helmerateshusa* was in the year 944.

Panoramic View of Bad Karlshafen

Known for its illuminated manuscripts and goldsmithing, the important Benedictine cloister of Helmarshausen, which received coin, customs and market rights in 997 from Emperor Otto III (996–1002), was given by Emperor Henry II to Bishop Meinwerk of Paderborn in

Panaromic View of Helmarshausen

1017. From 1215–20, Archbishop Engelbert of Cologne built the Krukenburg that towers high over Helmarshausen. After long feuds between Hesse and Paderborn, the town fell to the landgrave of Hesse in the 16th century. In 1536, the abbey was closed and fell into disrepair. In an attempt to bypass the economically disadvantageous customs and storage yards of Hann. Münden, Landgrave Karl of Hesse-Kassel (1677–1730) set out in 1699 to build a canal from the Weser River to Kassel, but the work came to a halt in the village of Hümme. At the northernmost point of the proposed canal, at the spot where the Diemel flows into the Weser, Karl settled Reformed Huguenots and Waldensians. He founded a port town in 1699 that got its name from the old Germanic hill-fort Sieburg above the new town. In 1717, the town was renamed *Carlshafen* in honor of the landgrave.

Town Hall (18th century)

What to See and Do

1. Visit the structural center of the town, built according to the plan of the Huguenot architect Paul du Ry (a regular layout in the style of classical Baroque, its harbor flanked by two symmetrical *squares* and streets over 100 feet wide). The plan was carried out by the engineer Frederick Conradi. Start at the historical harbor and the 18th century **town hall** with its characteristic arcades on the ground floor and the massive roof over the upper level. While strolling around, notice the French-inspired archi-

The German Huguenot Museum Interior and Exterior

tectural clarity of the grid-pattern of blocks of white houses on both sides of the harbor, the *Frey House* (1723), the *Customs House*, the former *Thurn and Taxis Post Office* as well as the three-story *Invalidenhaus* (1704–10).

2. **The German Huguenot Museum** depicts the life and persecution of Reformed Protestants in France and their inclusion and integration into Germany. Of the approximately 44,000 French religious refugees who arrived in Germany, about 3,800 found their new home in northern Hesse.

3. Don't miss traveling to the one thousand year-old **Helmarshausen** whose landscape is

Helmarshausen: The ruins of the legendary Krukenburg (13th century)

still dominated by the castle ruin **Krukenburg** (13th century) with its castle keep on a mountain ridge above the Diemel, as well as to the ruins of the *Johanneskapelle* (12th century) modelled on the *Church of the Holy Sepulchre* over Christ's reputed grave in Jerusalem.

4. Finally, down in the valley you will encounter a series of *half-timbered buildings* (16th–18th centuries), the *parish church* and the **ruins of the cloister** of the former Benedictine abbey. Due to its artistic and scientific prowess, the abbey was among the most important monasteries of the empire during the 11th and 12th centuries. The so-called *Gospels of Henry the Lion*, one of the most valuable books in the world and considered the masterpiece of Romanesque book illumination, was created around 1188 by the painter monk Heriman in Helmarshausen. A facsimile of the precious Gospel is preserved in the museum in the Old Town Hall.

Weser Therme (Thermal Brine Baths)

5. Don't forget to relax in Bad Karlshafen's *Weser Therme* (thermal brine baths) with its graduation structure. The spring was discovered by the Huguenot apothecary Jacques Galland in 1730.

What is the Huguenot tradition?

Is it possible that neither Little Red Riding Hood nor Briar Rose (Sleeping Beauty) are really native to Germany? The Brothers Grimm tapped into the French fairy tale tradition so convincingly that what once was French soon became part of the very essence of German literary tradition. Behind it all is a remarkable set of historical circumstances that served to mingle the cultural traditions of Europe. It all began when the French Protestants adopted the religious teachings of Jean Calvin and thereby joined the Reformed branch of the Protestant Reformation. Called Huguenots, they quickly attained stature in France. This was not a welcome development in Catholic France and led to the St. Bartholomew's Day Massacre (1572) when thousands of them were killed.

The adoption of the Edict of Nantes (1598) put Huguenots on an equal footing with the Catholics, so they were allowed to enter French public life and seemed to thrive – that is, until the Sun King, Louis XIV, renounced the Edict in 1685, making Protestantism illegal in France. What followed was a mass exodus of Huguenots from France to Germany, England, Switzerland, Holland, South Africa and America in search of religious freedom.

Just over a century later, the Grimms heard many of their fairy tales from women like Amalie, Jeanette and Marie Hassenpflug and Dorothea Viehmann, in whose French Huguenot ancestry the stories had been told and retold. In this way, the *Contes* of Charles Perrault entered the oral tradition through the Grimms. Instead of diminishing the Grimm tradition, the discovery of these stories enriched the German fairy tale tradition. Their continued circulation in French-German homes attests to the resilience of fairy tales.

Fürstenberg (Weser)

Saga and Story References

Two very old Fürstenberg sagas are *Heufass* (Hay Drum) and *The Eichelsaat* (Acorn Seed). Additionally, the Fürstenberger narrator and local chronicler, Hansulrich Kaste (*1932), contributed the stories *The White Knight, The Red Richard* as well as *A King to Visit.*

History

Shortly before 1350, the castle *vorstenberch* was built on the right side of the Weser River,

Fürstenberg Castle above the Weser River

where the high plateau of the Solling on Kathagenberg with its large quarries dominates the Corvey landscape. Due to its geographical location on the border between the Duchy of Brunswick, the Abbey of Corvey, and the bishopric of Paderborn, the castle frequently changed owners until it finally came to the Brunswick-Wolfenbüttel line of the Guelphs as part of the division of the Weser countries in 1495. After the destruction of the castle by the Hessians in 1545, it was rebuilt under Duke Henry Julius (1589–1613) into a Renaissance castle and seat of the Fürstenberg administrative district, which included the southern tip of the duchy.

Fürstenberg Castle

Duke Carl I founded the Fürstenberg porcelain factory in 1747, which then started production in the castle in 1750 under the leadership of Johann Georg von Langen. The place was built up in the second half of the 18th century, when large numbers of factory workers recruited by the factory owners settled in Fürstenberg.

Jerome Napoleon Bonaparte, King of Westphalia, once visited the Royal Porcelain Factory in Fürstenberg, but not without obstacles.

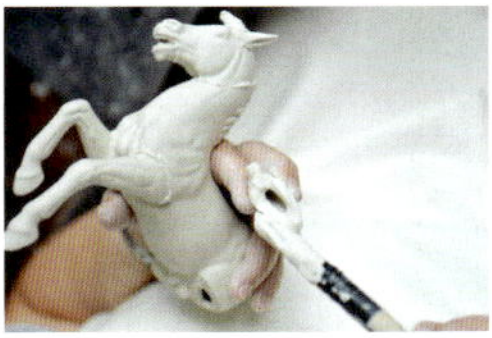

Tableware AUREOLE CLAIR DE LUNE

Precise craftsmanship

What to See and Do

1. **Fürstenberg** is known far beyond the borders of Germany for its **porcelain factory**. Visitors to the museum in the castle are informed about the history, development and current production program of the factory, as well as the production of fine porcelain in the factory's workshop in the museum. The exhibition, where three centuries of porcelain art are presented, is housed on three floors of the Weser Renaissance palace built under Duke Heinrich Julius and decorated with bay windows and rich curved-gables. The wooden staircase from about the middle of the 18th century, integrated into the inner courtyards of the castle, is remarkable for its truss construction. Built of rubble stone, the residential and commercial buildings of the factory were built partly at the end of the 18th century.

2. Children and adults can experience what it was like to live in the Middle Ages in the recreated **medieval village Bokenrode** (youth educational site Fürstenberg) built in 2004–08. Two residential barn houses and two pit

houses, a bakery, a kiln, a tavern as well as a blacksmithery are grouped around a village green dating from the early and late Middle Ages.

3. Also worth seeing are the church with free-standing bell tower executed in Solling sandstone in 1897–99, some half-timbered houses, as well as the statue of the bronze horse, Vollblut (Thoroughbred), created by Professor A. H. Hußmann from Berlin in 1936 and donated to the community by his wife in 1946.

Fürstenberg Castle with Museum and Restaurant

Polle

Fairy Tale and Saga References

When the weather is ideal, the picturesque ruins of Polle Castle, situated high above the Weser, offers visitors a breathtaking view of the Weser landscape. If you let your imagination run wild, Polle Castle becomes the home of Cinderella and, keeping with its theme on the German Fairy Tale Route, Grimm's fairy tale *Cinderella* is performed in the castle ruins at 2:45 pm every third Sunday from May to September.

There's more. According to an old north German legend, a large black dog called Klingehund (Jingle Dog), lives in the Polle Castle but occasionally hikes down to the Weser River. When he does, he jingles all the way.

On the Köterberg, only 12 km away from Polle, the boundaries of Lower Saxony and North Rhine-Westphalia come together. A small part of the Köterberg, a mountain asso-

Polle Castle (Performance Venue for Grimm's Fairy Tale Cinderella)

Polle Castle: Entrance Gate (Weser Renaissance Style)

ciated with a world full of fairy tales and sagas, lies in the region of Polle. In the summer of 1813, Wilhelm Grimm took a trip there where he heard a shepherd recite in Low German dialect the tale *De drei Vügelkens* (The Three Little Birds) and the saga *Die Springwurzel* (The Springroot) as well as *Der Köterberg*, all of which found their way into the *Children's and Household Tales* or the *German Sagas*.

History

First mentioned in records in 1285, the Polle Castle was probably built in the 12th century. It was the residence of the large land-holding

View from Polle Castle over the Weser Valley

counts of Everstein, who were responsible only to the emperor; their lands once encompassed nine castles and the broad Weserland from Holzminden to Hamelin. Their downfall proved to be the continual antagonism with the dukes of Brunswick that gradually brought large parts of the Everstein lands into Brunswick possession. Polle was conquered in 1407 and fell to the Guelph Duke Henry of Brunswick. The Polle Castle was often besieged during the Thirty Years War; the lower castle was set ablaze by Tilly in 1623 while the Swedes set the upper castle on fire in 1641. Shortly before the end of the Second World War, American and German forces met at Polle and engaged in a fierce skirmish that destroyed the west and north wings of the castle, the old administration building of the lower castle of 1656, and thirty-three houses, which went up in flames.

Cinderella

What to See and Do

1. Still a little market town with its narrow streets and squares, Polle spreads out beneath its castle ruins high on a Jurassic saddle above the Weser River. The **landmark of Polle is the former castle** of the counts of Everstein. Nowadays, the approach to the castle ruins includes a possible stop at Cinderella's room or a walk along the Cinderella path. From the castle ruins and the lookout tower in the castle keep, you have a wonderful panoramic view of the Weser Valley to the Lippe landscape and the forested areas of Vogler and Solling. A magnificent portal preserved from the era of the Weser Renaissance lies in front of the adminstrative building destroyed shortly before the end of World War II.

2. In the Burgstraße, Mittelstraße and Hintere Straße (Rear street) there is a series of handsome half-timbered houses partly from the 16th through 19th centuries with so-called *Utluchten* (small gables equipped with windows). The **parish church** of St. George, a hall building

Parish Church of St. George (16th century)

with flat beams, was built in the second half of the 16th century. Remaining of its one time interior is the entrance of red sandstone blocks, the stucco ceiling and epitaphs.

3. Also recommended is a 12km trip to saga and fairy tale-filled **Köterberg** (496 m), from which a magnificent panoramic view of the Weser River landscape is available on clear days.

Lügde

Town of the Burning Easter Wheels

Fairy Tale and Saga references

Lügde is a town with both a rich treasure trove of legends and interesting historical buildings. The Lügder Saga Treasury was collected and published in the 19th and 20th centuries: in the mid-19th century by the local poet and composer Josef Seiler (1823–77, *Legends and Fairy Tales from Homeland and Abroad* as well as *Folk Tales and Legends of the Paderborn Region*), by the end of the 20th century by his distant relative, the archivist and chronicler Manfred Willeke (*1964, *Lügder Saga Treasury. Legends and Mythical Stories from the Town of Lügde*). Oral tradition holds that Wilhelm Grimm, during a visit in nearby Bad Pyrmont where his wife and daughter went for treat-

An impressive old custom: on Easter Sunday burning Easter Wheels are rolled down the Easter Mountain (Osterberg)

ment at the spa, met Josef Seiler in July 1841 and supposedly encouraged the publication of his collections.

Southwest of Lügde rises the Herlingsburg (334 m), a rampart from pre-Christian times and an old Saxon stronghold, which sagas report to have been the residence of Arminius (that is Hermann, who defeated the Romans in the Battle of the Teutoburg Forest in 9 AD). Numerous legends and tales are set on and around the highest point of land, the Köterberg (496 m), which belongs for the most part to Lügde. Several of them can be found in the *Children's and Household Tales*, as well as in the *German Sagas* of the Brothers Grimm (see Polle).

The legendary Köterberg: Fairy Tale and Saga Location in the Brothers Grimm Collections

History

Even Charlemagne left some traces in Lügde. He celebrated his first Christmas in the land of the Saxons in *villa liuhidi* (estate Lügde) in 784. At this site, north of the present town center of Lügde, a church was built, later to be replaced by the Romanesque Church of St. Kilian from the 12th century.

Winter: Defensive Tower, Emmer Brook and Town Wall

As early as 1195 Lügde was a fortified castle locale where the counts of Pyrmont minted their first coins. After the construction of Pyrmont Castle (before 1184) by the Archbishop of Cologne, the relationship between the counts of Pyrmont and the archbishops of Cologne deteriorated.

Lügde was founded as a planned town and was the most prominent place of the county of Pyrmont; it was first referred to as a town in documents in 1255.

In 1494, Count Moritz, the last male ruler of the house of Pyrmont, died without an heir and during the following years there were repeated land disputes over the county. It was not until 1668 that the Pyrmont Accords divided the county between the Archbishopric Paderborn and the counts of Waldeck. Despite vigorous protests, Lügde fell to the Prince-Bishopric of Paderborn, while Pyrmont Fountain (Bad Pyrmont) and ten villages were awarded to the

GPS Adventure Path Fabeled Lügde: Young Women on Trail

house of the Waldeck counts. Even before that, in 1624, Lügde was re-catholicised against the will of the people.

From 1802–06, Lügde belonged to Prussia, and from 1806–13 to the Kingdom of Westphalia and was, after its termination, once again Prussian. After the Second World War, when Prussia was dissolved as a state in 1947 by the Allies, Lügde became part of the newly founded German state, North Rhine-Westphalia.

What to See and Do

The Old Town of Lügde has one of the best preserved historical centers in North-Rhine Westphalia.

1. The approximately 45 km long **GPS Adventure Path Fabeled Lügde** (see web-index)

Mittlere Straße: well-tended half-timbered gabled homes

leads from the historic Old Town through various districts of Lügde. On this route there are fantastic places and exciting adventure tours waiting to be discovered.

2. The **Mythenweg** (Myth Path) of Lügde runs around the Herlingsburg, along mystical sites and cultural historically significant places.

3. Lügde's **Old Town,** with its three dominant longitudinal streets and narrow cross roads, is bordered by the about 1.5 km long town wall with towers including the Brückentorturm (Bridge Tower), Wehrturm (Defensive Tower), Im Winkel (In the Corner, 13th century) and the defensive trench. The streetscape features a number of **half-timbered gabled homes** from the 18th century: Hintere Straße, Mittel Straße, Vordere Straße, Seilerstraße). The houses No. 12 (1612) and No. 14 (1669) in the Hintere Straße (Rear Street) are Lügde's oldest houses, having

escaped the great fire of 1797. In the town center are the Town Hall and the towering Neo-Gothic St. Mary's Church, built in 1894 to replace an earlier building dating from the 14th century (steeple 1353, retable early 16th century).

The Romanesque Church of St. Kilian (12th century)

Interior: bench of the executioner (16th century) who had to sit away from the congregation

4. The former Franciscan Monastery with its stately Baroque portal was erected between 1746-56. Three impressive half-timbered homes are in the Hintere Straße (numbers 84–88); the local museum is located in the middle building. Here you can find stimulating information about farm life, the former work environment and the Lügde town history. From here, you can reach the **St. Kilian Church** which is located about 400 meters beyond the Upper Gate. On a hill surrounded by a cemetery, the once fortified Romanesque church is regarded, due to its excellent state of preservation, a nearly perfect example of a small medieval church. The cruciform vaulted basilica was begun in 1135 in the architectural tradition of the Monastery Church of Lippoldsberg (see Wahlsburg). Its interior is established by the high central nave and the great transept; the arcades between the aisles are separated by columns with decorated capitals. The wall paintings in the main apse date from the time of the building of the church (12th century).

5. Thousands of visitors are attracted to Lügde on Easter Sunday when an old custom documented as early as 1743, the **Lügde Burning Easter Wheel Race,** is celebrated; Easter Fire was mentioned as early as 1629. After a procession, the Burning Easter Wheel Race involves huge oak wheels (1.7 m diameter, approximately 270 kg) being rolled burning down the Osterberg (Easter Mountain), an impressive spectacle!

Elbrinxen: Stork Station

6. The ancient **Wittekind linden tree**, which is about 900 years old, stands in the middle of the cemetery, next to the Romanesque church (12th century, pulpit of 1562) in the Elbrinxen district. The Stork Station in Elbrinxen is a place where many young storks come into the world each spring. On its idyllic grounds, nesting platforms have been built specifically for the storks.

7. The former **monastery church** of Falkenhagen (three remarkable stained glass windows) was built in the late 15th century. Preserved from the monastery are the east wing, the dormitory, an old half-timbered building of 1509 and the cloister.

Munchausen-Town of Bodenwerder

Munchausen's Cock-and-Bull Stories

The very interesting town of Bodenwerder has become widely known largely because of the adventures of her most famous son, the *Baron Hieronymus Carl Friedrich von Münchhausen* (1720–97).

Three men in particular have contributed to the global success of the book *Marvellous Travels on Water and Land: Campaigns and Comical Adventures of the Baron of Munchausen*:

– The Baron Münchhausen himself, who told his cock-and-bull stories in the company of friends in Bodenwerder.

– Rudolf Erich Raspe (1736–1794), fraudulent polymath of international standing and the writer who used various German sources to issue Münchhausen's tall tales under different titles in English after 1785, such as *Baron Munchausen's Narrative of his Marvellous Travels and Campaigns in Russia.* He paved the way for the great reputation the Münchhausen stories enjoy in the English-speaking world.

Baron von Münchhausen

– Gottfried August Bürger (1747–94), poet and professor of aesthetics at the University of Göttingen. He translated Raspe's texts back into German, edited them freely and added more: *Of Baron Munchausen's Wonderful Travels and Adventures at Sea and on Land,* just as he used to tell his circle of friends with the bottle. Bürger's last issue of 1794, shortly before his

The Münchhausen Museum: Interior and Exterior

death, forms the basis of modern German versions.

History

The market settlement *insula* (Werder) developed near the monastery of Kemnade (founded in 959). It came into the possession of Henry II of Homburg when it was purchased from the abbey of Corvey in 1245 and from whom it received town rights in 1287. The name of the town goes back to the lords of Homburg, one of whom was a knight named Bodo von Homburg, who became the first overlord of Bodenwerder (Bodo's island or Werder). After the Homburg line died out in 1409, the prosperous town came over to the Guelphs. Severe fires, floods, and the Thirty Years War inflicted serious damage to the town from which it recovered slowly in subsequent years.

What to See and Do

1. The great fabulist, Baron H.C.F. von Münchhausen, is remembered in Bodenwerder in nu-

Munchhausen Cock-and-Bull Stories: Munchhausen pulls himself out of the swamp and Half-Horse Fountain

merous ways: The former Münchhausen estate is a building complex consisting of a mansion, the former brandy distillery and the Schulenburg (stone house). The mansion built in 1603, now the Town Hall, is where Münchhausen was born, and where he died. The Schulenburg, whose core is a medieval stone house from 1300, is the home of the **Münchhausen Museum** (memorabilia, book editions, illustrations, etc.). In addition, the **Münchhausen grotto** from 1763, in whose upper level Münchhausen told many of his anecdotal tall tales, is located on the mountainside a short distance from town.

Other Münchhausen attractions in the town are a number of **Münchhausen sculptures** that successfully depict scenes from his fanciful tales, such as *The Ride on the Cannonball*, the *Half Horse* or *The Team of Ducks* and the **Münchhausen Play** (every first Sunday from May – October), and the **Münchhausen Musical** (Jun-Sep, every second and fourth Sunday at 3:00 pm), incidentally free!

2. At the marketplace of Bodenwerder stands the **St. Nicolai Church**, which was consecrated

Kemnade: The former Convent Church, where Baron von Münchhausen was buried, is almost 1000 years old

in 1410, and the oldest house of the town (built in 1484). In the immediate vicinity is **St. Gertrudis Chapel** from the 12th century. Worth seeing are a number of **half-timbered houses** with their well-kept gables in Homburg Street and King Street, including the Plate-Haus of 1550. In the Weser Street one can view the old pharmacy (1625), the former customs house, the old ferry house with humorous ornamental paintings and old high-water marks as well as a house from 1604 decorated with a large number of carvings.

3. The Münchhausen grave is located in the former convent **church** in the **Kemnade** district. In the beautiful triple-naved Romanesque church that is almost a thousand years old, many sacred treasures have been preserved including two crucifixes from the 13th and 16th

Hehlen: Weser Renaissance Castle

centuries, a carved wooden Pieta (c. 1500), a resplendent madonna (c. 1480), a Romanesque baptismal font and a small sacramental booth made from colorful sandstone.

4. Picturesquely situated on the Weser River in the town of Hehlen is a moated castle (private property). The builder of the four-winged **Weser Renaissance castle** (1579–84) was Fritz von der Schulenburg. On a hill of Hehlen is the **Immanuel Church**, built in 1697–99 as one of the earliest examples of a Protestant main room church in Germany.

What is the Munchausen Syndrome?

So strong is the connection between the name Münchhausen and the tendency to exaggerate that it is attached to medical conditions where patients suffer from imagined illnesses. The Munchausen Syndrome or the more insidious Munchausen Syndrome by Proxy, which often takes the form of a parent creating the appearance of illness or injury in their children, bear the name of this man who never suffered from anything like this medical condition.

Both conditions emerged in medical literature in the middle of the 20th century and are often cited in cases where young children are hospitalized for maladies that have no plausible explanation except for the involvement of a parent or caregiver. Ironically, while there is a strong tendency for children to be exploited by adult caregivers in the fairy tale literature, none of the narratives like *The Juniper Tree* or *Sleeping Beauty* would be considered examples of the Munchausen Syndrome by Proxy because they lack that sense of a feigned illness. Overt cruelty, on the other hand, is something completely different.

Baron Munchausen's Ride on the Cannonball

(Gottfried August Bürger/Rudolf Erich Raspe – English version: E. Michael Iba/Thomas L. Johnson)

Once we had besieged the fortress of a town whose name I cannot at the moment recall. According to the field marshal, it was of utmost importance that we should find out what was taking place inside the fortress. But the task of passing all the pickets, guards, and fortifications seemed to be extremely difficult, if not impossible. In fact, there was no suitable person who could possibly do it.

Full of courage and zeal, I rashly got close to one of the biggest cannons as it was being fired in the direction of the fortress and quickly sprang onto the cannonball intending to let it carry me inside the fortress. But when I was half-way there, riding through the air on the cannonball, all kinds of misgivings arose in my head. "You can get inside the fortress but how will you ever get out afterwards? And what will happen to you in there? You will be taken for a spy and hanged on the nearest gallows." Too much honor for me.

As these and similar thoughts passed through my head, I quickly made up my mind and, when a cannonball directed from the fortress against our camp passed just a few feet from me, I took a chance. I leaped from my cannonball onto the one heading into the other direction and thus returned to our camp without, it is true, having accomplished my project. But at least I was safe and sound.

Pied Piper-Town of Hamelin

Saga and Literary References: The Pied Piper Saga

The *Pied Piper Saga* is one of history's great mysteries that gives Hamelin its continuing fame: what happened to the children of Hamelin in 1284? Located in the sumptuous *Leisthaus* and in the *Stiftsherrenhaus* in the Oster Street, the Hamelin Museum holds countless documents, drawings, sculptures as well as an extensive library covering the Pied Piper Saga. The most plausible reason for the disappearance of 130 *children of Hamelin* on June 26, 1284 is the eastward German colonization occurring in the Middle Ages. Territorial chiefs recruited or conscripted settlers for open land in Moravia, Pomerania, East Prussia and in the district of the Teutonic Order. This view holds that

Open Air Performance of the Pied Piper Saga (Terrace of the Wedding House)

The magnificient Leisthaus: Location of the Hamelin Museum with its important collection of the Pied Piper Saga

the children from Hamelin became willing émigrés from the town of Hamelin.

Other than the piper, famous people associated with Hamelin include Karl Philipp Moritz (1756–93), a close personal friend of Goethe. Moritz's major work, *Anton Reiser*, a pietistic-shaded autobiographical novel, is considered the first developmental novel in German literary history.

Also born in Hamelin were both the folk tale writer Elsa Sophia Baronin von Kamphoevener (1878–1963) – *At the Night Fires of the Serail Caravan* – and the Grimm researcher, Ludwig Denecke (1905–96, see Hann. Münden).

Pied Piper Carillon: Enacting the Pied Piper Saga in the gables of the Wedding House

History

The starting point for the development of Hamelin was the donation of a private church in the year 812 that was made into a cloister of the imperial abbey of Fulda in 826. By the 11th century, Hamelin had developed into a market center and has its first documented reference around 1200. After the Battle of Sedemünder in 1260, Hamelin joined the Duke of Guelph, Albrecht von Braunschweig, who sanctioned the freedoms and rights of the town.

Pedestrian Zone: Fine Buildings in the Weser Renaissance Style

Because of its favorable location as an important river crossing over the navigable Weser, Hamelin achieved significant prosperity especially through trade in grains and millstones. From 1426 until 1572, Hamelin was part of the Hanseatic League. After the Thirty Years War and the Seven Years War, Hamelin became an impregnable fortified town and was considered the *Gibraltar of the North*. Most of the fortifications were pulled down in 1808 by the forces of Napoleon after the town surrendered to him without a fight.

What to See and Do

Hamelin is the home of the **Pied Piper Saga** and the center of the unique architectural style of the 16th and 17th centuries called the **Weser Renaissance.**

1. There are reminders of the **Pied Piper** throughout the town. There is a *Pied Piper Fountain* in the Town Hall Square and another in Osterstraße, a *glass window* in the Market Church as well a historical inscription on the *Pied Piper House, a Pied Piper relief* in the Bür-

Today's Pied Piper guides visitors

gergarten and naturally a display about the Pied Piper Saga in the excellent *Hamelin Museum.*

2. The **Wedding House** (Hochzeitshaus) was constructed by the citizens of Hamelin in 1610–17 as a festival house and represents the last building in town built in the Weser Renaissance style.

The short **musical** entitled **Rats** is performed at 4.30 p.m. every Wednesday afternoon from May until September on its terrace; the ancient saga of the Pied Piper is performed by amateur actors in historical costumes every Sunday at noon in the summer months (mid-May to mid-September). All year around, one can listen to the Pied Piper carillon in the gables of the Wedding House (and watch wooden figures enacting the story of the Pied Piper as it plays

Details of the Façade of Stiftsherrenhaus (1556–58)

three times a day (1.05 p.m., 3.35 p.m., 5.35 p.m.).

3. Take a foot tour around the picturesque **old town** of Hamelin. In the old town, the homey half-timbered buildings and superb examples of the Weser Renaissance with their rich decorations and striking façades create an unforgettable impression.

On your walk, pay particular attention to the Rattenfängerhaus (1602/3), the house at 12 Osterstraße, the Leisthaus (1585–89) and Stiftsherrenhaus (1556–58), the Market Church St. Nikolai (rebuilt after destruction in WW II using the original building materials), the two medieval towers, the Powder Tower (Pulverturm) and the Haspelmath Tower joining the old town wall, the Dempter Haus (1607/8), Hochzeitshaus (Wedding House 1610–17), the Rattenkrug Restaurant from 1250 (transformed between 1568–69), the Jerusalem curia, and the Redenhof.

4. On the Weser shore, the Romanesque-Gothic **Minster of St. Boniface** (11th–14th centuries) near the Weser Bridge is the heart of Hamelin. Among the oldest parts of the renovated church are the 11th century crypts and the

Schwöbber Castle (1754–1604) houses the prestigious Hilmar von Münchhausen Schlosshotel

eight cornered crossing tower (12th century). Worth seeing inside the Minster are the Gothic sacramental structure, a limestone relief of the crowning of Mary by the angels from the 15th century and gravestones and epitaphs spanning the 14th through 17th centuries.

5. A different perspective of Hamelin is gained through a walk or trip up the local mountain of Hamelin, the **Klüt**, which offers a splendid panorama of the town of Hamelin and the Weser Valley. This motivates one to take a bicycle trip along the Weser – or a canoe or boat trip on the river.

Recommended side trips include visiting several important Weser Renaissance castles, namely Hämelschenburg and Schwöbber, 11 and 10 km from Hamelin respectively.

6. The moated **castle Hämelschenburg** is the most representative building of the Weser Renaissance. The picturesque three-winged structure was begun in 1588. The courtyard with its octagonal stair towers can be reached through a magnificent gate from 1600. Highlights of the interior are the Pilgrims Hall, nu-

Hämelschenburg Castle: the most representative building of the Weser Renaissance Style of the whole region

merous pieces of furniture (16th–19th centuries), the collection of portraits of German princes and the ballrooms in the style of the era (19th century).

7. The gorgeous, three-winged and moated **castle Schwöbber** came into existence in three phases over the period between 1754–1604. Schwöbber Castle now houses a prestigious hotel with a restaurant and bears the name of its builder, Hilmar von Münchhausen, Schlosshotel Münchhausen. In the middle wing of the castle high quality stucco work on the ceiling beams and charming fireplaces from the 16th century are preserved.

The Children of Hamelin

(Brothers Grimm – English version:
Thomas L. Johnson)

In the year 1284 a mysterious man appeared in Hamelin. He was wearing a multi-colored coat of bright cloth, which led to his being called the Pied Piper. He claimed to be a rat catcher, and he promised that for a certain sum he would rid the town of all mice and rats. The citizens struck a deal, promising him a certain payment.

The rat catcher then took a small fife from his pocket and began to blow on it. Rats and mice immediately came from every house and gathered around him. When he thought that he had them all, he led them to the Weser River where he pulled up his clothes and walked into the water. The animals all followed him, fell in, and drowned.

Once the citizens had been freed of their plague, they regretted having promised him so much money, so, using all kinds of excuses, they refused to pay him. Finally he went away, bitter and angry. He returned on June 26, Saint John's and Saint Paul's Day, early in the morning at seven o'clock (others say it was at noon), now dressed in a hunter's costume, with a dreadful look on his face and wearing a strange red hat.

He sounded his fife in the streets, but this time it wasn't rats and mice that came to him, but rather children: a great number of boys and girls, four years old and older. Among them was the mayor's grown daughter. The swarm followed him, and he led them into a mountain, where they all disappeared with him.

All this was witnessed by a babysitter who, carrying a child in her arms, had followed them from a distance but had then turned around and carried the news back to the town. The anxious parents ran in droves to the town gates seeking their children. The mothers cried out and sobbed pitifully. Within the hour messengers were sent everywhere by water and by land inquiring if the children – or any of them – had been seen, but it was all in vain.

A total of one hundred thirty were lost. Two, as some say, had lagged behind and came back. One of them was blind and the other mute. The blind one was not able to point out the place, but was able to tell how they had followed the piper. The mute one was able to point out the place, although he (or she) had heard nothing. One little boy in shirtsleeves had gone along with the others, but had turned back to fetch his jacket and thus escaped the tragedy, for when he returned, the others had already disappeared into a cave within a hill. This cave is still known.

Until the middle of the eighteenth century, and probably even today, the street through which the children were led out to the town gate was called the quiet street, because no dancing or music was allowed there. Indeed, when a bridal procession on its way to church crossed this street, the musicians would have to stop playing.

The mountain near Hamelin where the children disappeared is called Poppenberg. Two

stone monuments in the form of crosses have been erected there, one on the left side and one on the right. Some say that the children were led into a cave and that they came out again in Transylvania.

The citizens of Hamelin recorded this event in their town register, and they came to date all their proclamations according to the years and days since the loss of their children.

According to Seyfried, the 22nd rather than the 26th of June was entered into the town register.

The following lines were inscribed on the town hall:

In the year 1284 after the birth of Christ
From Hamelin were led away
One hundred thirty children, born at this place
Led away by a piper into a mountain.

And on the new gate was inscribed:

Centum ter denos cum magus ab
urbe puellos
duxerat ante annos CCLXXII condita
porta fuit.

(This gate was built 272 years after the magician led the 130 children from the town.)

In the year 1572 the mayor had the story depicted in the church windows. The accompanying inscription has become largely illegible. In addition, a coin was minted in memory of the event.

Hessisch Oldendorf

Fairy Tale and Saga References

Numerous tales and legends have been handed down in and around Hessisch Oldendorf. The notorious Ratskeller landlord, merchant and town pillar, Cord Baxmann (1599–1690), who gained considerable wealth through cunning, deceit and diligence, is remembered in Hessisch Oldendorf in both sagas and in many other ways: Four hundred years after his birth, *Baxmann* often returns to lead visitors to the Baxmann sites, such as the *Baxmann-Haus* (Volksbank, Lange Str. 85), the *Baxmann Fountain* at the market, the *Baxmann Memorial*, the *Baxmann spring*, the *Bax-*

Münchhausen Court, 1583 (Weser Renaissance Style)

The legendary Baxmann explaining things

The fabled Hohenstein

manngrave (in the cemetery) etc., and tells them his gruesome story: "After his death, the greedy Baxmann was welcome neither in heaven nor in hell and was relegated to drawing water with a thimble until the end of time."

Less well known is the fact that four very noteworthy tales originate in the Weibeck district, one of which, namely *Dwarf Holzrührlein Bonneführlein*, has parallels to the Grimm's *Rumpelstiltskin*.

A number of legends have grown up around the *Hohenstein* with its 164 foot high cliffs and around the *Dachtelfeld*, a 250-acre plateau.

History

To better distinguish from other places of the same name, Oldendorf was given the designation Hessisch in 1905 though it was likely already founded by the counts of Schaumburg in the 13th century. Hessisch Oldendorf was recognized with town rights in the 14th century. In the important Battle of Hessisch Oldendorf (between Segelhorst and Barksen in 1633) during the Thirty Years War, the Protestant army defeated the Catholic imperial troops.

After the death of the last count of Schaumburg in 1640, Oldendorf fell by inheritance to the landgrave of Hesse-Kassel and was, as was the whole of Hesse-Kassel, in the Kingdom of Westphalia between 1807 and 1813. Hessisch Oldendorf became Prussian in 1866 (an enclave in the district of Kassel) and joined the Prussian governmental district of Hannover in 1932.

The district of Fischbeck, mentioned as early as 892 in a charter of King Arnulf and the donation of a royal estate to the Saxon Earl Egbert, is older than the core town of Hessisch Oldendorf. A convent was founded on this property by the noble lady Helmburg in 995. With the introduction of the Reformation in 1559, the convent was converted into a home for women.

Collegiate Church of Fischbeck, one of the most important Romanesque buildings in the Weser region

What to See and Do

1. Already evident in the engraving by Merian from 1647, the skyline of Hessisch Oldendorf is still dominated today by the Münchhausen Court and the town church. The **Münchhausen Court** was built in the 13th century. The current double-wing facility was built in 1583 in the Weser Renaissance style by Borries von Münchhausen (not to be confused with Baron Münchhausen at Bodenwerder) and is one of the largest courts in the Weser mountain country. The south façade facing the Weser River is particularly typical of this style with its stepped gables decorated with spirals.

2. The triple-naved **town church** was built from the end of the 14th to the beginning of the

Half-timbered, gabled-ended houses

15th centuries. Its décor includes, among others, a magnificent bronze font (1590), a picture of the Last Supper (1590) and two crucifixion plates (early 17th century).

3. Very worth seeing in the inner town is a row of lovingly restored **half-timbered, gable-ended houses** (Lange Straße, Schulstraße, Kirchplatz).

4. The 12th century Stiftskirche (**Collegiate Church**) of **Fischbeck** is one of the most important **Romanesque buildings** in the Weser region. The crypt under the choir is a triple-nave crypt. The three-sided cloister and western parts of the enclosed wing are what remain of the medieval buildings. Fortunately, a significant number of religious treasures of the facility were saved despite extensive looting during the Thirty Years War. Among the most valuable treasures are the *Triumphal Cross* (1250), the life-size *wooden statue* of the convent founder Helmburg (circa 1300), a head *reliquary* (12th century copy), the expressive wooden figure of Christ in distress (15th century) and the famous **Fischbeck tapestry**.

Kids enjoying their visit to Schillat Cave

5. Worthwhile excursions in the area include a visit to the fabled cliffs of **Hohenstein** in the Süntel mountains, a nature reserve that is of particular significance because of its rare plants and natural history as well as the Schillat Cave in the Langenfeld district and the Langenfeld Waterfall, a natural waterfall at the Hollen Mill. Anybody who would like to know how the earth came into being, where seas once were and why the dinosaurs disappeared is well served by visiting the **Schillat Cave**. A journey into the cave begins with a glass elevator that carries visitors through millions of years of geological history. Passing rock paintings, the tour enters a 180 m long cave room where a fairy tale "forest" reveals itself. Sparkling crystals and luminous stones lend the cave a mystical atmosphere.

Bad Oeynhausen

Bad Oeynhausen, a renowned spa, is also one of those uniquely European places whose combination of warm springs and natural salt make it a destination for people seeking a curative rest.

Fairy Tale, Saga and Literary References

In this stop on our journey through the German Fairy Tale Landscape, we visit one of the finest fairy tale museums in all of Germany, read one short piece from the forgotten Grimm brother, Ferdinand, and prepare to follow the Bremen Town Musicians through this enchanted landscape.

The German Fairy Tale and Weser Saga Museum

View into the interior of the German Fairy Tale and Weser Saga Museum

According to legends, the hoof of the horse of the Saxon Duke Wittekind is said to have miraculously caused the *Wittekind Spring* to bubble up in the town section *Bergkirchen* by the Wiehen range.

The *German Fairy Tale and Weser Saga Museum* at the edge of the Kurpark has information about fairy tales and of Wittekind as well as about the general sagas of the Weser region. The museum has a library of over 14,000 volumes. Founder and first leader of the museum was the fairy tale and saga researcher, Karl Paetow (1903–92), who authored *The Most Beautiful Weser Sagas* and *The Wittekind Saga*.

The writer and editor Walther Victor (1895–1971, *The General and the Women*) and the journalist, writer and historian Rudolf Pörtner (1912–2001) were born in Bad Oeynhausen.

Victor, an editor of Social Democratic newspapers, was an employee from 1919 to 1933 of the leftist weekly publication, the Weltbühne. Its illegal anti-fascist activities forced him to flee abroad when the periodical was banned by the Nazis in 1933. In 1947 he returned to Germany, namely East Germany, where he was awarded the National Prize in 1961.

Pörtner was widely known for his popular science books.

History

The region around the Rehme section of Bad Oeynhausen, not far from where the Werre River joins the Weser, was already settled as early as the early Stone Age.

Kaiserpalais (1905–08)

The first time it is mentioned in documents, however, is the year 753 when the Franconian king, Pippin the Younger (714–68) and later his son, Charlemagne, come to the Saxon region during their military campaigns. Very early in the opening phase of the Christianization of Saxony, Rehme was allowed to build a church by the bishopry of Minden during the Middle Ages. This was a privilege granted almost exclusively to the oldest churches.

After the discovery of a salt source in the district of Rehme, the Prussian state permitted construction of a salt works (called New Salt Works) in 1750. In the first half of the 19th century, Karl Freiherr von Oeynhausen (1795–1865) drilled into thermal wells with natural carbonization near the New Salt Works; these were immediately put into use as healing baths. In 1848, the bath-area of Bad Oeynhausen was created and dedicated in the name of

The magnificent Theater (1913–15)

the Freiherr von Oeynhausen by King Frederick Wilhelm IV of Prussia (1840–61). Bad Oeynhausen was granted municipal rights in 1859.

In 1853, the garden architect and director of the royal Prussian gardens, Peter Joseph Lenné, created plans for the bath facilities of Bad Oeynhausen that still function. Developed primarily at the turn of the twentieth century, the dominating presence of the town bath with its classical and Jugendstil villas grew up all

Wandelhalle (1926)

around the Kurpark. In 1926, after the inspector of mines, Jordan, opened up the largest carbonated thermal brine well on earth, named *Jordan Sprudel* in his honor.

In the course of a recent communal restructuring in 1973, seven communities of Rehme and the town of Bad Oeynhausen merged.

What to See and Do

1. Spend some time in the enchanting **German Fairy Tale and Weser Saga Museum**, housed in the splendid neo-Renaissance Paul-Baehr-Villa. Its enthusiastic staff has assembled numerous interactive displays to bring fairy tales and sagas to life.

Sültemeyer Fountain

2. Meeting place for young and old in Bad Oeynhausen is the **Sültemeyer Fountain** in the pedestrian zone, designed to honor the discovery of mineral springs. Not far from the village of Rehme, the pigs of farmer Sültemeyer were wallowing on a June day in 1745 in puddles and muddy ground. As he later drove them away, Sültemeyer noticed that a silvery crust

Bali Spa

had attached itself to his pigs. An examination revealed that the puddles contained salt.

3. Take a wellness cure in the **Kurpark,** which belongs to the *European Garden Network.* Visit the bath house II (1883–85) with its richly-decorated neo-Renaissance dome in the rotunda, the Kaiserpalais (former Kurhaus, 1905–08) with the GOP Varieté and the Wandelhalle (1926) offering well water and spa concerts. Enjoy a program in the theater (1913–15) of the spa gardens. If it is a swimming experience you are looking for, the nearby Bali Spa might be perfect. You can also experience the power of water by stepping down into the aqua crater of the *Aqua Magica Park.*

4. In a southerly direction from the *Kurpark,* visit the the **Sieker Valley** with its museum featuring a traditional court yard of the region consisting of a main house (1739), barn (1803), bakery (around 1800), granary (1792), Heuerlingshaus (hired workers' residence, 1654) and park watermill (1772) that is very worth seeing.

5. Check out American-Canadian architect **Frank Gehry's** ultramodern Energy Center

Historic Granary (1792)

Building (1995) that blends architecture with modern energy technology. The *Wave Power* exhibition uses interactive displays to make various visual and audible forms of waves perceptible. Gehry also designed the *Ronald McDonald House* with its snail-shaped roof, a care facility for children with health challenges.

6. Also worth a visit are the parish church at **Rehme** (its core dates from the 12th century, while tower, the aisles and sacristy are from the 19th century) as well as the *moated castle* **Övelgönne**, built in the current form in 1740 at Eidinghausen. The history of the castle extends back to the 12th century.

The Fern Seed

(Ferdinand Grimm – English version: Thomas L. Johnson)

The seed of the fern has a wonderful characteristic, namely that it makes one invisible. It is difficult to find because it ripens only during the Midsummer Night between twelve and one and then falls immediately off and disappears. Something remarkable occurred once to a man from Bergkirchen. On precisely that night, he was looking for his lost foal and passed through a meadow exactly as fern seeds were ripening, and some of those seeds fell into his shoes. In the morning he returned home, walked into the parlor and sat down. It seemed to him rather unusual that neither his wife nor the other bedfellows seemed to notice him. At last he spoke: "I didn't find the colt."

Everybody in the parlor was terrified. They heard the man's voice but saw nobody. Then his wife called out to him by name with the idea that he might have hidden himself. But he stood up, moved to the center of the room and said: "Whom are you calling? I am standing here right next to you."

Now their fear increased because they heard him stand up and move but saw nothing. At that moment the man realized that he was invisible. It occurred to him that he must have collected fern seeds in his shoes, because they seemed as tight as they might if they had sand in them. As soon as he had taken his shoes off, he stood there visible for all to see.

Wiedensahl

Literary, Fairy Tale and Saga References

The great German humorist, illustrator, painter and poet Wilhelm Busch (1832–1908) was born in Wiedensahl. He spent more than forty years in his native village. He was less interested in seeking closeness to others than in the silence and solitude of the landscape, which he honored with more than a thousand oil paintings and two thousand drawings. More famous, however, are Wilhelm Busch's picture stories (including *Max and Moritz* – see Ebergötzen, *The Pious Helene, Hans Huckebein, the Unlucky Raven*), making them the pioneers of the comic book tradition. With his sharp pen, he impaled the weaknesses and errors, the absurdities and evils of the bourgeois world in pointed, laconic, short rhymes, sometimes mocking his readers, thereby adding to their annoyance.

Many of his works originated in Wiedensahl, including but not limited to *Plisch and Plum,*

Wilhelm Busch's Birth House, museum and meeting place for culture and communication

Fipps the Ape, Dideldum, the Knopp-trilogy as well as fairy tales and legends in his collection: *Ut ôler Welt* (From Old Times) posthumously published by his nephews. Wilhelm Busch had been told these tales and legends by informants in Wiedensahl (including his grandmother) and transcribed them without any major changes.

The central point of commemoration is his birth house designed as a modern museum in the middle of the market town Wiedensahl, in the historical border triangle of Schaumburg-Lippe, Prussia and Hanover.

Wilhelm Busch (1832–1908)

History

According to records of the former pastor Albert Hahn from the year 1898, Wiedensahl goes back to an old Saxon free royal farm, which was built on the west bank of a small rural lake, but the farm and fields were already terribly deteriorated by around 1200. The suggested date for the actual birth of Wiedensahl is at the beginning of the 13th century by the counts of Schaumburg as a so-called *Hagenhufendorf*. Extending out from the eponymous village pond *Sahl*, settlers cleared sections of the forest for their farms, fields and meadows (Hufe). In the case of Wiedensahl, individual farms with their properties lying behind them were created on both sides along the village road.

Drawing, entitled Volks-Märchen (folk tales), in his collection Ut ôler Welt

The first documented mention of the place as *widensole* is from in 1253, as Bishop Wedekind of Minden transferred the tithe of Wiedensahl to the Free Imperial Abbey of Loccum. In the 14th century, inhabitants of the small villa-

The Old Parsonage where Busch lived from 1872–79, note the Busch monument in front

ge of Wagenrode that lay between Loccum and Wiedensahl and had been destroyed by a severe storm, settled in Wiedensahl.

In the Middle Ages there were repeated disputes between the bishop of Minden, the counts of Schaumburg-Lippe, the Guelphs and the Free Imperial Abbey of Loccum. In 1640, Wiedensahl finally fell to Loccum, where it remained until 1841. In 1885, Wiedensahl became part of the county of Stolzenau which merged into the county of Nienburg in 1932. Since the territorial reform of Lower Saxony in 1974, Wiedensahl belongs to the newly created county of Schaumburg.

Wilhelm Busch: Fipps the Ape

What to See and Do

Wiedensahl, low German *Wiensaol*, writes Wilhelm Busch, "takes its name in part from the pond called *dat saol* (Sahl – remains of an ancient country lake) located in the center of the village so anyone who enjoys surmising about origins might assume that the meaning of the whole could be forest sea, willow sea or even holy sea."

Kids are reading and listening to stories about Wilhelm Busch in his birth house

1. The **birth house of Wilhelm Busch**, a meeting place for culture and communication, waits with an exhibition on the life and work of W. Busch. You can see the rooms of his childhood, personal photos, sketches, paintings and drawings, of equal interest to both young and old. From the birth house you can enjoy a walk through the village.

2. At the entrance to the **Museum Old Parsonage**, Wilhelm Busch welcomes the visitor in the form of an impressive monument (1913). W. Busch lived from 1872–79 in the Old Parsonage in two rooms with his sister Fanny and her husband Pastor Hermann Nöldeke. Housed upstairs in the Old Parsonage, whose residential wing dates from 1713, is the local museum (collection Oswald Klose with exhibits on regional history). The front barn wing was built

St. Nikolai Church and Sahl Pond

around 1550 and is one of the oldest preserved Lower Saxon parish farmhouses.

3. In the middle of the Wiedensahl cemetery with grave stones and Romanesque baptismal font from the 17th and 18th centuries, stands the medieval village **church of St. Nikolai**, the interior of which deserves attention: gallery, baptismal font, pulpit, organ, altar (between 1669–1701).

4. A curiosity is the Lower Saxon **Folding Ruler Museum**. In the basement of his house, Günter Uhlig displays 38,000 folding rulers from 37 countries. His name is listed in the Guinness Book of World Records, and in the Book of Superlatives.

5. On a **25 km cycling trail** in and around Wiedensahl are places that served as inspirations for the rural motifs of the draftsman and painter Wilhelm Busch.

6. Loccum Abbey lies about 10 km away from Wiedensahl and serves today as a seminary for the Hanoverian regional church and a venue for meetings and special events. The former Cistercian abbey with its collegiate church was founded in 1163. The monastery complex is uniquely well-preserved in rare unity. The majority of the buildings date back to the 13th century. Deserving special attention are the cloister and chapter house. Inside the Collegiate Church of Loccum, built from 1240–80, the wooden reliquary (13th century), remnants of the old choir stalls (13th century), a painted triumphal cross and grave stones are particularly worth seeing.

Wilhelm Busch: Plisch and Plum

7. A mere 5 km from Loccum is the **Dinosaur Park Münchehagen**, an open-air museum, which was built around the Münchehagen Natural Monument of dinosaur tracks (protected by a large glass hall). Huge dinosaurs left their footprints about 140 million years ago. On a 2.5 km long footpath through various geological eras, one encounters 230 lifelike dinosaur reconstructions.

Fine half-timbered houses in the historic Nienburg town center

Nienburg (Weser)

This sculpture reminds us of the northern German folk song 'I'm the little Nienburgerin'

Saga and Folk Song References

Several times a day (9:15 am, 1:15 pm, 6:15 pm) a carillon at the historic Post Office in downtown Nienburg chimes the famous northern German folk song *I'm the little Nienburgerin*. This tune reminds us in a humorous way of the contrast between the citizens of the town of Nienburg and the farmers of the Calenberger landscape. The folk song of the *Little Nienburgerin* and some Nienburger Sagas can be found in the collection of Hermann Ziegler, *The Gewekenstein. Legends and stories from the Nienburg/Weser district.*

A number of dwarf and giant legends are told about the *Giebichenstein* (Wilhelm Dismer, *Stories and Legends of the Old Days)*, the largest erratic boulder from glacial times in

According to Stiftung Lebendige Stadt (Living City Foundation) Nienburg holds the most beautiful Farmer's Market in Europe

northern Germany. The Giebichenstein lies in the Krähe (Crow), a state forest between Erichshagen and Stöckse.

History

First mentioned in documents in 1025, Nienburg was the seat of the lord of Roden. Named a town for the first time in 1225, Nienburg had come into the possession of the counts of Hoya ten years earlier. Likely erected in the 11th century, Nienburg Castle (the name means *new castle*) was the residence of the counts of Hoya from 1345 to 1582.

Because of its strategic location as a Weser crossing at the intersection of important military and trade routes, the counts of Hoya and, after their extinction, the Guelf dukes built Nienburg into a strong fortress. In 1625, during the Thirty Years War, forces of the Catholic League under Tilly besieged the fortress Nienburg with 40,000

Lange Straße 34: View of a house with overhanging Weser Renaissance Style Alcoves

Cozy restaurants invite you in

men but could not take it. The Nienburgers fought bravely, and only plague and famine in 1627 forced the town finally to surrender.

What to See and Do

Storied buildings are the *Hakenhof* in the Hakenstraße where the saga *The Glowing Embers in Nienburg* is staged. The *Fresenhof*, a former vassals residence in the Weser Renaissance style, is the scene of the legend of the *White Maiden of Nienburg.*

1. The **medieval character** of Nienburg, despite many renovations and new buildings, is still very well preserved in the town center. The Nienburger Bärenspur (Bear Trail), a 3.3 km long tour circuit unites sightseeing highlights in the old town of Nienburg.

The Weser River, Weser River Boat, bridge and church of St. Martin

2. The Lange Straße, Weserstraße, Mühlenstraße and the church square are lined with beautiful **half-timbered houses** (16th-19th centuries) of different types. Particularly interesting are the **Erker-Haus**, a powerful broad-gabled town house, the *house of Gödecke Schünemann* from the mid-16th century, and the *Posthof* (post office), frequently used by the kings of England and electors of Hanover, George I and George II, on their trips to Hanover in the 18th century. A **monument** to the **little Nienburgerin**, title character of the North German folk song of the same name and the symbol of Nienburg, stands at the front side of the Posthof.

3. Landmark of the town is the parish **church** of **St. Martin** that was dedicated in 1441 with its 72 m high tower; the late Gothic brick church (remains of the Romanesque early church from the 12th century are preserved) contains valuable grave markers and sculptures in its interior.

The Stock Tower where prisoners once lay in stocks

4. The charming **town hall** probably dates from the 14th century; the impressive gable front in the Weser Renaissance style in Lange Straße was added at the end of the 16th century.

5. The legendary *Fresenhof*, the former vassal residence built in the Weser Renaissance style, is now part of the **Nienburg Museum**. The museum also includes the decorative classical *Quaet-Faslem-Haus,* named after its builder, the royal architect Bruno Emanuel Quaet-Fas-

The legendary Fresenhof, setting of the saga "The White Maiden of Nienburg" (Die weiße Jungfrau von Nienburg)

lem (1785–1851) and the *Rauchhaus* (Smoke House), home of the Lower Saxon Asparagus Museum.

6. The only tower preserved from the former castle of the Counts of Hoya on the Weser Wall is the so-called **Stockturm** (stock tower), where prisoners once lay in stocks.

Hoya

The town of Hoya is located on a bend of the river Weser, which meanders through the region. The town is the place of administration of the joint community of Hoya County, which includes ten municipalities.

Saga References

The well-known dwarf saga, *The Count of Hoya*, was included in the *German Sagas* written by the Brothers Grimm. Their version dates back to an old source in the late 16th century.

Other sagas and legends from the region around Hoya tell from the goblin *Hinzelmann in Eystrup, The Construction of the Church of Hoyerhagen, the Poltergeist of the Parsonage* in Hoyerhagen, *The Golden Spinning Wheel on Kolks Farm* in the former mill of Hilgermissen, *The Foundation of the Collegiate Church in Bücken* or from the *Golden Barrel in the Wastelands* near Bücken.

Primary School: The Dwarf Fountain reminds young and old of the ancient dwarf saga. Entitled 'The Count of Hoya' the Brothers Grimm included it in their German Sagas

History

The location close to the river was of utmost importance for Hoya, which is first mentioned as a *wik*, a merchant settlement situated next to the river Weser. At the beginning of the 13th century, Count Henry I of Hoya (1202–35) had the fortified castle of Hoya built on an island in the Weser. The castle of Hoya was first mentioned in 1233; it became the residence of the

Aerial View of the River Weser, Weser Bridges and Hoya Castle

counts of Hoya who expelled the native aristocrats of Hodenberg in the years 1205–06 and took over their possessions located on the left side of the river Weser. The free County of Nienburg, downstream from Hoya, was also added to the County of Hoya in 1215.

In 1582 the Counts of Hoya died out and their lands went to the dukes of Brunswick-Lüneburg and, in 1705, to the Electorate of Hanover. In 1929, Hoya was granted town privilege.

In 1974, Hoya, the market town of Bücken and four other municipalities merged together to become the joint community of Hoya County; in 2011, the municipality Eystrup was added along with three other communities, so that the current joint community of Hoya consists of a total of ten communities.

What to See and Do

1. Nine fabulous bicycle routes (e.g. Poltergeist Route, Gold Barrel Route, Donkey Route,

The legendary Hoya Castle

Hoya town guides in historic costumes in front of Hoya Castle

Monks Route, and more) make their way across the County of Hoya and along the river Weser, they all are based on local legends and stories. The Count's Route leads to the scene of the *Dwarf Saga*, the moated castle built by the Counts of Hoya, located on the eastern bank of the Weser. The east and west wings were built on a layout dating back to the Middle Ages while the central structure was created in the 19th century.

2. Every year in September, the historical **Catherine's Fair** (Katharinenmarkt) brings Hoya back to the time when the counts of Hoya ruled. Jugglers, minstrels and aristocratic men and women come from all over the former County

Martin's Church

of Hoya. Merchants and artisans peddle their goods from stalls that are set up around the Dwarf Fountain and the Primary School of Hoya, in the park and around Martin's Church.

3. Built to its present form in 1750, **Martin's Church**, with its Gothic choir and the neo-Gothic west tower has been used as a cultural center since 1995. The church was the burial place of the Counts of Hoya (epitaphs from the Gothic period and the 16th–18th centuries, chancery pulpit altar from around 1750 with a baptismal font from 1592).

4. Around the Bakelberg there are some nice **half-timbered houses** preserved from the

Kirchstraße: Fine Half-timbered Houses

17th–19th centuries. Deserving special attention are the houses No. 11 (1616) and No. 13 (1658) in the Deichstraße, as well as the former *Staffhorst Manor* next to the park, where the *Museum of the County of Hoya* is situated. In the former rectory, built in 1758, the *Museum of Printing* is located.

A rarity of historical art can be found in the Great Hall of the apartments of Von Behr Manor: Thirty lengths of handprinted, exotic-looking picture wall paper with motifs from colonial Brazil made in 1829.

5. The legendary twin-towered **Collegiate Church of Bücken** was founded by the Archbishop Rimbert of Bremen (865–88). The impressive church was built in four constituent parts between the 11th and 14th centuries and was completely restored in the 19th century. The rich interior is worth mentioning: a great late-Gothic carved altar (around 1510), tabernacle (1500), stone pulpit (13th century), triumphant cross (1230), choir stalls (1340), and stained glass (before 1250).

Hanseatic Town of Buxtehude

Fairy Tale and Saga References

In Buxtehude, so it is said near and far, *the dogs bark with their tails*, and that came about in the following manner: The town of Buxtehude came into existence when the archbishop Giselbert hired Dutch dike builders to create the then modern harbor town of Buxtehude. As they were completing this town, they built a church with a very high steeple that was fitted out with bells. Although most of the towns in the area rang their bells by means of a simple hammer, these bells, soon called the dogs, were to be rung with ropes. It didn't take long for the ropes to be so frayed that they looked like the tails of dogs. From that point, 'the *dogs*' (bells) were rung by means of their *tails* (the frayed ropes): nowadays, the metaphor has be-

Monument: The Hare and the Hedgehog (Fairy Tale of the Brothers Grimm)

Fleth, part of the medieval harbor

Man on the Rail

come a reality as Buxtehude is known as the place where dogs literally "bark with their tails."

According to the *Children's and Household Tales*, the footrace between *the Hare and the Hedgehog* took place on the *Buxtehude Heath*. This legendary race is commemorated in countless ways in the picturesque old town: in the *Buxtehude Museum* (special exhibit on the theme of the Hare and the Hedgehog), at the Town Hall of Buxtehude, at the entrance to the *Ratskeller*, in the *monument* to the Hare and the Hedgehog, and in the *Hare and Hedgehog Walkway* among others. Wilhelm Schröder (1808–78) wrote this fairy tale in Low German and published it for the first time in the Volksblatt newspaper of Hanover on April 4th, 1840.

History

The Buxtehude Museum for Regional History and Art

The settlement built around a royal court of *buochstadon* (located in the contemporary subdivision of Altkloster) was mentioned for the first time in a document of Otto I in the year 959. The Archbishop Giselbert of Bremen founded the town of Buxtehude about one mile from the original settlement on a sandy island in the bottomlands of the Este River in 1285. It was the first systematically designed town built around a harbor basin in Germany. This newly built town, called New Town, assumed over time the name of the original settlement, Buxtehude. Overseas trade created a rapid boom for this town defended by a town wall and dikes. It received the town charter for the district of Stade in 1328 and was a member of the Hanseatic League as early as 1363. In the Thirty Years War, it was conquered by the Danes and the Swedes, passing over to Sweden as a result of the Treaty of Westphalia in 1648, then to Denmark in 1712, and finally to Hanover in 1715.

What to See and Do

The historic old Hanseatic town of Buxtehude, with its old town dike called *Viver* and its medieval harbor, the *Fleth*, is well-preserved.

1. Buxtehude is sometimes called the Fairy Tale Town, a title it shares with Kassel, and has civic events that underscore this fact including the naming of a Fairy Tale Story Teller as well as gatherings of fairy tale characters every other year. In the **Buxtehude Museum for Regional**

Gothic St. Petri Church: interior

History and Art on Stavenort, one finds a special exhibiton on the fairy tale theme of *the Hare and the Hedgehog*. The building also includes the Homeland Museum of 1913 with its beautiful ceramic ornamentation and a modern addition and also examples of local handicraft art, exhibit-pieces from the St. Petri Church including a Dutch passion altar from the 15th century.

2. The round outer ward of the old town wall, the **Marschtorzwinger** (Marsh Gate Outer Ward), erected in 1539, still stands on the feeder to the Fleth. A closed development with **historical private homes** is located in the *Abtstraße* and also in the *Lange Straße* and *Westfleth* with particularly beautiful examples at numbers 3 and 6 of the Abtstraße and 25 and 37 of the Lange Straße and at Westfleth 29, 35, and 45.

3. The medieval **Town Hall** in the Breite Straße 2 was destroyed by a fire in 1911 and replaced by an Art Nouveau reconstruction that absorbed the remains of the old décor.

4. The most meaningful structure of the Hanseatic town is the triple-nave Gothic **St. Petri Church**, which was encased in brick in the 19th century. The inside of the building retains its original character. Of particular note of the furnishings are the *Halepaghen Altar* (late Gothic with scenes of the passion), a crucifix, a choir stall from the beginning of the 15th century, the Baroque high altar as well as the pulpit of 1674. The most famous art object, the Buxtehude Altar (ca. 1400), is represented by a copy in the church itself as the original is displayed as a loan in the Kunsthalle (Art Hall) of Hamburg.

Climbing the 96 steps to the observation deck of the church tower provides a wonderful view of Buxtehude, the Old Land (marshland) and beyond the Elbe to the harbor facilities of the neighboring Hanseatic City of Hamburg.

Town Guide in historical Old Land costume and visitors in front of a typical Buxtehude half-timbered house

5. Out of town the **church of Neukloster**, built in 1903 with the rich furnishings from the dismantled abbey church, and the historic thatch-roofed water mill of Ovelgönne are worth seeing.

6. Outside the gates of Buxtehude is the **Old Land**, a rich and fruitful marshland. An excursion to the marshland is highly recommended as the Old Land is the largest enclosed fruit region in Germany and very magical when the apple and cherry blossoms turn the landscape into a sea of blossoms. Also impressive are the farm houses covered by picturesque thatched-roofs and onion patterns between the white half-timbered beams.

Bremen: the Free Hanseatic City

and World Heritage Site

Fairy Tale, Saga and Literary References

Once you begin travelling the *Fairy Tale Route*, the next to last destination is Bremen. *We are going to Bremen*, is the word on the road in the famous tale of the *Bremen Town Musicians*, but even if we aren't going to Bremen for musical reasons, we now begin to feel the air of the northern seas.

Although the donkey, dog, cat, and hen never quite reached Bremen in the Brothers Grimm tale, they nevertheless belong to Bremen, where one encounters them in every nook and cranny. On the west side of the City Hall, not far from the Ratskeller, stands the bronze statue of the Bremen Town Musicians created by Gerhard Marcks. It has become a beloved photographic subject.

The Bremen Town Musicians

The famed Ratskeller of Bremen, renowned for the 650 different German wines stored in its wine cellar, is also a storied place. This subterranean kingdom of wine with the huge painted wine kegs from the 17th and 18th centuries has frequently inspired both famous and the not-so-famous writers. In his poem *In Harbor* from the second North Sea Cycle, Heinrich Heine writes, *"Lucky the man who reaches the harbor and then sits warm and relaxed in the good Bremen Ratskeller."* The *Hauff Cellar* re-

The famed Ratskeller of Bremen

minds us still today of the visit of the young Swabian writer, Wilhelm Hauff (1802–27), to the cellar in 1826. Hauff was personally accompanied by Mayor Smidt and assisted down the steep staircase by the Senators Droste and Gildemeister. In his story, *Fantasies in the Bremen Ratskeller, an Autumn Gift for the Friends of Wine,* Wilhelm Hauff left Bremen and the Ratskeller an enduring literary monument with his famous *Rose Wine.*

Mayor Smidt was a friend and patron of Jacob and Wilhelm Grimm. There were connections between Bremen and Kassel and (Jo-) Hanne Smidt, daughter of the mayor, probably contributed the Bremen variation of the Grimm fairy tale *Fair Katrinelje (Die schöne Katrinelje) and Pif Paf Poltrie* to the brothers.

Just across the City Hall, the Town Musicians decorate the official seal of the *German House.* Further appearances of the four are in the *Hauff Cellar* of the Ratskeller in a fresco by Max Slevogt and in the *Council Chamber* as well as in the historic *Böttcherstraße.* There the Town Musicians decorate the stair-case of the *St. Peter House* and, as small sculptures along with clay reliefs of the *Seven Lazybones* (Sieben Faulen), they festoon the fountain of the same name.

UNESCO World Heritage Site: Bremen City Hall

One well-known saga in Bremen is about the arsenic serial murderer, *Gesche Gottfried*, who was executed in Cathedral Square at a spot marked by stones that even today are covered with the *spit of disgusted citizens* of this northern city. Other sagas are *The Countess Emma and the Cripple* as well as *The Clucking Hen of Bremen.*

Also in the Böttcherstraße, a plaque reminds us of the *Robinson Crusoe House* honoring Daniel Defoe's English adventure novel, *Robinson Crusoe.* In the first paragraph of that novel, the reader is told that Robinson's father came from Bremen and his real name was *Kreutznaer*, although the family name became Crusoe in England.

For those interested in folklore, it is worth noting that the publisher of *Bremen's Folk Legends,* Friedrich Wagenfeld (1810–46), and the

Böttcherstraße

founder and publisher of the series *Fairy Tales of World Literature*, Friedrich von der Leyen (1873–1966) were both born in Bremen. The same is true for the story-teller Wilhelm Scharrelmann (1875–1950, his *Cottage in the Devil's Moor* is a continuation of the *Bremen Town Musicians*, and Johann von Harten who edited the well-known collection, *Lower Saxony's Wellspring of Legends*, with Karl Henniger.

History

The year 782 is the first documented mention of Bremen with respect to the battles that the Saxon Duke Wittekind was conducting against Charlemagne. Five years later, Charlemagne established a bishopric in Bremen and the Anglo-Saxon Willehad was Bremen's first bish-

Bremen Cathedral: interior

op. After the destruction of Hamburg by the Normans in 845, Archbishop Ansgar (801–65) settled in Bremen, which became increasingly important as the launching point of the Christian mission work extending into Scandinavia. In 888, King Arnulf granted the first market privileges to Bremen and Emperor Otto I granted additional privileges including courts, customs, and currency rights in 965.

For a long time, the archbishop's mission activities aided the expansion of trade and transportation with foreign lands for Bremen, but eventually the citizenry gained so much autonomy that it developed its own trade relations with the north, the east, the Netherlands, and England. Bremen joined the Hanseatic League in 1358 and

Three-masted Vessel on the Weser River in Bremen

in the following years became a crucial member of this important mercantile association.

The last decade of the 18th century held major significance in Bremen's flowering into a modern world-class seaport. The impetus for this came from the United States, which later became one of the most important trading partners of Bremen. The first requirement for a burgeoning overseas trading presence is the existence of a first-class harbor. While it might be warlike neighbors or sea pirates who normally threaten trade, for Bremen the danger since the 16th century was its slow separation from the sea due to the continued silting up of the lower Weser River.

From 1619 to 1622, Bremen created the new regional port 18 km below the city in Vegesack where the Lesum flows into the Weser River. But this provided only a temporary reprieve. Soon ships couldn't even reach Vegesack and Bremen saw itself forced to use the communities of Elsfleth and Brake in the competing principality of Oldenburg as anchorages. The forward-thinking mayor, Johann Smidt, was successful in acquiring a strip of land 70 km north of Bremen from the Kingdom of Hanover and building a new harbor there for Bremen. Known as Bremerhaven, this permanent seaport secured and still secures for Bremen a competitive position in world shipping.

UNESCO World Heritage Site: The Roland Figure, Symbol of Justice and City Freedom

What to See and Do

1. Every Sunday from May to October, **the Bremen Town Musicians** tell their story at 12 o'clock on the cathedral square near the City Hall. Also recommended is a guided tour of the historic city center with the Bremen Town Musicians.

2. Situated on the marketplace are two proud structures of Bremen that have been recognized as **World Heritage Sites** by UNESCO: **the statue of Roland and the City Hall.** Its centerpiece is the monumental 800-year-old **City Hall** with its Weser Renaissance façade from the early 17th century. In the middle of the marketplace stands the symbol of justice and city freedom, the **Roland** figure from 1404. Of course, there is the famous Ratskeller in the City Hall with its wine cellar, popular restaurant, and the Bremen Town Musicians near the entry. Across the square is the Schütting, the Merchants' Guild House (1536) and proud houses from the 17th to 19th centuries as well as **St. Peter's Cathedral** (11th century).

3. Afterwards, slip into the **Böttcherstraße** next to the Schütting, a quaint lane with shops and museums and a panoply of traditional and expressionistic homes including the Paula Becker-Moderson House, the Roselius House, the St. Peter House, and even the Robinson Crusoe House. This street leads down to the Weser that has riverside walkways leading to the Schnoor and beyond.

Schnoor, Bremen's oldest quarter

4. A walk through Bremen's oldest quarter, **the Schnoor**, with its picturesque seafarer's and artisan's homes demonstrates what Bremen was like during the 14th and 15th centuries. Other things to see include windmills, the Oversea Museum, the famous **Kunsthalle** (art hall) and its masterworks from the 16th-21th centuries, and the *Weserburg Museum* with its collection of modern art.

5. Another important museum is the **Bremer Landesmuseum** for Art and Cultural History, named Focke-Museum located in an area surrounded by old oak trees in the noble district Schwachhausen, with its collections of art and cultural history, the history of the shipping industry and the economy, for pre- and early history as well with its puppet and glass collection.

Haus Riensberg - Focke Museum, officially called Bremer Landesmuseum for Art and Cultural History

6. The strikingly designed **Universum Science Center** in Bremen permits children, adolescents and adults to go on an exciting expedition through the imaginary continents – mankind, earth and cosmos – where different scientific phenomena are explored through the senses.

7. To get the flavor of Bremen's first artificial harbor at Vegesack, it is worth a trip to see this town with its seafarer's homes and the Havenhaus from 1645.

What is a *Hanseatic City*?

Although most appropriately attached to Bremen, this information could apply to a surprising number of places on the Fairy Tale Route. For about two centuries (1241–1441) during the Middle Ages, the Hanseatic League, a loose confederation of towns and cities around northern Germany and the Baltic Sea, existed to allow a network of towns and cities to band together to ensure the relatively free and safe movement of goods in their domain. Because there was no central German government, this league provided merchants with an element of security and exclusivity, but the Hanseatic League met only intermittently after reaching its peak of influence in the 14th century and gradually waned in importance, holding its last Diet in 1669.

In our era, with the collapse of the Soviet Union and the continued expansion of the European Union into the Baltic Region, it is not unusual to read once again about the emergence of a single market to permit the free movement of goods, capital, as well as people, between the trading partners. The idea of the Hansa has re-emerged since the 1980's and has particularly grown in scope following the collapse of the Warsaw Pact in 1990. Annual meetings focus on contemporary issues such as environmental protection and historical preservation.

For most, however, the single most visible remnant of the Hanseatic League is the HL (Lübeck), HH (Hamburg), and HB (Bremen) on the license plates of those cities to identify each as a former Hansestadt (Greifswald, HGW, Wismar, HWI and Rostock, HRO, also retain the H).

Of course, it's absolutely unclear whether Bremen's reputation as a Hanseatic city has anything to do with the idea of the Town Musicians of this famous tale to make Bremen their destination. But these were very sophisticated animals.

Seaside City of Bremerhaven

Saga References

The drum rolls marking the inclusion of the Seaside City of Bremerhaven into the German Fairy Tale Route stirred up the hobgoblin known as the *Klabautermann*. According to tradition, he is a good ship spirit who only leaves a vessel if it is going down.

Fountain: The Ship's Goblin Klabauter Man

Another notable character is the sailor *Hein Mück*, of whom it is reported in a shanty song that he ships out into the world from Bremerhaven to visit diverse ports where he thrills the world of women.

Other legends, such as *The Giant Rik* and the *Sandbar of Red Sand* or *The Devil in the*

Skyline Bremerhaven
© Gross

Sail Ship Seute Deern, on board a homey restaurant

Wulsdorfer Parish Garden as well as the shanty song *Hein Mück* are found in the small collection *The Klabautermann and Other Legends and Stories In and Around Bremerhaven* by E.M. Iba.

History

Bremerhaven, located where the Geeste River flows into the Weser, was founded at the beginning of the 20th century through the merger of three Lower Weser towns: Bremerhaven, Lehe, and Geestemünde along with some surrounding villages. The founding of Bremerhaven itself occurred in 1827, when the visionary mayor of Bremen, Johann Smidt (see Bremen),

Old Harbor

acquired a 220 acre site belonging to Lehe on the Weser estuary from the Kingdom of Hanover. He then commissioned a native of Amsterdam, hydraulic engineer Jacobus Johannes van Ronzelen (1800–65), to construct a new port for Bremen and lay out a new attached town to be named Bremerhaven. Other territorial concessions were necessary to allow for the expansion of the growing town and harbor as they had increased ten times their original scope by 1939.

Climate House Bremerhaven 8° East

New Lock in the New Harbor

After the founding of Bremerhaven, the Kingdom of Hanover built the port and town Geestemünde (1845–47) on the land of the village of Geestendorf on the opposite side of the Geeste. The rapidly growing community was merged with Geestendorf under the name Geestemünde in 1889 and received town rights in 1913.

The market town of Lehe was for many centuries the most important settlement at the mouth of the Weser. That place, whose first documented mention was as early as 1270, was granted a market privilege in the 16th century by the Bremen Council. After the founding of Bremerhaven, Lehe developed more and more into a sleeping and living community for the port workers of Bremen. In 1880, Lehe received a town-like constitution and was given town rights in 1920. In 1924 it was united with Geestemünde as the city of Wesermünde into which Bremerhaven was also incorporated in 1939 with the international ports remaining under the ownership of Bremen. After World War II, the city of Wesermünde became an American supply base under the sovereignty of city state Bremen and was renamed Bremerhaven in 1947.

The German Emigration Center Bremerhaven

What to See and Do

1. Highlights of the tourist-magnet **Havenwelten** (Harbor Worlds) composed of the historical *Old* and the *New Harbor* include the award-winning **German Emigration Center Bremerhaven** (Europe's largest hands-on mu-

The National German Maritime Museum

seum on the topic of migration. From 1830 to 1974 over seven million people emigrated from Bremerhaven to overseas locations. The museum also features 300 years of immigration to Germany), the futuristic **Klimahaus** (Climate House) Bremerhaven 8° Ost (visitors travel one time around the world along the 8th degree of longitude from Bremerhaven and experience nine different climatic zones of the world), the **Atlantic Hotel SAIL City** (hotel, observation deck, etc.) and the new im-jaich **Lloyd Marina**.

2. The **Old Harbor**, laid out by JJ van Ronzelen in the years 1827–30, is now used as an open air museum, where among others, the three-masted *Seute Deern* (sailing ship of 1919 – on board is a restaurant), the submarine *Wilhelm Bauer Technical Museum*, the light ship *Elbe 3* and the *whaling steamer Rau IX* are moored and can be visited.

3. Located just behind the Weser Dike in the Old Harbor is the **National German Maritime Museum**, the final project of the German architect Hans Scharoun (1893–1972) who grew up in Bremerhaven. To be seen in the main building are the centerpieces – the *paddle steamer MEISSEN*, the parlor and a whaling commander as well as the Bremen **Hanse Kogge**, the most important German sailing ship from the time of the Middle Ages (around 1380).

4. Located on the Weser and the New Harbor is the **Zoo at the Sea** with its collection of northern-focused species and aquatic animals (500 animals of 50 species) as well as the *Simon Loschen Lighthouse* built in Neo-Gothic style in 1854.

Zoo at the Sea

5. Extended between the Overseas Harbor and the Weser is the internationally known *Columbuskaje* and the *Columbus Cruise Center*. Worth seeing is the large international port located north of the city center with the **container terminal** and to the south the **Shop Window Fishery Harbor** – the historic fishing harbor now a maritime strolling mile focused on fish and the sea with restaurants, a smoking

Container Terminal Bremerhaven

house and the museum ship FMS Gera, a floating offshore fishing museum.

6. On the banks of the Geeste is the **Historical Museum of Bremerhaven** (opened for the first time in Geestemünde in 1906), a modern designed regional museum of history, shipping, art and culture of the coast and right across the Geeste River you can find Germany's oldest dry dock – the *Wenckedock.*

Located nearby in the city center on the other side of the Geeste are historic buildings of the former *emigrant boarding house* (now part of the campus of the University of Bremerhaven) and the *Mayor Smidt Memorial Church,* built from 1853–70 according to plans by Simon Loschen in Neo-Gothic style.

The Ship's Goblin Klabauter Man

(Johann J. Cordes/ Ferdinand Müller – English version: E. Michael Iba/Thomas L. Johnson)

Not far from the National German Maritime Museum in Bremerhaven across from the radar tower stands a fountain with a dwarflike little man, the *Klabauter Man*. In the popular belief, the Klabauter Man is a goblin who lives on wooden ships; he is known everywhere on the coast. He takes his name from *kalfatern*, a maritime word having to do with the sealing of cracks and seams between the ship and deck planks with oakum and pitch.

The Klabauter Man, described by some as a gray and by others as a red little man with a thick head and fine hands, is barely two feet tall, but of a compact stature. He is supposed to be the spirit of a dead man whose soul had originally taken residence in a tree. If this tree is selected to be the mast of a ship, the spirit of the Klabauter Man comes into existence as protector of the ship and its crew. In order to keep him in good humor, the crew places a keg full of milk on the deck. When that happens, he sews and cleans, hammers and knocks like a good fairy for the sailors. May God have mercy on them when he is in a bad mood; then spars and other shipboard equipment fly around, he makes noise, loosens hawsers and sails and, taking invisible form, boxes the sailors' ears. If he sits high above on the mast or on the spreaders between the sails, then earnest concerns creep into the hearts of the shippers. Then the weather-hard seamen know that their ship is in great danger. In the hour of sinking, the Klabauter Man appears next to the captain on the command bridge, extends him a hand of farewell and flies away before the eyes of those doomed to die in storm and waves.

Once the Klabauter Man appeared before an easily upsettable and hot-tempered ship carpenter. He had become offended by the noise that the Klabauter Man made nights in the cargo bay of the ship that cost him so many hours of sleep. In his anger, he reached for a stick of wood and hurled it against the little man. His throw unfortunately hit the Klabauter Man on the thigh and broke his leg.

Several days later, the carpenter stumbled over an unseen hindrance. Murmuring a blasphemous curse, he tried to raise himself, but oh woe, it didn't happen. At that very moment a shrill mocking laughter rang out from the ship's compartment and the carpenter knew immediately who had played the trick on him.

Göttingen

Major Brothers Grimm Locale

The Göttingen Seven

From 1830–37, Jacob and Wilhelm Grimm served as professors and librarians at the University of Göttingen and seemed on track to establish sterling academic careers. That all ended when they and five others were caught up in the vehement protests occurring as the new king, Ernst August, violated the legal constitution and dissolved the parliament. Known thereafter as the *Göttingen Seven*, these professors were illegitimately removed from their positions and forced to leave both the city of Göttingen and the Kingdom of Hanover.

Market Square: The Town Hall

Wilhelmsplatz: University Building (1835–37)

Fairy Tale and Literary References

The Göttingen years had been productive years for Jacob and Wilhelm; they had produced the volume *Teutonic Mythology*; new editions of *Freidank*, a Middle High German didactic poet of the early 13th century whom Wilhelm hypothesized was really Walther von der Vogelweide; *Reynard the Fox*; and the *Rosengarten Saga*.

In 1838, because of their banishment from the Kingdom of Hanover, the Brothers Grimm agreed to begin work on the *German Dictionary*, a task they were destined to never see finished in their lifetimes. Indeed, this completed work appeared for the first time in 1961 in a sixteen-volume edition including more than 67,000 separate entries and about 320,000 key words.

Completely in keeping with the Brothers Grimm is the work of Georg Schambach (1811–97) and Wilhelm Müller (1812–90), who became acquainted with each other in one of the lectures of Jacob Grimm. They subsequently published their volume, *Lower Saxon Sagas and Fairy Tales*, "directly from the voices of the people" in Göttingen in 1854.

Wilhelmsplatz: Assembly Hall (Universitätsaula)

Today, the editorial office of the *Encyclopedia of the Fairy Tale*, a reference work presenting the results of almost two centuries of international research in the field of folk narrative, is located in Göttingen. Its founder was the narrative researcher, Kurt Ranke, successor to Will-Erich Peuckert as the chair of folklore at Göttingen. With titles like *The Spider in the Yucca Palm* and *The Mouse in the Jumbo Jet*, Rolf Wilhelm Brednich (1935–) continues the saga tradition of the Grimms in a decidedly more modern context.

History

Göttingen, a great German university city in Lower Saxony, provides the purest example of how an old town can be revived through the founding of a university. Though the first docu-

Interior of Pauliner Church (14th century), since the 19th century University Library; working place of the Brothers Grimm

mented mention of Göttingen comes from a land deed of Emperor Otto I in 953, it received its municipal charter in the early 13th century. Its membership in the Hanseatic League in the 14th and 15th centuries allowed it to thrive, but the subsequent war years saw it revert back into a listless provincial town.

Georgia Augusta University was founded in 1734 by the appropriately named Georg August, Elector of Hanover – known also as George II, King of Great Britain and Ireland (1683–1760). The growth of that university into one of the major academic institutions of Europe brought Göttingen a stature it continues to enjoy to this day. It celebrates more than 40 Nobel laureates, placing it alongside only Cambridge.

Otto von Bismarck, the first chancellor of modern Germany, studied in the city in 1833, living in the old fortress tower on the Wall now called the *Bismarck Cottage*.

The 19th century American writer Henry Wadsworth Longfellow also spent time studying in Göttingen as did Edward Everett, who was the other speaker on the day Abraham Lincoln delivered his *Gettysburg Address*. Even Ben Franklin spent a day in Göttingen on July

A freshly baked doctor is kissing Gänseliesl (goose girl)

19, 1766, taking a seat in the Society of the Sciences.

What to See and Do

1. Kiss (or at least take a picture of) **Gänseliesel**, the little goose girl, whose bronze likeness in front of the historical Town Hall has earned her the reputation of the most kissed girl in the world because each academic with a freshly baked doctorate is obliged to give her a kiss. So rampant was the practice that the city council proclaimed a short lived kissing ban in 1926.

2. Walk through the **Old Town Hall** behind Gänseliesel with its Gothic porch and ancient heating system. Then have a look at the numerous half-timbered houses of the city: Pauliner Straße 6 (1495), Ratsapotheke (1480), Schrödersches Haus (1549) and Gasthaus Schwarzer Bär (1590).

3. St. Johannis Church. Built in the early 14th century, this church has a nave and two aisles of Gothic design, while the north portal displays a Romanesque style. Other noteworthy churches from the 14th to 15th centuries include St. Albani and St. Jacobi (1350–1433). The Marienkirche from the 13th to 15th centuries is known for its winged altar (1524).

View towards St. Johannis Church (14th century)

4. Visit the **Old Assembly Hall** inside the University Classical Building (1835–37), a gift to the university on the occasion of its 100th birthday by King William IV. The Brothers Grimm worked at the university library that is still housed in the Pauliner Church (14th century).

5. Somewhat outside downtown on the Nikolausberg is the imposing former **Augustinian cloister church Nikolausberg** (first mentioned in 12th century). This former cloister church was a pilgrimage site until into the 17th century.

Who exactly is Gänseliesel?

If you're not careful, you can quickly assume that the picturesque little bronze girl with the flowers and a goose in the center of Göttingen is yet another depiction of a Grimm fairy tale character. After all, there are over 200 Grimm fairy tales and many do feature geese and girls and at least one is named the Goose Girl, so it all seems natural. In fact, until an author named Hans A. Piper produced a Gänseliesel Fairy Tale in 2003, there was just the century-old sculpture (the first Gänseliesel sculpture by Paul Nisse was placed in front of the Town Hall in July 1901) and the tradition of newly-degreed graduate students planting a kiss on this most kissed girl in the world.

Berlin

Major Brothers Grimm Locale

Jacob and Wilhelm Grimm Center: Glass door of the Central Library of the Humboldt University

The capital city of Germany is not considered part of the German Fairy Tale Route and is actually quite distant from it. Kassel, the major hub of that route, is 380 kilometers from Berlin. Nevertheless, in a book that subtitles itself *The Storied World of the Brothers Grimm*, we considered it important to include Berlin as this was the place where the Brothers Grimm spent the final two decades of their lives, where they conducted their research, and where they were ultimately buried. For that reason, we have chosen to briefly include a summary of their time in Berlin and to also include visual references to the fairy tale landscape of Berlin. To discover more about Berlin's attractions for tourists who are English-speakers, look under www.visitberlin.de.

Fairy Tale References

Fairy Tale Fountain in Volkspark Friedrichshain

In Berlin, there are two streets and a narrow lane that bear the name of the Brothers Grimm. Much more evident than their authors' names, however, are the many pathways and streets in Berlin that get their names from fairy tales. In the fairy tale district of Köpenick, for example, one finds seven streets including the Star-Money Street (Sterntalerstraße) and Tom Thumb's Way (Däumlingsweg). Several foutains are decorated with motifs from fairy tales of the Brothers Grimm, including the large Fairy Tale Fountain in the public park of Friedrichshain,

Brandenburg Gate

the Neukölln Fairy Tale Fountain, the Goose Girl Fountain in Wilmersdorf, and the Frog Prince Fountain in Pankow.

Along with Kassel, Hanau, Steinau and other places of the German Fairy Tale Route, Berlin is a mecca for fans of fairy tales. From Berlin, the association *MÄRCHENLAND – German Center for Fairy Tale Culture*, organizes more than 1,500 events for children and adults throughout Europe every year. During the Berlin Fairy Tale Days in November, a significant number of fairy tale events are presented.

Biographical and Research History of the Brothers Grimm in Berlin

The Brothers Grimm spent roughly twenty years of their lives in Berlin; their life journey ended there (Wilhelm died on December 16, 1859 – Jacob on September 20, 1863). In March

1841, the Brothers Grimm moved with their family from Kassel to Berlin, where they continued their work on the German Dictionary. Because of royal family alliances (King Frederick William IV of Prussia was a nephew of King Ernst August of Hanover who had removed Jacob and Wilhelm Grimm from their university posts – see Göttingen Seven), the Brothers Grimm were not appointed to the University of Berlin, but received a special salary from the personal assets of the king. As members of the Academy of Sciences, however, it was possible for them to give lectures at the university (today Humboldt University of Berlin). Between the years 1841–46, the Grimms lived with their family in the Lennéstraße (adjacent to the Tiergarten), 1846–47 in Dorotheenstraße and from 1847 in the Linkstraße (near the former Potsdamer Bahnhof).

Humboldt University

In addition to new editions of the Children's and Household Tales and publication of the history of the German language (J. Grimm), the principal occupation of the Brothers Grimm was working on the gigantic task that was the German Dictionary (see also Göttingen). Part of their extensive library of more than 5,500 vol-

Berlin Cathedral

Gendarmenmarkt (Square)

umes is housed today in the University Library. Original documents related to the German Dictionary are kept in the Berlin-Brandenburg Academy of Sciences and the confidential State Archives.

All of their residences in Berlin were destroyed in the Second World War. In addition to street and fairy tales names, the Grimms are remembered today in Berlin with a commemorative plaque at the house Potsdamer Straße 5, near Potsdamer Platz, their honorary graves at the old St. Matthew's Cemetery in Schöneberg and the Jacob and Wilhelm Grimm Center (Central Library of the Humboldt University).

Graves of the Brothers Grimm

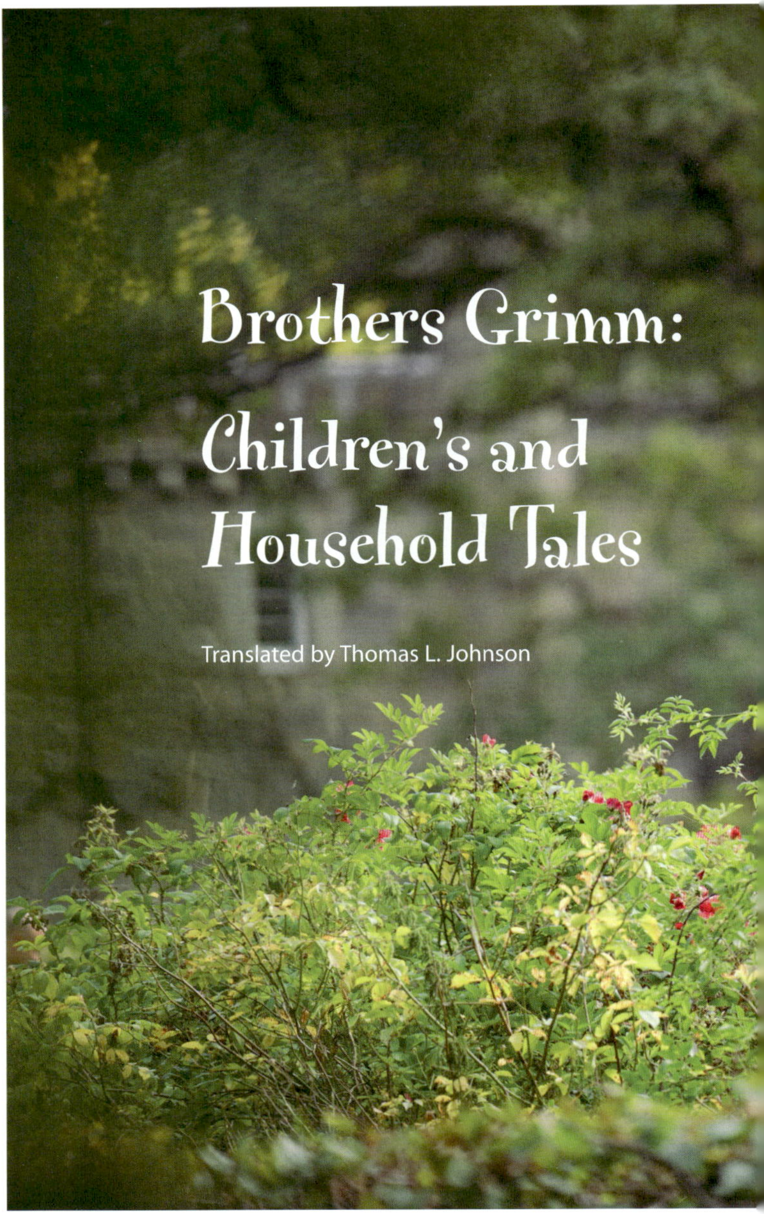

Brothers Grimm: Children's and Household Tales

Translated by Thomas L. Johnson

The Wolf and the Seven Little Kids

(Brothers Grimm)

Once up on a time an old nanny goat had seven little kids whom she loved with all the love a mother has for her children. One day she wanted to go into the forest to get some food, so she called all seven to her and said, "Dear children, I have to go into the forest, so be on your guard against the wolf; if he comes in, he will devour you completely – skin and hair. The villain often disguises himself, but you can always recognize him by his gruff voice and his black feet."

The kids said, "Dear mother, we will take good care of ourselves; you can leave without worrying." So the old one bleated and went on her way with an easy mind.

It wasn't long before someone knocked at the door and called, "Open the door, dear children; mother is here and has brought back something for each of you."

But the little kids knew by the gruff voice that it was the wolf. "We will not open the door," they cried. "You aren't our mother. She has a soft, pleasant voice, but your voice is rough; you are the wolf!"

So the wolf went off to a shopkeeper and bought himself a large lump of chalk and ate it to soften his voice. Then he came back, knocked at the door of the house, and cried, "Open the door, dear children, your mother is here and has brought back something for each of you."

But the wolf had laid his black paws onto the windowsill, and when the children saw them they cried, "We won't open the door. Our mother doesn't have black feet like you; you are the wolf."

Then the wolf ran to a baker and said, "I have stubbed my toes, rub some dough over them for me." And when the baker had rubbed his paws, he ran to the miller and said, "Sprinkle some white meal over my feet for me."

The miller thought to himself, "The wolf wants to deceive someone," so he refused; but the wolf said, "If you won't do it, I'll eat you up!" At that point the miller was fearful enough to make his paws white for him. That is how people are.

So now the villain approached the house the third time, knocked at the door and said, "Open the door for me, children; your dear little mother has come home and has brought back with her something for each one of you from the forest."

The little kids cried, "First show us your paws so that we may know if you are our dear little mother." So he put his paws in through the window, and when the kids saw that they were white, they believed that what he said was true, and opened the door. But who should come in but the wolf! They were terrified and wanted to hide themselves. One sprang under the table, the second into the bed, the third into the stove, the fourth into the kitchen, the fifth into the cupboard, the sixth under the washing bowl, and the seventh into the clock cabinet.

The wolf found them all and unceremoniously swallowed one after the other. The youngest, hidden in the clock cabinet, was the only one he didn't find. Once the wolf had satisfied his appetite, he took off, lay down under a tree in the green meadow outside and began to sleep.

Soon afterwards the nanny goat came home again from the forest. Oh! What a shock she had! The house door stood wide open. The table, chairs, and benches were thrown down, the washing-bowl lay broken in pieces, and the quilts and pillows were pulled off the bed. She looked for her children, but they were nowhe-

re to be found. She called them one after another by name, but no one answered. At last, when she came to the youngest, a soft voice cried, "Dear mother, I am in the clock cabinet." She took him out, and he told her that the wolf had come and had eaten all the others. You can only imagine how she wept over her poor children.

Finally, in her grief she went out, and the youngest kid ran with her. When they reached the meadow, they saw the wolf beneath the tree snoring so loudly that its branches shook. She looked at him from every angle and saw that something was wriggling and struggling in his gorged belly. "Oh, dear God," said she, "is it possible that my poor children whom he has swallowed for his supper might still be alive?"

Then she told the kid to run home to fetch scissors and a needle and thread. The goat then cut open the monster's stomach, but hardly had she made one cut when one little kid thrust its head out, and when she cut farther, all six sprang out one after another. They were all still alive and had suffered no injuries at all, for in his gluttony the monster had swallowed them all whole. What joy there was! They embraced their dear mother and jumped like a tailor at his wedding.

The mother, however, said, "Now go and look for some big stones, and we will fill this godless beast's stomach with them while he is still asleep." Then the seven kids quickly dragged the stones to her and put as many of them into his stomach as they could; and the mother sewed him up again in the greatest haste, so that he was not aware of anything and never once stirred.

When the wolf finally had his full nap, he got up, and because the stones in his stomach made him very thirsty, he wanted to go to a well to drink. But when he began to walk and move about, the stones in his stomach knocked against each other and rattled. Then he cried,

"What rumbles and tumbles
Against my poor bones?
I thought it was kids,
But it's nothing but stones."

When he reached the well and bent over the water for a drink, the heavy stones pulled him down and he drowned miserably. After the seven kids saw that, they came running past the spot and cried loudly, "The wolf is dead! The wolf is dead!" and danced for joy around the well with their mother.

Rapunzel

(Brothers Grimm)

Once upon a time there were a man and a woman who had wished in vain very long for a child. Finally, the woman believed that God was about to grant her wish. Now these people had a little window at the back of their house from which a splendid garden full of the most beautiful flowers and herbs could be seen. There was a high wall surrounding it, however, so no one dared enter it because it belonged to an enchantress, who had great power and was dreaded by all the world.

One day as the woman was standing at this window and looking down into the garden, she saw a bed that was planted with the most beautiful rampion (rapunzel), and it looked so fresh and green that she began to crave it. After several days, her craving caused her to waste away, and she began to look pale and miserable. At that point, her husband became concerned and asked: "What is wrong with you, dear wife?"

"Oh," she replied, "if I can't eat some of the rapunzel that is in the garden behind our house, I shall certainly die."

The man, who loved her deeply, thought: "Rather than let my wife die, I'll bring her some of the rapunzel myself, cost what it may."

So at dusk he climbed over the wall into the garden of the enchantress, hastily grabbed a handful of rapunzel, and took it to his wife. She quickly made herself a salad with it and ate it greedily. It tasted so good to her – so very good in fact, that the next day she craved it three times as much as before. If she were to have any peace, her husband knew he would have to enter the garden one more time.

So he set out at dusk again, but just when he had climbed down to the other side, he received a terrible scare when he saw the enchantress standing in front of him. "How dare you sneak into my garden like a thief to steal my rapunzel?" she said with an angry look. You will suffer for this!"

"Oh please," he answered, "let mercy take the place of justice; I only made up my mind to do this out of necessity. My wife saw your

rapunzel from the window and felt such a craving for it that she would have died if she had not gotten some to eat."

Then the enchantress allowed her anger to soften a bit, and said to him: "If the situation is exactly as you say, I will allow you to take away as much rapunzel as you need on one condition only: you must give me the child that your wife will bring into the world; it will be treated well as I will care for it like a mother." In his terror, the man agreed to everything, and when his wife had the baby, the enchantress appeared at once, gave the child the name of Rapunzel, and took it away with her.

Rapunzel grew into the most beautiful child under the sun. When she was twelve years old, the enchantress locked her up in a tower out in a forest. The tower had neither stairs nor a door, but had a little window at its top. When the enchantress wanted to enter, she placed herself beneath it and cried:

"Rapunzel, Rapunzel,
Let down your hair."

Rapunzel had magnificent long hair, as fine as spun gold, and when she heard the voice of the enchantress, she unfastened her braided tresses, wound them around a window hook, and then dropped the braid down seventy five feet to the ground so the enchantress could climb up on it.

After several years, it just so happened that a prince rode through the forest and passed by the tower. From above, he heard a song that was so beautiful that he stood still and listened. This was Rapunzel, who passed her time of solitude in the tower by letting her sweet voice resound. The prince wanted to climb up to her and looked for the door of the tower, but couldn't find one. He rode home, but the singing had touched his heart so deeply that he went out into the forest every day to hear it. Once, when he was standing behind a tree listening, he saw that an enchantress arrived and heard how she cried:

"Rapunzel, Rapunzel,
Let down your hair."

Then Rapunzel lowered the braids of her hair, and the enchantress climbed up to her. "If that is the ladder by which one climbs, I will also try my luck", he said. As it began to get dark the next day, he went to the tower and called out:

"Rapunzel, Rapunzel,
Let down your hair."

Immediately the hair fell down and the prince climbed it.

Because she had never seen a man before, Rapunzel was at first terribly afraid each time the prince came up to her; but he began to talk to her quite like a friend. He told her that his heart had been so stirred by her singing that it had let him have no rest, and he had no choice but to see her. Rapunzel lost her fear eventually, and when the prince asked her if she would take him as her husband, and she saw that he was young and handsome, she thought: "He will love me more than old Frau Gothel (godmother) does; and she said yes, and laid her hand in his. She said: "I will gladly go away with you, but I do not know how to get down. Bring a skein of silk with you every time that you come, and I will weave it into a ladder and when it is ready, I will climb down and you will take me away on your horse." They agreed that until that time he should come to her every evening, for the old woman came during the day.

The enchantress was unaware of everything until the day Rapunzel said to her: "Tell me, Frau Gothel, how does it happen that you are so much heavier for me to pull up than the young prince–he comes up in just seconds."

"Oh! You godless child," cried the enchantress. "What did I just hear you say! I thought I had cut you off completely from the world, and yet you have deceived me!" In her anger she grabbed Rapunzel's beautiful tresses, wrapped them twice round her left hand, seized a pair of scissors with the right, and snip, snap, they were cut off, and the lovely braid fell to the ground. And then the heartless enchantress took poor Rapunzel into a desolate wasteland where she had to live in great grief and misery.

The very day that she banished Rapunzel, the enchantress fastened the braid of hair that she had cut off to the hook of the window, and when the prince came and cried:

"Rapunzel, Rapunzel,
Let down your hair."

she let the hair down. The prince climbed up, but instead of finding his dearest Rapunzel, he found the enchantress, who gazed at him with evil and venomous looks. "Aha!" she cried mockingly, "you want to fetch your dearest, but the beautiful bird no longer sits singing in her nest; the cat has got her, and will scratch out your eyes as well. Rapunzel is lost to you; you will never see her again."

The prince was beside himself with pain, and in his despair he leapt down from the tower. He escaped with his life, but the thorns into which he fell pierced his eyes. After that, he wandered completely blind around the forest, eating nothing but roots and berries, and did nothing but grieve and weep over the loss of his dearest wife. He roamed blind and in misery for some years, and came at length to the wasteland where Rapunzel lived in wretchedness with the twins, a boy and a girl, to which she had given birth. He heard a voice that seemed so familiar to him that he went towards it, and, when he approached, Rapunzel recognized him and wrapped her arms around his neck and wept. Two of her tears fell into his eyes and they grew clear again, and he could see with them as before. He led her back to his kingdom where he was joyfully received, and they lived happy and contented for a very long time.

Cinderella

(Brothers Grimm)

The wife of a rich man fell ill, and as she felt that her end was drawing near, she called her only daughter to her bedside and said, "Dear child, stay good and pious, and then the good Lord will always stand by you, and I will look down on you from heaven and surround you." Then she closed her eyes and departed. Every day the maiden went out to her mother's grave and wept but remained pious and good. When winter came, the snow spread a white sheet over the grave, and before the spring sun had drawn it away, her husband had taken another wife.

That woman had brought two daughters into the house with her who were beautiful and fair of face, but vile and black of heart. The poor stepchild entered a difficult time.

"Does the stupid goose get to sit in the parlor with us?" they asked. "Whoever wants to eat bread must earn it; out with the kitchen maid." They took away her pretty clothes, put an old gray outfit on her, and gave her wooden shoes. "Just look at the proud princess, how decked out she is!" they cried, laughed and led her into the kitchen. There she had to do hard work from morning till night, get up before daybreak, carry water, light fires, cook and wash.

Besides this, the sisters did everything they could to bring her pain – they mocked her and emptied her peas and lentils into the ashes, so that she was forced to sit and pick them out again. In the evening when she had worked till she was exhausted, she had no bed to go to, but slept instead in the ashes by the fireside. And as that led to her always looking dusty and dirty, they called her Cinderella.

It just so happened that once as the father was going to the fair, he asked his two stepdaughters what he should bring back for them. "Beautiful dresses," said one. "Pearls and jewels," said the other. "And you, Cinderella," he asked. "What do you want?"

"Father, break off the first branch that knocks against your hat on your way home for me." So he bought beautiful dresses, pearls and jewels for his two stepdaughters, and on his way home, as he was riding through a green thicket, he brushed against a hazel branch that knocked off his hat. Then he broke off the branch and took it with him. When he reached home, he gave his step-daughters the things that they had wished for, and to Cinderella he gave the branch from the hazel-bush. After thanking him, Cinderella went to her mother's grave and planted the branch on it and wept so much that her tears fell down on it and watered it. And it grew and became a handsome tree. Three times a day Cinderella went and sat beneath it and wept and prayed, and a little white bird always flew onto the tree, and if Cinderella expressed a wish, the bird threw down to her what she had wished for.

It happened, however, that the King announced a festival that was planned to last three days, and he invited all the beautiful young girls in the country with the idea that his son might select a bride from their number. When the two stepsisters heard that they too were to appear among the number, they were delighted, called Cinderella and said, "Comb our hair for us, brush our shoes and fasten our buckles, for we are going to the festival at the King's palace." Cinderella obeyed, but wept, because she too would have liked to go with them to the dance and begged her stepmother to allow her to go.

"You, Cinderella!" said she. "As dusty and dirty as you are, you want to go to the festival? You have neither clothes nor shoes, and yet you want to dance!"

As, however, Cinderella went on asking, the stepmother at last gave in. "I have emptied a dish of lentils into the ashes for you; if you can pick them out in two hours, you can go with us." The girl went through the back door into the garden and called, "You tame pigeons, you turtle-doves, and all you birds beneath the sky, come and help me to pick -

"The good into the pot,
The bad into the crop."

Then two white pigeons came in through the kitchen window, and afterwards the turtledoves, and eventually all the birds in the sky came whirring and crowding in and landed in the ashes. And the pigeons nodded with their heads and began pick, pick, pick,

pick, and the rest began also pick, pick, pick, pick, and gathered all the good grains into the dish. Barely one hour passed before they had finished, and all flew out again. Then the girl took the dish to her stepmother, and was glad, and believed that now she would be allowed to go with them to the festival.

But the stepmother said, "No, Cinderella, you have no clothes and you can't dance; you would only be laughed at." And because Cinderella wept at this, the stepmother relented, "If you can pick two dishes of lentils out of the ashes for me in one hour, you may go with us." And she thought to herself, "That she most certainly cannot do."

When the stepmother had emptied the two dishes of lentils into the ashes, Cinderella went through the back door into the garden and cried, "You tame pigeons, you turtledoves, and all you birds under heaven, come and help me to pick -

"The good into the pot,
The bad into the crop."

Then two white pigeons came in by the kitchen window, and afterwards the turtledoves, and eventually all the birds in the sky came whirring and crowding in and landed in the ashes. And the doves nodded with their heads and began pick, pick, pick, pick, and the others began also pick, pick, pick, pick, and gathered all the good seeds into the dishes, and before half an hour was over, they were already done, and all flew out again. Then the maiden carried the dishes to the stepmother and was delighted and believed that she might now go with them to the festival. But the stepmother said, "None of this will help you. You can't go with us because you have no clothes and can't dance; we would be ashamed of you!" At this, she turned her back on Cinderella and hurried away with her two proud daughters.

As no one was now at home, Cinderella went to her mother's grave beneath the hazel-tree, and cried,

"Shiver and quiver, little tree,
Silver and gold throw down over me."

Then the bird threw a gold and silver dress down to her and slippers embroidered with silk and silver. She hastily put on the dress and went to the festival. Her stepsisters and the stepmother, however, did not recognize her and thought she must be a foreign princess, for she looked so beautiful in the golden dress. They never once thought of Cinderella, believing that she was sitting at home in the dirt, picking lentils out of the ashes. The prince went to meet her, took her by the hand and danced with her. He wouldn't dance with any other maiden and never let go of her hand, and if anyone else came to invite her to dance, he said, "She is my partner."

She danced till it was evening, and then she wanted to go home. But the King's son said, "I will go with you to provide you company," for he wanted to see where the beautiful maiden lived. She escaped from him, however, by jumping into the pigeon-house. The King's son waited until Cinderella's father came, and then he told him that the foreign maiden had leaped into the pigeon-house. The old man thought, "Can this be Cinderella?" and they brought him an axe and a pickaxe so that he could chop the pigeon-house to pieces, but no one was inside it. And when they got home, Cinderella lay in her dirty clothes among the ashes, and a dim little oil lamp was burning on the mantle-piece, for Cinderella had jumped quickly down from the back of the pigeon-house and had run to the little hazel-tree, and there she had taken off her beautiful clothes and laid them on the grave, and the bird had taken them away again, and then she had returned to the kitchen to lie in the ashes in her gray smock.

The next day, when the festival began all over again and her parents and the stepsisters had once again gone, Cinderella went to the hazel-tree and said -

"Shiver and quiver, my little tree,
Silver and gold throw down over me."

Then the bird threw down a much more beautiful dress than on the previous day. And when Cinderella appeared at the festival in this dress, everyone was astonished at her beauty. The King's son had waited until she came, and he instantly took her by the hand and would dance with no one but her. When others came and invited her, he said, "She is my partner."

When evening came, she wished to leave, but the King's son followed her and wanted to see which house she went into. But she pulled away from him and fled into the garden behind the house. There stood a beautiful tall tree that held in its branches the most magnificent pears. She clambered so nimbly between the branches like a squirrel that the King's son did not know where she had gone. He waited until her father came and said to him, "The foreign maiden has escaped from me, and I believe she has climbed up the pear-tree."

The father wondered, "Can it be Cinderella?" and had an axe brought and cut the tree down, but no one was on it. And when they got into the kitchen, Cinderella lay there in the ashes, as usual, for she had jumped down on the other side of the tree, had taken the beautiful dress to the bird on the little hazel-tree, and put on her gray smock.

On the third day, when the parents and sisters had gone away, Cinderella went once more to her mother's grave and said to the little tree -

"Shiver and quiver, my little tree,
Silver and gold throw down over me."

And now the bird threw down to her a dress that was even more splendid and magnificent than any she had yet had, and the slippers were golden. And when she went to the festival in the dress,

everyone was astonished to the point of speechlessness. The King's son danced only with her, and if any one invited her to dance, he said, "She is my partner."

When evening came, Cinderella wanted to leave, and the King's son was anxious to go with her, but she escaped from him so quickly that he could not follow her. The King's son had, however, used a stratagem, and had covered the whole staircase with pitch, so that when she ran down, Cinderella's left slipper stuck to the step. The King's son picked it up, and it was small and dainty and all golden.

Next morning, he went with it to the father and said to him, "No one else shall be my wife but the one whose foot fits into this golden slipper." Then the two sisters were glad because they had pretty feet. The eldest went with the shoe into her room and wanted to try it on as her mother stood by. But the shoe was too small for her and she couldn't get her big toe into it. Then her mother gave her a knife and said, "Cut the toe off; when you become queen you won't need to go anywhere by foot." The maiden cut the toe off, forced the foot into the shoe, swallowed the pain, and went out to the King's son. Then he took her on his horse as his bride and rode away with her.

They were, however, obliged to pass the grave, and there on the hazel-tree sat the two pigeons who cried,

"Look, look, you'll see it too,
Blood flows inside the shoe;
The shoe was much too tight,
Go back for your true bride."

So he looked at her foot and saw how the blood was streaming from it. He turned his horse around and took the false bride home again, and said she was not the true one, and that the other sister was to put the shoe on. Then this one went into her room and got her toes safely into the shoe, but her heel was too large. So her mother gave her a knife and said, "Hack a bit off your heel; when you become queen you won't need to go anywhere by foot." The maiden cut a bit off her heel, forced her foot into the shoe, swallowed the pain, and went out to the King's son. He took her on his horse as his bride and rode away with her, but when they passed by the hazel-tree, two little pigeons sat on it and cried,

"Look, look, you'll see it too,
Blood flows inside the shoe;
The shoe was much too tight,
Go back for your true bride."

He looked down at her foot and saw how the blood was running out of her shoe and how it had stained her white stocking. Then he turned his horse and took the false bride home again. "This also is not the right one," he said. "Do you have another daughter?"

"No," said the man, "The only one left is a little stunted kitchen maid that my late wife left behind, but she cannot possibly be the bride." The King's son said he was to send her up to him, but the mother answered, "Oh, no, she is much too dirty; she can't show herself!" He absolutely insisted on it, and Cinderella had to be called.

First, she washed her hands and cleaned her face, and then went and bowed down before the King's son, who gave her the golden shoe. Then she seated herself on a stool, drew her foot out of the heavy wooden shoe and put it into the slipper, which fit like a glove. And when she rose up and the King's son looked into her face, he recognized her as the beautiful maiden who had danced with him and cried, "That is the true bride!"

The stepmother and the two sisters were terrified and became ashen with rage; he, however, took Cinderella on his horse and rode away with her. As they passed by the hazel-tree, the two white doves cried -

"Look, look, you'll see it too,
No blood is in the shoe,
The shoe fits just right;
This is your true bride."

After they had cried that, the two came flying down and placed themselves on Cinderella's shoulders, one on the right, the other on the left, and remained sitting there.

When the time came to celebrate the wedding with the King's son, the two false sisters came and wanted to get into favor with Cinderella and share her good fortune. When the betrothed couple went to church, the elder was at the right side and the younger at the left, and the pigeons pecked out one eye of each of them. Afterwards, as they came back, the elder was at the left, and the younger at the right, and then the pigeons pecked out the other eye of each. And thus, for their wickedness and falsehood, they were punished with blindness as long as they lived.

Frau Holle

(Brothers Grimm)

A widow had two daughters, one of whom was pretty and hard working while the other was ugly and idle. But she favored the ugly and idle one, because she was her true daughter while the other was forced to do all the work and be the Cinderella of the house. Every day the poor girl had to sit next to the street by a well and spin and spin till her fingers bled.

Now it happened that one day the shuttle was completely covered with her blood so she dipped it in the well to wash it off, but it dropped out of her hand and fell to the bottom. She began to weep and ran to her stepmother and told her of the mishap. But she scolded her sharply and was heartless enough to say, "Since you have let the shuttle fall in, you must fish it out again."

So the girl went back to the well and did not know where to start. In the sorrow of her heart she jumped into the well to get the shuttle. She fainted and when she awoke and came to herself again, she was in a lovely meadow where the sun was bright and many thousands of flowers were growing. Along this meadow she went and came at last to a baker's oven full of bread; the bread cried out, "Oh, take me out! Take me out or I'll burn. I have been baked a long time!" So she went up to it and took out all the loaves one after another. After that she went on till she came to a tree covered with apples, which called out to her, "Oh, shake me! Shake me! We apples are all too ripe!" So she shook the tree till the apples fell down like rain and went on shaking till they were all down, and when she had gathered them into a mound, she went on her way.

At last she came to a little house, out of which an old woman peeped; but she had such large teeth that the girl was frightened and was about to run away.

The old woman, however, called out to her, "What are you afraid of, dear child? Stay with me. If you will do all the work in the house properly, you will be the better for it. Only you must take care to make my bed well and shake it so thoroughly that the feathers fly — for then it snows up on the earth. I am Frau Holle."

Because the old woman spoke so kindly to her, the girl took courage and agreed to enter her service. She did her jobs to the satisfaction of her mistress and always shook her bed so vigorously that the feathers flew about like snowflakes. So she had a pleasant life with her -- never an angry word -- with boiled or roast meat every day.

She stayed some time with Frau Holle but eventually became sad. At first she did not know what it meant but came to realize that it was homesickness. Although she was many thousand times better off with Frau Holle than at home, she nevertheless had a longing to return. At last she said to the old woman, "I have a longing for home; and however well off I am down here, I cannot stay any longer. I must go up again to my own people." Frau Holle said, "I am pleased that you long for your home again, and because you have served me so truly, I will take you there again myself." At that point she took her by the hand and led her to a large door. The door was opened, and just as the maiden was standing beneath the doorway, a heavy shower of golden rain fell and all the gold stuck to her so that she was completely covered over with it.

"You can have that because you have been so industrious," said Frau Holle, and at the same time she gave her back the shuttle that she had dropped into the well. Then the door closed, and the maiden found herself once again on earth, not far from her mother's house.

And as she came into the yard the cock was standing by the well side, and cried -

"Cock-a-doodle-doo!
Your golden girl's come back to you!"

So she went in to her mother, and because she arrived completely covered with gold, she was well received by both her and her sister.

The girl told all that had happened to her, and as soon as the mother heard how she had come by so much wealth, she was very anxious to obtain the same good luck for the ugly and lazy daughter. She had to seat herself by the well and spin, and in order that her shuttle might be stained with blood, she stuck her hand into a thorn bush and pricked her finger. Then she threw her shuttle into the well and jumped in after it.

Like the other, she came to the beautiful meadow and walked along the very same path. When she got to the oven the bread again cried, "Oh, take me out! Take me out or I shall burn; I have been baked a long time!" But the lazy thing answered, "Do you think I want to get myself dirty?" and on she went. Soon she came to the apple-tree, which cried, "Oh, shake me! Shake me! We apples are all ripe!" But she answered, "I'm sure! One of you might fall on my head," and so went on.

When she came to Frau Holle's house, she was not afraid, for she had already heard of her big teeth, and she hired herself to her immediately.

The first day she forced herself to work diligently and obeyed Frau Holle when she told her to do anything, for she was thinking of all the gold that she would give her. But on the second day she began to laze around, and on the third day still more so, and then she wouldn't get up in the morning at all. Neither did she make Frau Holle's bed as she should, nor did she shake it hard enough to make the feathers fly. Frau Holle was soon tired of this and gave her notice to leave. The lazy girl was willing enough to go and figured that now the golden rain would fall. Frau Holle led her to the same large door; but while she was standing beneath it, instead of the gold, a big kettle full of pitch was emptied over her. "That is the reward you get for your service," said Frau Holle, shutting the door.

So the lazy girl went home completely covered with pitch, and the cock by the well-side, as soon as he saw her, cried out -

"Cock-a-doodle-doo!
Your dirty girl's come back to you!"

But the pitch stuck tightly to her and would not come off as long as she lived.

Little Red Riding Hood

(Brothers Grimm)

Once upon a time there was a sweet little girl who was loved by all who laid eyes on her, but most of all by her grandmother whose feelings for the child were limitless. Once she gave her a little red velvet cap that suited her so well that the little girl would never wear anything else. After that, she was always called Little Red Riding Hood.

One day her mother said, "Come, Little Red Riding Hood. Here is a piece of cake and a bottle of wine to bring to grandmother. She is ill and weak and they will refresh her. Get on your way before it becomes hot, and, when you are walking, walk calmly and quietly. Don't stray from the path or you might fall and break the bottle, and then your grandmother will get nothing. And when you go into her room, don't forget to say good-morning, and don't peer into every corner before you do it."

"I'll do everything right," said Little Red Riding Hood to her mother, shaking hands on it.

The grandmother lived out in the woods half an hour from the village, but as soon as Little Red Riding Hood entered the forest, she met a wolf. Little Red Riding Hood did not know what a wicked creature he was and was not afraid of him at all.

"Good day, Little Red Riding Hood," he said.

"Thank you kindly, wolf."

"Where are you off to so early, Little Red Riding Hood?"

"To my grandmother's."

"What are you carrying in your apron?"

"Cake and wine. We baked yesterday so poor sick grandmother might have something good to strengthen her."

"Where does your grandmother live, Little Red Riding Hood?"

"Fifteen minutes deeper into the forest. Her house stands beneath three large oak-trees, the ones with the hazel-bushes just below. You surely know it," replied Little Red Riding Hood.

The wolf thought to himself, "What a tender young thing. A nice juicy mouthful, she would be better to eat than the old woman. If you are clever, you can get both of them." So he walked for a short time alongside Little Red Riding Hood and then said, "Little Red Riding Hood, have you seen how pretty the flowers are around here? Why don't you look around. I don't believe you've noticed how sweetly the little birds are singing. You walk as seriously as if you were going to school and yet everything else out here in the forest is so happy."

Little Red Riding Hood lifted her eyes and saw the sunbeams dancing here and there through the trees and how full everything was with pretty flowers and she thought, "If I bring grandmother a fresh bouquet, it will really cheer her up. It is so early in the day that I will still get there on time." So she ran from the path and headed into the forest to look for flowers. And whenever she had plucked one, she imagined that she saw a prettier one farther on, so she ran after it and penetrated deeper and deeper into the woods.

Meanwhile the wolf ran straight to grandmother's house and knocked on the door.

"Who is there?"

"Little Red Riding Hood," replied the wolf, "bringing you cake and wine. Open the door."

"Lift the latch," called out the grandmother, "I am too weak to get up."

The wolf lifted the latch and the door sprang open. Without saying a word, he went straight to grandmother's bed and swallowed her up. Then he put on her clothes, dressed himself in her nightcap, laid himself in bed and pulled the curtains shut.

Little Red Riding Hood, however, was still running around picking flowers, and when she had gathered so many that she could not carry any more, she remembered her grandmother and set out on her way again.

It surprised her to find the cottage-door unlatched so that when she went into the room, she felt so strange that she said to herself, "My word, how uneasy I feel today, and usually I like being with grandmother so much."

She called out, "Good morning," but received no answer. So she went to the bed and pulled back the curtains. There lay her grandmother with her nightcap pulled down over her face looking very strange.

"Oh, grandmother," she said, "what big ears you have."

"The better to hear you with, my child."

"But, grandmother, what big eyes you have," she said.

"The better to see you with, my dear."

"But, grandmother, what large hands you have."

"The better to be able to grab you."

"Oh, but, grandmother, what a terrible big mouth you have."

"The better to eat you with."

No sooner had the wolf said this, than he sprang out of bed and swallowed up Little Red Riding Hood, too.

When the wolf had satisfied his appetite, he laid himself down again in the bed, fell asleep and began to snore very loudly. A hunter was just passing the house and thought to himself, "How that old woman is snoring. I better see if she needs help."

So he went into the room, and when he came to the bed, he saw that the wolf was lying in it. "So I find you here, you old sinner," he said. "I've been looking for you a long time."

Just as he was going to fire at him, it occurred to him that the wolf might have devoured the grandmother, and that she might still be saved. So he did not shoot: instead he took a pair of scissors and began to cut open the belly of the sleeping wolf.

After two snips, he saw the Little Red Riding Hood shining, so he made two more snips and the little girl sprang out, crying, "Oh how frightened I have been. It was very dark inside the wolf."

After that, the old grandmother also came out alive, but scarcely able to breathe. Little Red Riding Hood quickly gathered some large stones. They sewed them into the wolf's belly so that when he awoke and tried to run away, he couldn't. The stones were so heavy that he instantly collapsed and fell dead.

Then all three were delighted. The hunter removed the wolf's pelt and went home with it. The grandmother revived as she ate the cake and drank the wine that Little Red Riding Hood had brought. Little Red Riding Hood, however, thought to herself, "As long as I live, I will never wander off the path to run into the forest when my mother has forbidden me to."

It is also said that once later on when Little Red Riding Hood was taking cakes to the old grandmother, another wolf spoke to her trying to tempt her from the path. Little Red Riding Hood, however, stood firm and went straightforward on her way. She told her grandmother that she had met the wolf, and how he had said good-morning to her, but with such a wicked look in his eyes, that if they had not been on the public road she was certain he would have eaten her up. "Well," said the grandmother, "we'll lock the door so he cannot come in."

Soon afterwards the wolf knocked, and cried, "Open up the door, grandmother, I am Little Red Riding Hood, and I am bringing you some cakes."

But they did not speak or open the door, so the graybeard circled two or three times around the house, and finally jumped onto the roof, intending to wait until Little Red Riding Hood went home that evening. He would then slink after her and devour her in the darkness. But the grandmother saw what he intended to do. In front of the house was a great stone barrel, so she said to the child, "Take the pail, Little Red Riding Hood. I made some sausages yesterday, so carry the water I cooked them in and fill up the barrel."

When the odor of the sausages reached the wolf, he sniffed and peeped down, and at last stretched out his neck so far that he lost his footing and began to slip, sliding down from the roof straight into the barrel and was drowned. But Little Red Riding Hood went merrily on her way home, and no one has ever tried to harm her since.

The Bremen Town Musicians

(Brothers Grimm)

A certain man had a donkey that had tirelessly carried corn sacks to the mill for many a long year, but his strength was fading, and he was growing more and more unfit for work. Then his master began to consider how he might best get rid of him to save on expenses, but the donkey, seeing that an ill wind was blowing, ran away and set out on the road to Bremen. "There," he thought, "I can certainly be a town musician." When he had walked some distance, he found a dog lying on the road, gasping like one who had run himself ragged. "What are you gasping like that for, you big fellow?" asked the donkey.

"Ah," replied the dog, "Because I am old and grow weaker each day and can no longer hunt, my master wanted to kill me, so I got out of there. But now how am I going to earn my bread?"

"I'll tell you what," said the donkey. "I am going to Bremen to be a town musician there. Join me and engage yourself as a musician with me. I'll play the lute, and you can beat the kettledrum."

The dog agreed, and off they went.

Before long, they came to a cat sitting on the path with a face as long as three rainy days. "Now then, old whiskers, what has gone wrong with you?" asked the donkey.

"Who can be happy when his neck is in on the line?" answered the cat. "Because I am now getting old, and my teeth are worn to nubs, and I prefer to sit by the fire and spin rather than hunt mice, my mistress wanted to drown me, so I ran away. But now good advice is scarce. Where do I go from here?"

"Go with us to Bremen. Anyone who understands night music can be a town musician."

The cat thought it made sense and went with them. After this, the three fugitives came to a farmyard where a rooster was sitting on the gate crowing for all he was worth. "Your crowing seems desperate," said the donkey. "What's the matter?"

"I have been predicting fine weather, because it is Our Dear Lady's Day when she washes the Christ Child's shirts and wants to dry them," said the rooster, "but guests are coming for Sunday, so the housewife has no pity and has told the cook that she intends to eat me in the soup tomorrow. This evening I am supposed to have my head cut off, so I am crowing my head off while I still can."

"Ah, but red-comb," said the donkey, "you had better come away with us. We're going to Bremen; you can find something better than death everywhere. You have a good voice, and if we make music together it must have some quality!"

The rooster agreed to this plan, and all four went off together. They could not, however, reach the city of Bremen in one day, so in the evening they came to a forest where they intended to pass the night. The donkey and the dog laid themselves down under a large tree, the cat settled himself in the branches, but the rooster flew to the very top where he was most safe. Before he went to sleep, he looked around on all four sides and thought he saw a little spark burning in the distance. He called out to his companions that there must be a house not far off, for he saw a light. The donkey said, "If so, we had better get up and go on, for the shelter here is bad." The dog thought that a few bones with some meat on them would do him good, too!

So they made their way towards the place where the light came from and saw it shining brighter and growing larger until they came to a well-lighted robber's house. The donkey, as the biggest, went to the window and looked in.

"What do you see, my gray steed?" asked the rooster.

"What do I see?" answered the donkey. "A table covered with good things to eat and drink, and robbers sitting around it enjoying themselves."

"That would be the sort of thing for us," said the rooster.

"Yes, yes; ah, how I wish we were there!" said the donkey.

Then the animals met together to figure out how they could drive away the robbers, and at last they thought of a plan. The donkey was to place himself on the window- ledge with his front

hooves, the dog was to jump onto the donkey's back, the cat was to climb up onto the dog while the rooster was to fly up and perch upon the head of the cat.

When this was done, at a given signal, they began to perform their music together: the donkey brayed, the dog barked, the cat meowed, and the rooster crowed. Then they shattered the glass and burst through the window into the room. In this horrible racket, the robbers sprang up, thinking that a ghost had come in, and fled totally frightened out into the forest. The four companions now sat down at the table, well content with what was left, and ate as if they were going to fast for a month.

As soon as the four minstrels were done, they turned out the light and each looked for a sleeping place according to his nature and to what suited him best. The donkey laid himself down upon some straw in the yard, the dog behind the door, the cat on the hearth near the warm ashes, while the rooster perched himself upon a beam of the roof. Tired from their long walk, they soon went to sleep.

When it was past midnight, the robbers saw from afar that the light was no longer on in their house and all appeared quiet, so the captain said, "We shouldn't have allowed ourselves be frightened out of our wits" and ordered one of them to go back and examine the house.

Finding everything still, the messenger went into the kitchen to light a candle, and, mistaking the glistening fiery eyes of the cat for live coals, he held a match up to them to light it. But the cat didn't understand the joke and flew into his face, spitting and scratching. He was dreadfully frightened and ran to the back door, but the dog, who was lying there, sprang up and bit his leg; and as he ran across the yard by the straw pile, the donkey gave him a smart kick with its hind foot. The rooster, who had been awakened by the noise and had become lively, then cried down from the beam, "Cock-a-doodle-doo!"

Then the robber ran back as fast as he could to his captain and said, "Ah, there is a horrible witch sitting in the house, who spat on me and scratched my face with her long claws; and by the door stands a man with a knife, who stabbed me in the leg; and in the yard there lies a black monster, who beat me with a wooden club; and above on the roof, sits the judge, who called out, 'Bring the rogue here to me!' so I got away as well as I could."

After this, the robbers didn't dare return to the house again, but it suited the four musicians of Bremen so well that they did not bother to leave it any more. And the mouth of the one who last told this story is still warm.

The Devil with the Three Golden Hairs

(Brothers Grimm)

There was once a poor woman who gave birth to a baby boy; and as he came into the world with a lucky skin (caul), it was predicted that in his fourteenth year he would take the king's daughter for his wife. It just so happened that soon afterwards the king himself came into the village although no one recognized who he was, and when he asked the people what the latest news was, they answered, "A child has just been born with a lucky skin; that means that whatever he does will turn out well. It is also prophesied that in his fourteenth year he will take the king's daughter as his wife."

The king, who had an evil heart, was angry about the prophecy, so he went to the parents, and, feigning friendliness, said, "You poor people, let me have your child, and I will take care of him." At first they refused, but when the stranger offered them a large amount of gold for him, they thought, "He is a luck-child, and everything must turn out well for him." They eventually agreed to give away the child.

The king put him into a box and rode away with him until he came to a deep stretch of water; then he threw the box into it and thought, "I have freed my daughter from an undesirable suitor."

The box, however, didn't sink but floated like a boat, and not a drop of water made its way into it. It floated to within two miles of the king's capital city, where there was a mill, and it came to rest at the mill dam. A miller's boy, who luckily was standing there, noticed it and pulled it out with a hook, thinking that he might have found a great treasure. But when he opened it, there lay a pretty boy inside, quite fresh and lively. He took him to the miller and his wife, and because they had no children, they were overjoyed and said, "God has given us a son." They took great care of the foundling, and he grew up in all goodness.

It just so happened that once during a storm, the king sought refuge in the mill, and he asked the mill folk if the tall boy was their son. "No," they answered, "he's a foundling. Fourteen years ago he floated down to the mill dam in a box, and the mill boy pulled him out of the water."

The king immediately recognized that this was none other than the luck-child that he had thrown into the water and said, "My good people, could your boy deliver a letter to the queen? I will give him two gold pieces as a reward." "Just as the king commands," they answered, and they told the boy to get ready. Then the king wrote a letter to the queen in which he said, "As soon as the boy arrives with this letter, let him be killed and buried, and all must be done before I come home."

The boy set out with this letter, but he lost his way, and in the evening came to a large forest. In the darkness he saw a small light; he went towards it and reached a cottage. When he went in, he saw an old woman sitting quite alone by the fire. She startled when she saw the boy and said, "Where do you come from, and where are you going?"

"I come from the mill," he answered, "and wish to go to the queen, to whom I am carrying a letter. But because I have lost my way in the forest, I would like to stay here over night."

"You poor boy," said the woman, "you have blundered into a den of thieves, and when they come home, they will kill you."

"Let them come," said the boy." I am not afraid, but I am so tired that I cannot go any farther." And he stretched himself upon a bench and fell asleep.

Soon afterwards, the robbers returned and angrily asked what strange boy was lying there. "Ah," said the old woman, "it is an innocent child who has lost himself in the forest, and out of pity I have let him come in. He is carrying a letter to the queen." The robbers opened the letter and read it, and read that as soon as the boy arrived, he would be put to death. Then the hard-hearted robbers felt pity, and their leader tore up the letter and wrote another, saying that as soon as the boy came, he should be married at once to the king's daughter. Then they let him lie quietly on the bench until the next morning, and when he awoke, they gave him the letter and showed him the right way.

And when the queen had received the letter and read it, she did as the letter instructed and had a splendid wedding feast prepared, and the king's daughter was married to the luck-child, and as the youth was handsome and agreeable, she lived with him in joy and contentment.

Some time later the king returned to his palace and saw that the prophecy had been fulfilled, and the luck-child was married to his daughter. "How did that come to pass?" he asked. "I gave quite another order in my letter."

So the queen gave him the letter and said that he might see for himself what was written in it. The king read the letter and saw quite clearly that it had been exchanged for another. He asked the youth what had become of the letter entrusted to him, and why he had brought another instead of it.

"I know nothing about it," he answered. "It must have been exchanged in the night when I slept in the forest."

The king said passionately, "You will not have everything quite so much your own way; the one who marries my daughter must bring me back from hell three golden hairs from the head of the devil. Bring me what I want and you may keep my daughter." In this way the king hoped to get rid of him forever.

But the luck-child answered, "I will fetch the golden hairs; I am not afraid of the devil." He immediately left them and began his journey.

The road led him to a large town where the watchman by the gates asked him what his trade was, and what he knew. "I know everything," answered the luck-child. "Then you can do us a favor," said the watchman, "if you can tell us why our market fountain, which once flowed with wine, has gone dry and no longer gives even water."

"I can tell you that," he answered. "Only wait until I come back."

Then he went further and came to another town where there was also a gatekeeper who asked him what his trade was and what he knew. "I know everything," he answered. "Then you can do us a favor and tell us why a tree in our town that once bore golden apples doesn't even grow leaves now."

"I can tell you that," he answered. "Only wait until I come back."

Then he went on and came to a wide river that he had to cross. The ferryman asked him what his trade was and what he knew. "I know everything," he answered. "Then you can do me a favor," said the ferryman, "and tell me why I must always row back and forth and am never set free."

"I can tell you that," he answered. "Only wait until I come back."

When he had crossed the water, he found the entrance to hell. It was black and sooty inside and the devil was not at home, but his grandmother was sitting in a large armchair. "What do you want?" she asked him, but she did not look so very wicked.

"I would like to have three golden hairs from the devil's head," he answered, "or else I cannot keep my wife."

"That is a lot to ask for," she said. "If the devil comes home and finds you, it will cost you your life, but because I pity you, I will see if I can help you."

She changed him into an ant and said, "Creep into the folds of my dress; you will be safe there."

"Yes," he answered, "so far, so good; but there are three things besides that I want to know: why a market fountain that once flowed with wine has become dry, and no longer gives even water; why a tree that once bore golden apples doesn't even grow leaves now; and why a ferryman must always row back and forth and is never set free."

"That is a tall order," she answered, "but only be silent and still and pay attention to what the devil says when I pull out the three golden hairs."

As evening came on, the devil returned home. No sooner had he entered than he noticed that the air was not pure. "I smell human flesh," he said. "Something is wrong here." Then he poked into every corner and searched, but he could not find anything.

His grandmother scolded him. "It has just been swept," she said, "and everything put in order, and now you are upsetting it again; you've always got human flesh in your nose. Sit down and eat your supper."

When he had eaten and drunk, he was tired and laid his head in his grandmother's lap, and before long he was fast asleep, snoring and breathing heavily. Then the old woman took hold of a golden hair, yanked it out and laid it down near her.

"Oh!" cried the devil, "what are you doing?"

"I had a bad dream", answered the grandmother, "so I grabbed hold of your hair."

"What did you dream then?" said the devil.

"I dreamed that a fountain in a market place from which wine once flowed was dried up so that not even water would flow from it. What would be the cause of that?"

"Oh, ho! If they only knew," answered the devil. "There is a toad sitting under a stone in the well. If they killed it, the wine would flow again."

He went to sleep again and snored until the windows shook. Then she pulled the second hair out. "Ha! What are you doing?" cried the devil angrily.

"Don't take offense," she said. "I did it in a dream."

"What have you dreamed this time?" he asked.

"I dreamed that in a certain kingdom there stood an apple tree that had once borne golden apples but now would not even grow leaves. What do you think the reason is?"

"Oh! If they only knew," answered the devil. "A mouse is gnawing at the root; if they killed it, they would have golden apples again, but if it gnaws much longer the tree will die altogether. But leave me alone with your dreams: if you disturb me in my sleep again you will get a slap on the ear."

The grandmother spoke gently to him until he fell asleep again and snored. Then she took hold of the third golden hair and pulled it out. The devil jumped up, roared out, and would have treated her badly if she had not quieted him once more and said, "Who can help bad dreams?"

"What was the dream, then?" he asked, and was quite curious.

"I dreamed of a ferryman who complained that he must always ferry from one side to the other and was never released. What is the cause of that?"

"Ah! The fool," answered the devil, "when anyone comes and wants to go across, he needs to put the oar in his hand, and the other man will have to ferry and he will be free." As the grandmother had plucked out the three golden hairs and the three questions were answered, she let the old serpent alone, and he slept until daybreak.

When the devil had gone out again, the old woman took the ant out of the folds of her dress and restored the luck-child to his human shape again. "Here are the three golden hairs for you," she said. "I suppose you heard what the devil said to your three questions."

"Yes," he answered, "I heard and will take care to remember."

"You have what you want," she said, "and now you can be on your way." He thanked the old woman for helping him in his need and left hell fully content that everything had turned out so fortunately.

When he came to the ferryman, he was expected to give the promised answer. "Ferry me across first," said the luck-child, "and then I will tell you how you can be set free." When he reached the opposite shore, he gave him the devil's advice: "Next time any one comes to be ferried over, just put the oar in his hand."

He went on and came to the town where the unfruitful tree stood, and the watchman wanted an answer there, too. So he told him what he had heard from the devil: "Kill the mouse that is gnawing at its root, and it will again bear golden apples." Then the watchman thanked him and gave him two donkeys loaded with gold as a reward.

At last he came to the town whose well was dry. He told the watchman what the devil had said: "A toad is in the well beneath a stone; you must find it and kill it and the well will again give plenty of wine." The watchman thanked him and also gave him two donkeys loaded with gold.

At last the luck-child got home to his wife, who was truly glad to see him again and to hear how well he had prospered in everything. To the king he took what he had asked for, the devil's three golden hairs. When the king saw the four donkeys loaded with gold, he was quite content, and said, "Now all the conditions are fulfilled and you can keep my daughter. But tell me, dear son-in-law, where did all that gold come from? That is tremendous wealth!"

"I was rowed across a river," he answered, "and got it there; it lies on the shore instead of sand."

"Could I also get some of it?" asked the king, who was quite eager about it.

"As much as you wish," he answered. "There is a ferryman on the river; let him ferry you over, and you can fill your sacks on the other side."

The greedy king set out as fast as he could, and when he came to the river, he called to the ferryman to carry him across. The ferryman came and asked him to get in, and when they got to the other shore, he put the oar in his hand and jumped out. So from this time forth the king has had to ferry as a punishment for his sins. Perhaps he is ferrying still. If he is, it is because no one has taken the oar from him.

Sleeping Beauty or Briar Rose

(Brothers Grimm)

A long time ago there were a king and queen who said every day, "Oh, if only we had a child!" but they never had one. But it happened that once when the queen was bathing, a frog crept out of the water onto the land and said to her, "Your wish shall be fulfilled; before a year has passed, you shall have a daughter."

What the frog said would happen did, and the queen had a little girl who was so pretty that the king could not contain himself for joy and ordered a great feast. He not only invited his kindred, friends and acquaintances, but also the wise women, so that they might be kind and well disposed towards the child. There were thirteen of them in his kingdom, but because he had only twelve golden plates for them to eat from, one of them was not invited.

The feast was held with all manner of splendor and when it came to its end, the wise women bestowed their magic gifts upon the baby: one gave virtue, another beauty, a third riches, and so on with everything in the world that one could wish for.

When eleven of them had made their promises, suddenly the thirteenth came in. She wished to avenge herself for not having been invited and without greeting or even looking at anyone, she cried with a loud voice, "In her fifteenth year the king's daughter will prick herself on a spindle and fall down dead." And, without saying a word more, she turned around and left the room.

They were all shocked, but the twelfth, whose good wish still remained unspoken, came forward, and because she could not undo the evil sentence, only soften it, she said, "It shall not be death, but a deep sleep of a hundred years into which the princess shall fall."

The king, who dearly wished to keep his dear child from the misfortune, gave orders that every spindle in the whole kingdom should be burned. Meanwhile the gifts of the wise women were all fulfilled in the young girl, for she was so beautiful, modest, good-natured, and wise, and everyone who saw her was fond of her.

It happened that on the very day when she turned fifteen years old, the king and queen were not at home, and the maiden was left in the palace quite alone. So she went around into all sorts of places, looking into rooms and bedchambers just as she liked, and at last came to an old tower. She climbed up the narrow winding staircase and reached a little door. A rusty key was in the lock, and when she turned it, the door sprang open and there in a little room sat an old woman with a spindle, busily spinning her flax.

"Good day, old grandma," said the king's daughter, "what are you doing there?" "I am spinning," said the old woman, and nodded her head. "What sort of thing is that, that jumps round so merrily?" said the girl, and she took the spindle and wanted to spin too. But scarcely had she touched the spindle when the magic decree was fulfilled, and she pricked her finger on it.

And in the very moment when she felt the prick, she fell down upon the bed that stood there and lapsed into a deep sleep. And this sleep extended over the whole palace; the king and queen who had just come home and had entered the great hall began to go to sleep, and the whole royal court with them. Even the horses went to sleep in the stable, the dogs in the yard, the pigeons upon the roof, the flies on the wall; even the fire that was flaming on the hearth became quiet and slept, the roast meat stopped sizzling, and the cook, who was just going to pull the hair of the scullery boy who had forgotten something, let him go, and went to sleep. And the wind subsided, and on the trees before the castle not a leaf moved.

A hedge of thorns began to grow around about the castle and every year it grew higher until at last it encircled the castle and covered it, so that there was nothing of it to be seen, not even the flag upon the roof.

But the story of the beautiful sleeping "Briar Rose" - for such was the princess' name - circulated around the country, so that from time to time kings' sons came and tried to penetrate through the thorny hedge into the castle. But they found it impossible, for the thorns held fast together as though they had hands, catching the youths so that they could not get loose again, leading to a miserable death.

After long, long years, a king's son came again to that country and heard an old man talking about the thorny hedge, and that a castle was said to stand behind it in which a wonderfully beautiful princess named Briar Rose had been asleep for a hundred years and that the king and queen and the whole court were likewise asleep. He had also heard from his grandfather that many kings' sons had already come and had tried to get through the thorny hedge, but that they had had gotten stuck in it, dying pitiful deaths. Then the youth said, "I am not afraid; I will go to see the beautiful Briar Rose." The good old man might dissuade him as he would, but he did not listen to his words.

By this time, the hundred years had passed, and the day had come when Briar Rose was to waken again. As the king's son approached the thorny hedge, he saw only large and beautiful flowers that parted from each other of their own accord and let him pass through unhurt before they closed again behind him like a

hedge. In the castle yard, he saw the horses and the spotted hounds lying asleep; on the roof sat the pigeons with their heads under their wings. And when he entered the house, the flies were asleep upon the wall, the cook in the kitchen was still holding out his hand to seize the boy, and the maid was sitting by the black hen, which she was going to pluck.

He went on farther, and in the great hall he saw the whole of the court lying asleep, and up by the throne the king and queen.

Then he went still farther, and everything was so quiet that mere breathing could be heard, and at last he came to the tower and opened the door into the little room where Briar Rose was sleeping. There she lay, so beautiful that he could not avert his eyes, so he stooped down and gave her a kiss. But as soon as he kissed her, Briar Rose opened her eyes and awoke and looked at him quite sweetly.

Then they went down together, and the king awoke, then the queen, and the whole court, and all looked at each other with huge eyes. And the horses in the court yard stood up and shook themselves; the hounds jumped up and wagged their tails; the pigeons upon the roof pulled out their heads from under their wings, looked around and flew into the open country; the flies on the wall crawled again; the fire in the kitchen flared up and flickered and cooked the meat; the roast began to turn and sizzle again; the cook gave the boy such a box on the ear that he screamed, and the maid plucked the chicken clean.

And then the marriage of the king's son with Briar Rose was celebrated in total splendor and they lived happily ever after.

Snow White

(Brothers Grimm)

Once upon a time, when snowflakes fell like feathers from heaven in the middle of winter, a queen sat sewing at a window that had a frame of ebony wood. And as she sewed and looked at the snow, she stuck a needle into her finger and three drops of blood fell into the snow. And because the red looked so beautiful in the white snow, she thought to herself: If only I had a child as white as snow, as red a blood, and as black as the wood in the frame.

Soon afterwards, she gave birth to a little daughter who was as white as snow, and red as blood with hair as black as ebony. The queen died after the birth of her child and the girl was known from that time forward as Snow White.

After a year had passed, the king took a second spouse. She was a beautiful woman, but she was proud and high-spirited and could not tolerate that anyone might rival her beauty. She had a remarkable mirror that she spoke to each time she walked over and looked into it:

"Mirror, mirror on the wall,
who in this land is the fairest of all?"

Thus answered the mirror:

"You, queen, are the most beautiful of all."

She was satisfied because she knew that the mirror always told the truth. Snow White, however, continued to grow up and was ever more beautiful and, by the time she was seven years old, she was as beautiful as a clear day and more beautiful than the queen herself. When the queen asked her mirror one day:

"Mirror, mirror on the wall,
who in this land is the fairest of all?"

The mirror answered:

"You, my queen, are the most beautiful here
but Snow White is a thousand times more fair."

This shocked the queen and she became yellow and green with envy. From that moment on, she hated the girl so much that her heart thumped and turned around in her body whenever she caught sight of Snow White. She found no peace either night or day as envy and pride grew ever higher like weeds in her heart. So she called a huntsman and said: "Bring the child out into the forest and kill her because I do not want to have to look at her anymore. You are to bring me her lungs and liver as proof of your deed."

The huntsman obeyed her and led Snow White out into the forest, and, once he had drawn the hunting knife with the intention of piercing her innocent heart, she began to cry and said: "Oh, dear huntsman, spare my life and I will run around in the woods and never return home."

Because the girl was so beautiful, the huntsman felt pity for her and said: "So take off, you poor child." The wild animals will have consumed her before long, he thought, but it seemed to him that a heavy stone had been lifted from his heart because he didn't need to kill her. And when a young boar bounded towards him, he stabbed it and took out the lungs and liver and brought them as proof to the queen. The cook was told to cook them in salt and the evil woman ate them and assumed that she had eaten Snow White's lungs and liver.

Now the poor child was completely alone in the huge forest and was so nervous when she looked at all the leaves of the trees that she had no idea what to do to save herself. She started to run and jumped over the sharp stones and through the thorns. Wild animals bounded past her but left her alone. She ran as far as her legs could carry her until she saw a small little cottage and entered it to find a place to rest as evening arrived. Everything in the little house was small but so unimaginably dainty and pure. A small table with a white tablecloth was set with seven small plates. Each setting included a little spoon, a small knife and fork and a small beaker. Arranged next to each other along the wall were seven small beds covered with snow white sheets. Because she was so hungry and thirsty, Snow White ate a little of the vegetables and bread from each little plate and sipped a little wine from each little cup in order to not take everything away from a single one. Afterwards, because she was so tired, she laid herself down into each little bed, but none fit; one was too long, another too short, until finally the seventh was perfect, and she stayed in that bed, prayed to God and fell asleep.

Once it was completely dark, the owners of the little house, seven dwarfs, came home from the mountains where they had been hacking and digging for ore. They lit their seven little lamps, and once it was light in the house, saw that someone was in it, and that everything was not exactly as they had left it.

The first dwarf said, "Who has been sitting in my chair?"
The second said, "Who has been eating off my plate?"
The third said, "Who has been eating my bread?"
The fourth said, "Who has been eating my vegetables?"
The fifth said, "Who has been jabbing with my fork?"
The sixth said, "Who has been cutting with my knife?"
The seventh said, "Who has been drinking from my cup?"

Then the first one saw that there was a little impression in his bed, and said, "Who has been lying in my bed?" The others came running up and shouted, "Someone has been lying in mine as well." But the seventh one, looking at his bed, found Snow White lying there fast asleep. The seven dwarfs all came running up, crying out with amazement. They fetched their seven lamps and focused the light onto Snow White. "Oh dear God! Oh dear God!" they cried. "What a beautiful child!"

They were so happy, that they did not wake her up, but let her continue to sleep there in the bed. The seventh dwarf had to sleep for one hour with each one his companions until the night passed.

When Snow White woke up in the morning, she saw the seven dwarfs and was frightened. But they were friendly and asked, "What is your name?"

"My name is Snow White," she answered.

"How did you find your way to our house?" the dwarfs continued.

Then she told them that her stepmother had tried to kill her and how the huntsman had spared her life, and how she had run the entire day before finally finding their cottage. The dwarfs said, "If you promise to keep house for us, and cook, make beds, wash, sew, and knit, and keep everything neat and clean, then you can stay with us, and we will make sure you will have everything that you want."

"Yes," promised Snow White, "with all my heart." So she kept the house orderly for them. Every morning they went into the mountains in search of ore and gold, coming home in the evening expecting their meal to be ready. Because Snow White remained alone during the day, the good dwarfs warned her, saying: "Be careful about your stepmother. She will soon know that you are here so do not let anyone in."

Since the queen believed that she had eaten Snow White's lungs and liver, she could only imagine that she was once again the first and the most beautiful woman of all. She stepped before her mirror and said:

"Mirror, mirror on the wall,
who in this land is the fairest of all?"

It answered:

"You, my queen, are most fair; tis true.
But beyond the mountains, Snow White

Lives with the seven dwarfs and is, despite,
Still a thousand times fairer than you."

This startled the queen, for she knew that the mirror never lied; so she realized that the huntsman had deceived her, and that Snow White was still alive. Then she pondered, and pondered again, how she might kill Snow White, for as long as long as she was not the most beautiful woman in all the land her envy would give her no rest. At last she came up with a plan. Coloring her face, she disguised herself as an old peddler woman, so that no one would re-

cognize her. In this disguise she crossed the seven mountains to the house of the seven dwarfs. Knocking on the door, she called out, "Beautiful wares for sale, for sale!"

Snow White peered out the window and said, "Good day, dear woman, what do you have for sale?"

"Good wares, beautiful wares," she answered. "Lace straps in all colors." And she took out one that was braided in colorful silk. "Would you like this one?"

"I can let this honest woman in," thought Snow White, who then unbolted the door and bought the pretty lace.

"Child," said the old woman, "how unkempt you look! Come, let me lace you up properly for once." Unsuspecting, Snow White stood before her and let her do up the new lace, but the old woman pulled so quickly and so tightly that Snow White could not breathe and collapsed as though dead.

"You used to be the most beautiful one," said the old woman as she hurried away.

Shortly afterward, the seven dwarfs came home at dinnertime. They were horrified when they saw their dear Snow White lying motionless on the ground as though she were dead. They lifted her up, and, seeing that she was too tightly bound, they cut the lace in two. Then she began to breathe a little, and little by little she became more animated. When the dwarfs heard what had happened they said, "The old peddler woman was no one else but the godless queen. Be careful and let no one in when we are not with you."

In the meantime, the wicked woman returned home, went to her mirror and asked:

"Mirror, mirror on the wall,
Who in this land is the fairest of all?"

It answered:

"You, my queen, are most fair; tis true.
But beyond the mountains, Snow White
Lives with the seven dwarfs and is, despite,
Still a thousand times fairer than you."

When she heard that, the shock caused all her blood to run to her heart because she knew that Snow White had recovered.

"This time," she said, "I will come up with something that will destroy you." Using the art of witchcraft, which she understood, she made a poisoned comb. Then she disguised herself in the shape of a different old woman. Thus she crossed the seven mountains to the cottage of the seven dwarfs, knocked on the door, and called out, "Good wares for sale, good wares!"

Snow White looked out and said, "Go away. I am not supposed to let anyone in."

"You are certainly allowed to take a look," said the old woman, pulling out the poisoned comb and holding it up. It pleased Snow

White so much that she let herself be deceived, and she opened the door. After they had agreed on the price, the old woman said, "Now give your hair a proper combing." No sooner had she stuck the comb into Snow White's hair than the poison took effect, and the girl fell down unconscious.

"You paragon of beauty," said the wicked woman, "now you are finished." And she walked away.

Fortunately, it was almost evening, and the seven dwarfs returned home. When they saw Snow White lying on the ground as though she were dead, they immediately suspected her stepmother. They examined her and found the poisoned comb. They had scarcely removed it when Snow White came to herself and told them what had happened. Once again they warned her to be her guard and to not to open the door for anyone.

Back at home the queen stepped in front of her mirror and said:

"Mirror, mirror on the wall,
who in this land is the fairest of all?"

It answered:

"You, my queen, are most fair; tis true.
But beyond the mountains, Snow White
Lives with the seven dwarfs and is, despite,
Still a thousand times fairer than you."

When the queen heard the mirror saying this, she shuddered and shook with anger, "Snow White must die," she shouted, "even if it costs me my life!" Then she went into her most secret and most private chamber where nobody was allowed to enter and there she made a poisoned apple. On the outside it was beautiful, white with red cheeks, and anyone who saw it desired it. But anyone who ate even a little piece of it would die. Then, coloring her face, she disguised herself as a peasant woman, and once again went across the seven mountains to the cottage of the seven dwarfs. She knocked on the door. Snow White stuck her head out the window and said, "I am not allowed to let anyone in. The dwarfs have forbidden it."

"That's fine with me," answered the peasant woman. "I'll easily get rid of my apples. Here, I'll give you one of them."

"No," said Snow White, "I cannot accept anything."

"Are you afraid of poison?" asked the old woman. "Look, I'll cut the apple in two. You eat the red half, and I'll eat the white half." Now the apple had been so skillfully made that only the red half was poisoned. Snow White looked at the beautiful apple, and, when she saw that the peasant woman was eating part of it, she could no longer hold herself back, and she stuck her hand out and took the poisoned half. She barely had a bite in her mouth when she fell to the ground dead. The queen looked at Snow White with a gruesome stare, burst into laughter and said, "White as snow, red as blood, black as ebony wood! This time the dwarfs cannot revive you."

Back at home she asked her mirror:

"Mirror, mirror on the wall,
who in this land is the fairest of all?"

It answered:

"You, dear queen, are now the fairest of all."

At last her envious heart was at rest, at least as well as an envious heart can be at rest.

Arriving home that evening, the dwarfs found Snow White lying on the ground and she was no longer breathing at all. She was dead. They lifted her up and looked for something poisonous. They undid her laces. They combed her hair. They washed her with water and wine. The dear child was dead, and, no matter what they did, she remained dead. They laid her on a bier, and all seven sat next to her and mourned for her and cried for three days. They were going to bury her, but she still looked as fresh as a living person, and still had her beautiful red cheeks. So they said, "We cannot bury her in the black earth."

So they had a transparent glass coffin made, so she could be viewed from all sides. They laid her inside, and wrote her name and that she was a princess on it with golden letters. Then they put the coffin outside on a mountain, and one of them always stayed with it and watched over her. Animals too came and mourned for Snow White, first an owl, then a raven, and finally a dove.

Snow White lay there in her coffin for an exceedingly long time and did not decompose, but looked like she was asleep, for she was still as white as snow and as red as blood with hair as black as ebony. Now it just so happened that a prince entered these woods and happened on the dwarfs' house, where he hoped to spend the night. He saw the coffin on the mountain with beautiful Snow White in it and read what was written in gold letters. Then he said to the dwarfs, "If you let me have the coffin. I will give you anything you want for it."

But the dwarfs answered, "We would not sell it for all the gold in the world."

Then he said, "Give it to me as a gift then, for I cannot live without being able to see Snow White. I will honor her and respect her as my dearly beloved one."

After they heard this, the good dwarfs felt pity on him and gave him the coffin. The prince had his servants carry it away on their shoulders. But when one of them stumbled over a shrub, the piece of poisoned apple that Snow White had bitten off was dislodged from her throat. Soon afterwards, she opened her eyes, lifted the lid from her coffin, sat up, and was alive again.

"Dear God, where am I?" she cried out.

The prince joyfully said, "You are with me." He told her everything that had happened, and then said, "I love you more than anything else in the world. Come to my father's castle with me where you will become my wife." Snow White was in complete agreement with that, so she went with him. Their wedding was planned with great splendor and majesty.

Snow White's godless stepmother was also invited to the celebration. After putting on her beautiful clothes she stepped before her mirror and said:

"Mirror, mirror on the wall,
who in this land is the fairest of all?"

The mirror answered:

"You, my queen, are the most beautiful here
but the new queen is a thousand times
more fair."

The godless woman uttered a curse and became so anxious, so frightened, that she did not know what to do. At first she did not want to go to the wedding, but she knew there would be no peace for her until she had seen the young queen. Arriving to the celebration, the evil woman recognized Snow White, and full of terror and fear, she stood there as though petrified. A pair of iron slippers were laid onto burning coals and then carried with tongs and placed in front of her. She had to step into the red-hot slippers and was forced to dance until she fell down dead.

Goose Girl

(Brothers Grimm)

Once upon a time there was an old queen whose husband had been dead for many years, and she had a beautiful daughter. When the princess grew up, she was betrothed to a prince who lived far away. When the time came for her to be married and journey forth into a distant kingdom, the aged queen packed up for her many costly vessels of silver and gold and also trinkets of gold and silver and cups and jewels — in short, everything that belonged to a royal dowry, for she loved her child with all her heart. She likewise sent her maid in waiting, who was to ride with her, and present her to the bridegroom, and each had a horse for the journey, but the horse of the King's daughter was named Falada and could speak. When the hour of departure arrived, the aged mother went into her bedroom, took a small knife and cut her finger with it until it bled. Then she held a white handkerchief beneath it into which she let three drops of blood fall, gave it to her daughter and said, "Dear child, preserve this carefully for it will be of service to you on your way."

So they took sorrowful leave of each other. The princess put the piece of cloth in her bosom, mounted her horse, and then went away to her bridegroom. After she had ridden for a while, she felt a burning thirst and said to her waiting-maid, "Dismount, and take my cup that you have brought with you for me, and get me some water from the stream, for I should like to drink."

"If you are thirsty," said the waiting-maid, "get off your horse yourself, and lie down and drink out of the water. I don't want to be your servant." So in her great thirst the princess alighted, bent down over the water in the stream and drank and was not allowed to drink out of the golden cup. Then she said, "Oh, Heavens!" and the three drops of blood answered, "If your mother knew, her heart would break." But the King's daughter was humble, said nothing, and mounted her horse again.

She rode some miles further, but the day was warm, the sun scorched her, and she was thirsty once more, and when they came to a stream of water, she again cried to her waiting-maid, "Dismount, and give me some water in my golden cup," for she had long ago forgotten the girl's ill words. But the waiting-maid said still more haughtily, "If you wish to drink, drink as you can; I don't want to be your maid." Then in her great thirst the King's daughter dismounted, bent over the flowing stream, wept and said, "Oh, Heavens!" and the drops of blood again replied, "If your mother knew, her heart would break." And as she was thus drinking and leaning right over the stream, the handkerchief with the three drops of blood fell out of her bosom and floated away with the water without her observing it, so great was her trouble. The waiting-maid, however, had seen it, and she rejoiced to think that she now had power over the bride. Once the princess had lost the drops of blood, she became weak and powerless. So now when she wanted to mount her horse again, the one that was called Falada, the waiting-maid said, "Falada is more suitable for me, and my nag will do for you" and the princess had to be content with that. Then the waiting-maid, with many hard words, made the princess exchange her royal apparel for her own shabby clothes. At length she was compelled to swear by the clear sky above her that she would not say one word of this to any one at the royal court, and if she had not taken this oath, she would have been killed on the spot. But Falada saw all this and observed it well.

The waiting-maid now mounted Falada and the true bride the bad horse, and thus they traveled onwards until at length they entered the royal palace. There was great rejoicing over her arrival, and the prince sprang forward to meet her, lifted the waiting-maid from her horse, and thought she was his consort. She was conducted upstairs, but the real princess was left standing below. Then the old King looked out of the window and saw her standing in the courtyard and how dainty and delicate and beautiful she was, and instantly went to the royal apartment and asked the bride about the girl she had with her who was standing down below in the courtyard, and who she was. "I picked her up on my way for a companion; give the girl something to work at, that she may not stand idle." But the old King had no work for her and knew of none, so he said, "I have a little boy who tends the geese, she may help him." The boy was called Conrad and the true bride had to help him to tend the geese.

Soon afterwards, the false bride said to the young king, "Dearest husband, I beg you to do me a favor." He answered, "I will do so most willingly." "Then send for the flayer, and have the head of the horse on which I rode here cut off, for it vexed me on the way."

In reality, she was afraid that the horse might tell how she had behaved to the King's daughter. Then she succeeded in making the King promise that it should be done, and the faithful Falada was to die; this came to the ears of the real princess, and she secretly promised to pay the flayer a piece of gold if he would perform a small service for her. There was a great dark-looking gateway in the town, through which morning and evening she had to pass with the geese: would he be so kind as to nail Falada's head onto it, so that she might see him again, more than once. The flayer's man promised to do that and cut off the head, and nailed it fast beneath the dark gateway.

Early in the morning, when she and Conrad drove out their flock beneath this gateway, she said in passing,

"Alas, Falada, hanging there!"

Then the head answered,

"Alas, young Queen, how ill you fare!
If this your tender mother knew,
Her heart would surely break in two."

Then they went still further out of the town and drove their geese into the country. And when they had come to the meadow, she sat down and unbound her hair, which was like pure gold, and Conrad saw it and delighted in its brightness and wanted to pluck out a few hairs. Then she said,

"Blow, blow, thou gentle wind, I say,
Blow Conrad's little hat away,
And make him chase it here and there,
Until I have braided all my hair,
And bound it up again."

And there came such a violent wind that it blew Conrad's hat far away across the fields and he was forced to run after it. When he came back, she had finished combing her hair and was putting it up again, and he could not get any of it. Then Conrad was angry and would not speak to her, and thus they watched the geese until the evening, and then they went home.

Next day when they were driving the geese out through the dark gateway, the maiden said,

"Alas, Falada, hanging there!"

Falada answered,

"Alas, young Queen, how ill you fare!
If this your tender mother knew,
Her heart would surely break in two."

And she sat down again in the field and began to comb out her hair, and Conrad ran and tried to clutch it, so she said in haste,

"Blow, blow, thou gentle wind, I say,
Blow Conrad's little hat away,
And make him chase it here and there,
Until I have braided all my hair,
And bound it up again."

Then the wind came and blew his little hat off his head and far away, and Conrad was forced to run after it, and when he came back, her hair had been put up a long time, and he couldn't get any of it; so they looked after their geese till evening came.

But in the evening after they had gone home, Conrad went to the old king, and said, "I won't tend the geese with that girl any longer!" "Why not?" inquired the aged king. "Oh, because she vexes me the whole day long." Then the aged king commanded him to relate what it was that she did to him. And Conrad said, "In the morning when we pass beneath the dark gateway with the flock, there is a sorry horse's head on the wall, and she says to it,

"Alas, Falada, hanging there!"

And the head replies,

"Alas, young Queen how ill you fare!
If this your tender mother knew,
Her heart would surely break in two."

And Conrad went on to relate what happened on the goose pasture, and how when there he had to chase his hat.

The aged king commanded him to drive his flock out again next day, and as soon as morning came, he placed himself behind the dark gateway and heard how the maiden spoke to the head of Falada, and then he too went into the fields and hid himself in the thicket in the meadow. There he soon saw with his own eyes the goose girl and the goose boy bringing their flock and how after a while she sat down and unplaited her hair, which shone with radiance. And soon she said,

"Blow, blow, thou gentle wind, I say,
Blow Conrad's little hat away,
And make him chase it here and there,
Until I have braided all my hair,
And bound it up again."

Then a blast of wind came and carried off Conrad's hat, so that he had to run far away while the maiden quietly went on combing and braiding her hair, all of which the king observed. Then, quite unseen, he went away, and when the goose girl came home in the evening, he called her aside and asked why she did all these things. "I may not tell you that, and I dare not lament my sorrows to any human being, for I have sworn not to do so by the heaven which is above me. If I had not done that, I should have lost my life." He urged her and left her no peace, but he could not draw anything from her. Then he said, "If you don't wish to tell me anything, tell your sorrows to the iron stove there," and he went away. Then she crept into the iron stove and began to weep and lament and emptied her whole heart and said, "Here am I deserted by the whole world, and yet I am a king's daughter, and a false waiting-maid has by force brought me to such a point that I have been compelled to take off my royal apparel, and she has taken my place with my bridegroom, and I have to perform menial service as a goose girl. If my mother only knew that that, her heart would break."

The aged king, however, was standing outside by the pipe of the stove and was listening to what she said and heard it. Then he came back again and asked her to come out of the stove. And royal garments were placed on her, and it was marvelous how beautiful she was! The aged king summoned his son and revealed to him that he had gotten the false bride who was only a waiting-maid, but that the true one was standing there, as the supposed goose girl. The young king rejoiced with all his heart when he saw her beauty and youth, and a great feast was made ready to which all the people and all good friends were invited. At the head of the table sat the bridegroom with the King's daughter at one side of him, and the waiting-maid on the other, but the waiting-maid was blinded, and did not recognize the princess in her dazzling array.

When they had eaten and drunk and were merry, the aged King asked the waiting-maid as a riddle what a person deserved who had behaved in such and such a way to her master, and at the same time related the whole story and asked what sentence such a person merited. Then the false bride said, "She deserves no better fate than to be stripped entirely naked and put into a barrel which is studded inside with pointed nails, and two white horses should be harnessed to it that will drag her along through one street after another till she is dead."

"It is you," said the aged King, "and you have pronounced your own sentence and thus shall it be done unto you." And when the sentence had been carried out, the young King married his true bride and both of them reigned over their kingdom in peace and happiness.

Doctor Know-It-All

(Brothers Grimm)

Once upon a time a poor farmer named Crabbe drove his two oxen to town with a load of wood and sold it for two dollars to a doctor. As the money was being paid to him, when the farmer saw the doctor sitting at table and how well he ate and drank, his heart was filled with longing and he would gladly have been a doctor. So he stood there for a while and finally asked if he could also be a doctor. "Oh yes," said the doctor, "and soon."

"What must I do?" asked the farmer.

"First you need to buy an ABC book, the kind which has a rooster inside, and second, convert your cart and your two oxen into money and get yourself some clothes and whatever else pertains to doctoring; third, have a sign painted with the words: 'I'm the Doctor Know-It-All', and nail it over your door!" The farmer did everything that he had been told.

After he had doctored people awhile, but not long, a rich, great nobleman's money was stolen. Someone told him about the Doctor Know-It-All who lived in such and such village and would certainly know where the money had gone. So the nobleman drove out to the village, and asked him if he was the Doctor Know-It-All.

"Yes, I am."

"Then you must come with me and recover my stolen money."

"O yes, but Grete, my wife, would have to come along also."

The nobleman agreed and had them both sitting in his carriage and they rode off together. When they came to the noble castle, the table was spread and he was invited to sit down and eat.

"Yes, but Grete must eat too," he said, and he sat down with her at the table. And when the first servant came with a dish of delicate fare, the peasant nudged his wife, and said, "Grete, that was the first," meaning that it was the first course.

The servant, however, imagined that he had really said: "This is the first thief," as he actually was. So he was afraid, and he said to his comrades: "The doctor knows everything; he said I was the first." The second servant did not want to enter, but when he did with his dish, the farmer looked to his wife and said, "Grete, that is the second."

This servant was terrified, and he quickly left the room. The third did not do any better, as the farmer again said: "Grete, that is the third."

The fourth had to carry in a covered bowl, and the nobleman told the doctor that he should show his skill by guessing what was inside – there were crabs. The farmer looked at the dish, and, feeling helpless, said, "Ah, poor Crabbe!" When the Lord heard this, he cried, "So if you know that you must also know who has the money."

The servants looked terribly uneasy and signaled that he should go outside. There all four of them confessed to him that they had stolen the money. They offered to give it all to him along with an additional handsome sum if he didn't turn them in. Otherwise they would all hang. They showed him where the money was hidden. The doctor was satisfied with this and he went back inside and sat down at the table again and said, "Sir, now will I search in my book to discover where the gold is hidden."

The fifth servant, however, crept into the stove in order to hear if the doctor knew still more. But the doctor sat and thumbed through his ABC book looking for the rooster. Unable to find it, he said, "I know that you're here so show yourself."

Believing the doctor meant him, the man in the oven jumped out in terror and cried: "The man knows everything."

So Doctor Know-It-All showed the nobleman where the money was, but he did not tell who had stolen it. He was rewarded with money from both sides and proceeded to become a famous man.

The Hare and the Hedgehog

(Brothers Grimm)

This story is completely made up, children, but it must be true since my grandfather, who gave it to me, informed me each and every time he told it to me, "It must be true, my lad, otherwise one certainly couldn't tell it." Anyway, here is how the story goes:

It was on a Sunday morning in autumn, just at that time when the buckwheat bloomed. The sun had risen brightly in the sky, the morning wind moved freshly over the stubble, the larks sang in the air, the bees buzzed in the buckwheat, and the people went to church in their Sunday clothes, and all God's creatures were satisfied, even the hedgehog.

The hedgehog stood in front of his door with his arms crossed, looked out at the morning wind and hummed a song to himself, as well and as bad as a hedgehog is able to sing on a perfect Sunday morning. As he sang half-lightly to himself, it occurred to him that he might as well take a walk in the field to see how his turnips were doing while his wife washed and dressed the children.

The turnips were very close to his house and he was used to eating them with his family which made him regard them as his own. The hedgehog closed the door behind him and set off out into the field.

He was not very far from home and wished to go directly around the blackthorn bush lying there before the field, and ramble over to the turnip patch, when he met the hare, who had gone

out with the same intentions, namely to tend to his cabbage. As the hedgehog became aware of the hare, he wished him a friendly good morning. The hare, however, who was in his own manner a completely distinguished gentleman, and terribly highfalutin about it, did not respond to the hedgehog's greeting, but said, in a clearly sarcastic voice, "How does it occur that you are running around the field so early in the morning?"

"I am taking a walk," said the hedgehog.

"A walk?" laughed the hare. "It seems to me that you could use your legs for better things." This response irritated the hedgehog beyond all measure for he could stand almost anything except remarks about his legs, which were naturally crooked.

"Do you imagine," the hedgehog said at that moment to the hare, "that you can accomplish more with your legs? I bet that if we had a footrace, I would pass you by."

"That is laughable, you with your crooked legs," said the hare, "but for all I care, let's do it if you really feel like doing it so much. What do you want to bet?"

"A golden Louis d'or and a bottle of brandy," said the hedgehog.

"Accepted," said the hare, "Shake hands and we can take right off!"

"No, there's no reason to hurry," said the hedgehog. "My stomach is still empty; first, I want to go home and have a little breakfast. I will be back here again in a half an hour."

The hare agreed to that and the hedgehog left. The hedgehog thought to himself as he was underway: "The hare trusts in his long legs but I will take care of him. He is certainly a distinguished fellow, but also clearly a dumb bozo, and he must pay for it."

When the hedgehog arrived home, he said to his wife, "Wife, get dressed, you have to go out into the field. I have wagered a golden Louis d'or and a bottle of brandy with the hare. I want to run against him to win the bet and you should be there with me."

"Dear God, husband," the hedgehog began to cry to her husband, "Are you stupid? Have you completely lost your senses? How could you make a wager to race with the hare?"

"Be quiet, wife," said the hedgehog, "that is my problem. Don't get involved in men's business. Hurry up and get dressed and come with me then." What could his wife do to the hedgehog? She had to follow him whether she wanted to or not.

As they were finally underway, the hedgehog spoke to his wife: "Now pay attention to what I tell you: look at the long field; that is where we want to have our footrace. The hare will run in one furrow and I in the other and we start to run from above. Now you have nothing more to do than to set yourself down here in the furrow and, when the hare arrives on the other side, you call out to him from your furrow, "I am already here!"

With that, they arrived at the field. The hedgehog showed his wife her place and then he went to the top of the field. The hare was already there when he arrived.

"Can we start?" asked the hare.

"Yes, indeed," said the hedgehog. "On your mark!" And each one took his place in his furrow.

The hare counted "One, two, three," and he tore down the field like a windstorm. But the hedgehog ran only about three steps and then ducked down in the furrow and remained there sitting quietly.

When the hare, in full run, arrived at the bottom of the field, the hedgehog's wife called out to him, "I'm already here!"

The hare hesitated and, more than a little surprised, believed it was the hedgehog himself, for, as everyone knows, a female hedgehog looks just like her husband.

The hare thought, "Something is not right here." He called out, "Let's run back again!" And he took off again like a windstorm, with his ears pinned back to his head. But the hedgehog's wife remained quietly in her place.

When the hare arrived at the top, the hedgehog called out to him, "I'm already here!"

The hare, beside himself with anger, shouted, "Let's run back again! One more round."

"It's all right with me," answered the hedgehog. "As often as you wish."

So the hare ran seventy-three more times, and the hedgehog always kept up with him. Each time the hare reached the top or the bottom of the field, the hedgehog or his wife said, "I am already here!"

But the hare did not finish the seventy-fourth time. He fell to the ground and died in the middle of the field, blood flowing from his neck.

The hedgehog took the Louis d'or and the bottle of brandy he had won, called his wife from her furrow, and they went back home happy. And if they have not died, then they are still alive.

So it happened that the hedgehog ran the hare to death on the Buxtehude Heath, and since that time no hare has ever agreed to run a race with a Buxtehude hedgehog.

The moral of this story is, first, that no one, no matter how distinguished he thinks he is, should make fun of a lesser man, even if that man is only a hedgehog. And second, that when a man marries, it is advisable that he choose a wife from his own class, one who looks just like him. In other words, a hedgehog should always make sure that his wife is also a hedgehog, and so forth.

E. Michael Iba

Eberhard Michael Iba, senior teacher, lives at the present time with his wife Elisabeth in Saarbrücken. Born on May 6, 1948, in the north Hessian village of Obermeiser near Hofgeismar, he spent his childhood and student years in Hofgeismar, where he achieved his Abitur from the Albert Schweitzer School. From 1969–1975 he studied English and French at the Universities of Marburg, Poitiers, Exeter, Bordeaux, and Trier, where he added an additional major in German as a foreign language. He taught from 1976–1994 in Bremerhaven and then moved to Luxembourg, where he was a teacher of German as a foreign language at the European School of Luxembourg. From 2003–2012 he taught English and French at the tradition-rich Albert-Einstein-Gymnasium in Völklingen; he is now retired.

Since his time as a student, E. Michael Iba has collected source texts and has assembled an extensive collection of sagas and fairy tales. He has published a series of books, including among others:

- Sagas and Histories from North Hessia, 7th Edition, 1998.
- On the Trail of the Brothers Grimm from Hanau to Bremen, 2nd Edition 1981.
- The Green Coastal Road from Emden to Westerland, 1981.
- From the Treasure Chest of the German Fairy Tale Route, Part I, 1987 – Part II, 1993.
- The German Fairy Tale Route: a Saga-filled Excursion from the River Main to the North Sea. (Die Deutsche Märchenstraße – Eine sagenhafte Reise vom Main zum Meer, 2011)

Thomas L. Johnson

Thomas L. Johnson, Professor Emeritus, lives at the present time with his wife Sheryl McRoberts in Plymouth, Minnesota. Born May 29, 1947 in northern Minnesota, he spent his youth in International Falls, Minnesota. He graduated from Wheaton College in Illinois with a degree in English Literature and completed graduate studies at the University of Minnesota (MA Comparative Literature) and the University of Wyoming. Until his retirement, he was a faculty member for 25 years at Bethel University in St. Paul, Minnesota and has published numerous poems and short stories including one, "The Glass-Eyed Winger", that has been anthologized in the USA and Canada.

He met Mr. Iba his very first day at the University of Trier-Kaiserslautern while on a Fulbright Grant in Trier (1973–74). This meeting developed into a decades-long friendship that continues to this day and includes both wives. Thomas L. Johnson and Sheryl McRoberts have developed a great affinity to Germany partly leading to the edition of this book. While her husband and E.M. Iba are responsible for the English texts, Sheryl McRoberts, who teaches studio art at Normandale College in Minnesota, took numerous photos during their visits at the German Fairy Tale Route. Quite a number of the lovely photos in this book were taken with her camera.

Bibliography

Arnim, Bettina von/Arnim, Gisela von
Das Leben der Reichsgräfin Gritta von Rattenzuhausbeiuns, Berlin 1926

Baudrillard, Jean
Simulations, Semiotext(e), Inc: New York, 1983

Baumgärtner, Ingrid (Hg.)
Kunigunde – eine Kaiserin der Jahrtausendwende, Kassel 1997

Bechstein, Ludwig
Deutsches Märchenbuch, Leipzig 1850

Bechstein, Ludwig
Deutsches Sagenbuch, Leipzig 1853

Beckett, Samuel
Dream of Fair to Middling Women, New York 1992

Benzel, Ulrich
Herbstein, die Stadt auf dem Berge. Sagen – Märchen. Schwänke, Lauterbach 1993

Bergengruen, Werner
Die Schwestern aus dem Mohrenland, Zürich 1963

Bindewald, Theodor
Oberhessisches Sagenbuch, Frankfurt/M. 1873

Boette, Ludwig Friedrich Werner
Volksdichtung in Hessen. Nach Märchen, Sage und Lied, dargestellt von L.F.W. Boette. Aus dem Nachlass herausgegeben und bearbeitet von Charlotte Oberfeld, Siegfried Becker und Andreas C. Bimmer, Frankfurt/M. 1993

Bolte, Johannes
Volkslieder aus Hessen, gesammelt von den Brüdern Grimm, in: Zeitschrift des Vereins für Volkskunde, 18. Jahrgang 1908, S. 84 ff.

Bolte, Johannes
Jacob Grimm als Volksliedersammler, Berlin 1928, 1. Jg., S. 157 ff.

Brednich, Rolf Wilhelm
Die Maus im Jumbo-Jet. Neue sagenhafte Geschichten von heute, München 1991

Brednich, Rolf Wilhelm
Die Spinne in der Yucca-Palme. Sagenhafte Geschichten von heute, München 1990

Bürger, Gottfried August/ Raspe, Rudolf Erich
Des Freih. v. Münchhausen wunderbare Reisen und Abenteuer zu Wasser und zu Lande, wie er dieselben bei der Flasche im Zirkel seiner Freunde selbst zu erzählen pflegte. – Zuerst gesammelt und englisch herausgegeben von R.E. Raspe. Übersetzt und hier und da erweitert von G.A. Bürger. Siebente Originalausgabe der deutschen Bearbeitung, Göttingen 1855

Burmeister, Helmut
Begegnungen im Märchenwald. Der Maler Theodor Rocholl (1854–1933) und der Reinhardswald, Hofgeismar 2004

Busch, Wilhelm
Gesammelte Werke I, 85. Auflage, München 1922

Busch, William
Max and Maurice: A Juvenile History in Seven Tricks, Roberts Brothers, Boston 1871

Busch, Wilhelm
Ut ôler Welt. Volksmärchen, Sagen, Volkslieder und Reime, München 1910

Cammann, Alfred
Deutsche Volksmärchen aus Russland, Göttingen 1967

Cammann, Alfred
Märchenwelt des Preußenlandes, Bleckede 1973

Cordes, Johann Jacob/ Müller, Ferdinand
Heimatbücher. Band I: Sagen, Lehe 1919

Curtze, Louis
Volksüberlieferungen aus dem Fürstentum Waldeck, Märchen, Sagen, Volksreime, Rätsel, Sprichwörter, Aberglauben, Sitten und Gebräuche, nebst einem Idiotikon, Arolsen 1860

Denecke, Ludwig
Jacob Grimm und sein Bruder Wilhelm, Stuttgart 1971

Denecke, Ludwig
Münden im Blickpunkt der Brüder Grimm, Hann. Münden 1987

Desel, Jochen
Französische Dörfer – deutsche Zuwanderer 1699–1779: 300 Jahre Kelze und Schöneberg, Band II, Hofgeismar 1999

Dreyer, Heinrich
Ein kleiner Heimatführer für alle Buschfreunde – Wiedensahl, Wilhelm Buschs Geburtsort und Heimatdorf, Wiedensahl 1952

Dismer, Wilhelm
Geschichte und Sage aus alten Tagen, II. Geschichten und Gestalten um den Giebichenstein, Nienburg o.J.

Eckhardt, Erika
Schwälmer Sagenborn, 2. Auflage Marburg, 1987

Ehrhardt, Holger (Hg.)
Dorothea Viehmann, Kassel 2012

Falckenheiner, Carl Bernhard Nicolaus
Sagen, in: Zeitschrift des Vereins für hessische Geschichte und Landeskunde. Erster Band, Kassel 1837, S. 356-360

Förderverein Gemeinschafts- und Kulturzentrum e.V. (Hg.)
Johann Heinrich Christian Bang, die Marburger Romantiker und die Märchen der Brüder Grimm, Lahntal 2014

Frau Holle ... weltberühmt Broschüre Naturpark Meißner - Kaufunger Wald, o.O./o.J. und doch unbekannt, www.frauholle.info

Glaser, Hermann/ Lehmann, Jakob/ Lubos Arno
Wege der deutschen Literatur. Eine geschichtliche Darstellung, 13. Auflage 1971

Grieser, Dietmar
Mit den Brüdern Grimm durch Hessen, Frankfurt/M. 1985

Grimm, Jacob
Deutsche Mythologie, Göttingen, 2. Auflage 1844

Brüder Grimm: Deutsche Sagen, Leipzig 1911

Brüder Grimm
Deutsche Sagen. Band I-III: Bände I+II: herausgegeben von Hans-Jörg Uther, Band III: herausgegeben von Barbara Kindermann-Bieri, München 1993

Brüder Grimm
Kinder- und Hausmärchen: Die handschriftliche Urfassung von 1810, herausgegeben und kommentiert von Heinz Rölleke, Stuttgart 2007

Brüder Grimm
Kinder- und Hausmärchen, Berlin 1812/15

Brüder Grimm
Kinder- und Hausmärchen: Große Ausgabe, 7. Auflage Göttingen, 1857

Brüder Grimm Gedenken
Herausgegeben von Ludwig Denecke u.a. (mehrbändige Forschungsreihe), Marburg 1963 ff.

Grimm, Ferdinand = Pseudonym
Philipp von Steinau: Volkssagen der Deutschen, Zeitz 1838

Grimm, Hans
Volk ohne Raum, München 1926

Grimm, Ludwig Emil
Erinnerungen aus meinem Leben, Leipzig 1911

Grüner, Gustav
Waldeckische Volkserzählungen, Arolsen 1963

Häger, Adolf
Der Schulschwänzer, Hofgeismar 1955

Hahn, Albert
Geschichte des im Stiftsbezirke Loccum gelegenen Fleckens Wiedensahl, Hannover 1898

Hauff, Wilhelm
Phantasien im Bremer Ratskeller. Ein Herbstgeschenk für Freunde des Weines, Stuttgart 1827

Hedwig, Andreas (Hg.)
Die Brüder Grimm in Marburg, Marburg 2013

Heidelbach, Paul
Kassel. Ein Jahrtausend hessischer Stadtkultur, Kassel 1957

Heine, Heinrich
Deutschland. Ein Wintermärchen, Hamburg 1844

Henniger, Karl/ Harten, Johann von
Niedersachsens Sagenborn, Hildesheim, Bd. I, 1907, Bd. II, 1909

Heßler, Carl
Hessischer Sagenkranz. Sagen aus Kurhessen, 4. Auflage Kassel, 1928

Hildebrandt, Irma
Es waren ihrer Fünf. Die Brüder Grimm und ihre Familie, Köln 1984

Hoffmann, Gerd/ Rölleke, Heinz
Der unbekannte Grimm. Deutsche Sagen von Ferdinand Philipp Grimm. Aus dem Nachlass herausgegeben von G. Hoffmann und H. Rölleke, Düsseldorf/Köln 1979

Hoffmeister, Philipp
Hessische Volksdichtung in Sagen und Märchen, Schwänken und Schnurren, Marburg 1869

Hoppe, Martin
Hanau und die Brüder Grimm, Hanau 2007

Huber, Jörg Adrian
Die Brüder Grimm in Kassel, Gudensberg 2007

Iba, Eberhard Michael
Auf den Spuren der Brüder Grimm von Hanau nach Bremen, unter Mitarbeit von Walter Iba, 2. Auflage Regensburg, 1981

Iba, Eberhard Michael
Auf den Spuren der Brüder Grimm: Eine literarische Reise entlang der Deutschen Märchenstraße mit Märchen, Sagen und Liedern. Band I: Von Hanau nach Höxter, 3. Auflage Hofgeismar/Strassen (Lux), 2000

Iba, Eberhard Michael
Aus der Schatzkammer der Deutschen Märchenstraße, Band I: Sagen, Geschichten, Märchen und Erzählungen aus Bremen, Bremerhaven, Verden und Nienburg, Bremen 1987

Iba, Eberhard Michael
Aus der Schatzkammer der Deutschen Märchenstraße, Band II: Nördliches Weserbergland, Hameln 1993

Iba, Eberhard Michael
Der Klabautermann und andere Sagen und Geschichten in und um Bremerhaven, 3. Auflage Bremerhaven 2010

Iba, Eberhard Michael
Die Deutsche Märchenstraße. Eine sagenhafte Reise vom Main zum Meer, Hameln 2011

Iba, Walter
Aus Großmutters Märchentruhe, in: Die Märchentruhe. Erzählungen für Kinder und Junggebliebene, Solingen 1946, S. 40-71

Iba, Walter/Meibert, Hildegard
Neue Kindermärchen, 2. Auflage Hofgeismar, 1957

Isaacson, Judith Magyar
Seed of Sarah, University of Illinois 1991

Justi, Karl Wilhelm
Die Vorzeit: Ein Taschenbuch für das Jahr 1826, Marburg und Kassel 1825

Kamphoevener, Elsa Sophia Baronin von
An Nachtfeuern der Karawan-Serail. Märchen und Geschichten alttürkischer Nomaden, Hamburg 1956/57

Keindorf, Gudrun
Wege der Überlieferung. Zu Funktions- und Bedeutungswandel der „Sagen" von der Burg Plesse, Plesse Archiv, Heft 10, Bovenden 1995

Kling, Burkhard
Die Brüder Grimm Leben und Wirken. Führer durch das Brüder Grimm-Haus in Steinau an der Straße, Steinau/Worms 2011

Kling, Burkhard
Die Brüder Grimm und die Märchenwelt. Führer durch das Brüder Grimm-Haus in Steinau an der Straße, Steinau/Worms 2011

Koch, Ernst
Prinz Rosa-Stramin, Marburg 1922

Koszinowski, Ingrid/ Leuschner, Vera
Ludwig Emil Grimm. 1790-1863. Maler - Zeichner - Radierer, Kassel 1985

Kuhn, Adalbert/ Schwartz, Wilhelm
Norddeutsche Sagen, Märchen und Gebräuche aus Mecklenburg, Pommern, der Mark, Sachsen, Thüringen, Braunschweig, Hannover, Oldenburg und Westfalen. Aus dem Munde des Volkes gesammelt, Leipzig 1848

Kurz, Carl Heinz
Bovender Sagen, Hann. Münden 1980

Lauer, Berhard
Die Brüder Grimm – Leben und Wirken, Kassel 2005

Lauer, Bernhard
Dorothea Viehmann und die Brüder Grimm, Sonderdruck aus der Chronik der Stadt Baunatal, herausgegeben im Auftrag der Stadt Baunatal von Heinrich Pflug, Baunatal 1997

Lauer, Bernhard/ Mayer, Andrea
Auf den Spuren der Brüder Grimm in Kassel, Kassel 2007

Lauer, Bernhard/ Mayer, Andrea
Auf den Spuren der „Märchenfrau" in Kassel und Baunatal, Kassel 2009

Lyncker, Karl
Deutsche Sagen und Sitten in hessischen Gauen, Kassel 1854

Märchen, Fliegen, Zeichenkreise. Die Liebhabereien des hessischen Predigers Philipp Hoffmeister (1804–1874), herausgegeben vom Förderverein Kultur- und Sozialzentrum Klosterkirche Nordshausen e.V. in Verbindung mit Karin Berkemann, Marburg 2013

magazin aus der mitte: Gute Seiten aus Nordhessen. Reiche Region: Märchen, märchenhafte Orte und Sagenhaftes, Herausgeber: Regionalmanagement Nordhessen GmbH, Kassel, Sommer 2010, Heft 4

Magistrat der Universitätsstadt Marburg – Fachdienst Kultur: Grimm-Stadt Marburg, Marburg 2012

Mascos, Werner
Großen Marburgern auf der Spur, 3. Auflage Marburg 1991

Martus, Steffen
Die Brüder Grimm. Eine Biographie, 2. Auflage Berlin 2010

Moritz, Karl Philipp
Anton Reiser. Ein psychologischer Roman, 5. Auflage Frankfurt/M. 1985

National Geographic
Deutschland. Hüter der Märchen: Die Brüder Grimm, Dezember 1999, S. 150-181

Nord, Rudolf
Plattdeutsche Volksmärchen aus Waldeck, Korbach 1939

Nord, Rudolf
Volksmärchen aus Waldeck, Korbach 1932

Oberfeld, Charlotte
Märchen des Waldecker Landes, Marburg 1982

Oberfeld, Charlotte
Volksmärchen aus Hessen, Marburg 1962

Oberfeld, Charlotte/ Bimmer, Andreas C.
Hessen. Märchenland der Brüder Grimm, Kassel 1984

Oberfeld, Charlotte/ Assion, Peter/ Denecke, Ludwig/ Röhrich, Lutz/Rölleke, Heinz
Brüder Grimm Volkslieder. Aus der Handschriftensammlung der Universitätsbibliothek Marburg, 3 Bd., Marburg 1985, 1987 und 1989

Oberhauser, Fred/ Kahrs, Axel
Literarischer Führer Deutschland, Frankfurt/M. und Leipzig 2008

Paetow, Karl
Die schönsten Wesersagen an der Märchenstraße von Kassel bis Bremen, 5. Auflage, Hameln 1989

Paetow, Karl
Die Wittekindsage, Hameln/Hannover 1960

Perrault, Charles
Histoires ou contes du temps passé, avec des moralités: Contes de ma mère l'Oye, Paris1697

Pfister, Hermann von
Sagen und Aberglaube aus Hessen und Nassau, Marburg 1885

Redeker, Wilhelm
Westphälische Sagen, meist aus mündlicher Überlieferung gesammelt und mitgeteilt. In: Westphalia. Beiträge zur vaterländischen Geschichte und Altertumskunde, Minden 1830, S. 35–69

Rölleke, Heinz
Die älteste Märchensammlung der Brüder Grimm. Synopse der handschriftlichen Urfassung von 1810 und der Erstdrucke von 1812, Cologny-Genève 1975

Rölleke, Heinz
Kinder- und Hausmärchen. Die handschriftliche Urfassung von 1810, Stuttgart 2007

Rölleke, Heinz
Die Märchen der Brüder Grimm. Eine Einführung, München 1985

Rölleke, Heinz (Hg.)
Die wahren Märchen der Brüder Grimm, Frankfurt/M. 1989

Rölleke, Heinz (Hg.)
Märchen aus dem Nachlass der Brüder Grimm, Bonn, 2. Aufl. 1979

Rölleke, Heinz/ Schindehütte, Albert
Es war einmal ... Die wahren Märchen der Brüder Grimm und wer sie ihnen erzählte, Frankfurt/M. 2011

Römer, Dorothee
Ludwig Emil Grimm in Carlshafen, HNA-Serie: Spuren der Hugenotten, in: HNA Hofgeismarer Allgemeine, 31.1.2013

Rohde, Heinrich
Weserwellen. Geschichten und Sagen aus dem Gebiet der Oberweser und der Diemel, 4. Auflage Hofgeismar, o.J.

Ruppel, Heinrich
Märchenstunde bei den Brüdern Grimm, Melsungen 1951

Ruppel, Heinrich/Häger, Adolf
Der Schelm im Volk. Einige Schock Schwänke, Schnurren und Schelmereien dem Volksmund nacherzählt, 3. Auflage Kassel, 1952

Sander, Eckhard
Schneewittchen, Märchen oder Wahrheit? Ein lokaler Bezug zum Kellerwald, Gudensberg 1994

Scharrelmann, Wilhelm
Wie es den Bremer Stadtmusikanten weiter erging, in: Worpsweder Märchen, Fischerhude 1984

Schede, Hans-Georg
Die Brüder Grimm, Hanau 2009

Schindehütte, Albert
Krauses Grimm'sche Märchen, Marburg 1991

Schneider, Emil
Hessisches Sagenbüchlein, 2. Auflage Marburg, 1905

Schoof, Wilhelm
Zur Entstehungsgeschichte der Grimm'schen Märchen, Frankfurt/M. 1931

Schwalm, Johann Heinrich
Der Kreis Ziegenhain. Ein Heimatbuch für Schule und Haus, Marburg 1908

Seidel, Ina
Drei Städte meiner Jugend, Stuttgart 1960

Seiler, Josef
Sagen und Märchen aus Heimat und Fremde, Kassel 1851

Seiler, Josef
Volkssagen und Legenden des Landes Paderborn 1848

Seitz, Gabriele Die Brüder Grimm. Leben-Werk-Zeit, 2. Auflage München, 1985

Storm, Theodor
Pole Poppenspäler, Braunschweig 1875

Strecker, Helmut (Hg.)
Wiedensahl früher und heute, Stolzenau 1975

Universität Kassel
Märchen, Mythen und Moderne. 200 Jahre Kinder- und Hausmärchen der Brüder Grimm. Internationaler Kongress vom 17. bis 20. Dezember 2012 an der Universität Kassel

Voges, Theodor
Sagen aus dem Lande Braunschweig, Braunschweig 1895

Vonjahr, Heinz
Der (un)glückliche Finder. Philipp Hoffmeister zum 125. Todestag..., in Jahrbuch 1999 Landkreis Kassel, S. 41 ff.

Vonjahr, Heinz
Grimm'sche Märchen aus Hoof ..., in: Jahrbuch 1985 Landkreis Kassel, S.155 ff.

Vonjahr, Heinz
Marie Hassenpflug und Friedrich von Dalwigk, in: Jahrbuch 1990 Landkreis Kassel, S. 37 ff.

Wagenfeld, Friedrich
Bremens Volkssagen, Bremen 1845

Walther, Victor
General und die Frauen. Vom Erlebnis zur Theorie, Berlin 1932

Wehrhan, Karl
Sagen aus Hessen und Nassau, Leipzig 1922

Weichelt, Hermann
Hannoversche Geschichten und Sagen, Leipzig 1908

Weiser, Karl
Hutten, Leipzig 1897

Weishaupt, Jürgen
Die Märchenbrüder. Jacob und Wilhelm Grimm – ihr Leben und Wirken, 2. Auflage Kassel, 1986

Wehrhan, Karl
Sagen aus Hessen und Nassau, Leipzig 1922

Wickenrode, Gemeinde
Festschrift zum 4. Dorftag der Gemeinde Wickenrode, 24.6.1938

wikimedia Foundation Inc. Wikipedia
Die freie Enzyklopädie

Willeke, Manfred
Eines der meistübersetzten Bücher. Prof. Wilhelm Grimm 1841 in Bad Pyrmont, in: Deister- und Weserzeitung, Hameln 31.8.2013

Willeke, Manfred
Lügder Sagen-Sammlung. Sagen und sagenhafte Geschichten aus der Stadt Lügde, 2. Auflage Lügde 1988

Winzentsen, Franz
Die Branntweinflasche von der Buxtehuder Heide, Buxtehude 2003

Wüstefeld, Karl
Obereichsfeldischer Sagenschatz, Heiligenstadt 1924

Zaunert, Paul
Hessen-Nassauische Sagen, Jena 1929

Zaunert, Paul
Deutsche Märchen seit Grimm, Köln 1984

Die ZEIT Geschichte
Die Brüder Grimm. 200 Jahre Märchen. Ein deutscher Welterfolg und seine Autoren, Hamburg Nr. 4/2012

Ziegler, Hermann
Der Gewekenstein. Sagen und Geschichten aus dem Landkreis Nienburg/Weser, Nienburg 1983

Ziegler, Hermann
Ich bin die kleine Nienburgerin (Lied), Manuskript Nienburg, 1975

Zipes, Jack
The Brothers Grimm. From Enchanted Forests to the Modern World, New York 2002

Zipes, Jack
The Golden Age of Folk & Fairy Tales from the Brothers Grimm to Andrew Lang, Indianapolis, 2013

Photo Credits

Cover:
Sababurg Castle: Tierpark Sababurg
Fairy Tale Characters: The Pied Piper of Hamelin and Little Red Riding Hood: Paavo Blafield – Sleeping Beauty: Familie Koseck, Dornröschenschloss Sababurg
Brothers Grimm: Hanauer Geschichtsverein e.V. 1844

On-page background vignettes: Markus Lefrançois.
p. 9 Paavo Blåfield
p. 11 Nationalpark Kellerwald-Edersee
p. 12 Paavo Blåfield
p. 14 Hanauer Geschichtsverein 1844 e.V.
p. 15 Paavo Blåfield
p. 17 Medienzentrum Hanau
p. 20 Hanauer Geschichtsverein 1844 e.V.
p. 21–25 Medienzentrum Hanau
p. 28 Above: Hanauer Geschichtsverein 1844 e.V. – Below: Museum Brüder Grimm Haus Steinau
p. 29, 30 Museum Brüder Grimm Haus Steinau
p. 31, 32 Stadt Steinau an der Straße
p. 35–37 Gemeinde Freiensteinau
p. 38 Kurbetriebsgesellschaft Herbstein GmbH
p. 39 Kurbetriebsgesellschaft Herbstein GmbH: N. Ruhl
p. 40 Kurbetriebsgesellschaft Herbstein GmbH: S. Wienold
p. 41 Kurbetriebsgesellschaft Herbstein GmbH: N. Ruhl
p. 42–44 Tourist Center Alsfeld
p. 45 Prof. Mc Roberts
p. 46 Left: Prof. McRoberts - Right:Tourist Center Alsfeld
p. 50 Tourismus und Marketing Gmbh Marburg: Above: Rainer Kieselbach – Below: Georg Kronenberg
p. 51 Prof. McRoberts
p. 52 Tourismus und Marketing Gmbh Marburg
p. 53–55 Tourismus und Marketing Gmbh Marburg: Georg Kronenberg
p. 56 Tourismus und Marketing Gmbh Marburg
p. 57 Tourismus und Marketing Gmbh Marburg: Georg Kronenberg
p. 59 Tourismus und Marketing Gmbh Marburg: Erhart Dettmering
p. 62 Karl Heinz Görmar
p. 63 Otto Ubbelohde
p. 64 Karl Heinz Görmar - Otto Ubbelohde
p. 65 Otto Ubbelohde
p. 66–69 Willingshausen Touristik GmbH
p. 70 Schwalm-Touristik e.V.
p. 71 Left: Prof. Mc Roberts – Right: Schwalm-Touristik e.V.
p. 72 Schwalm-Touristik e.V.
p. 73 Prof. McRoberts

p. 74 Schwalm-Touristik e.V.
p. 76 Prof. McRoberts
p. 77 Prof. McRoberts
p. 78 Kurbetrieb Bad Hersfeld
p. 79 Prof. McRoberts
p. 80 Prof. McRoberts
p. 81 Kurbetrieb Bad Hersfeld
p. 82 Prof. McRoberts
p. 83–85 Knüll Touristik e.V.
p. 86 Stadt Homberg(Efze): Jörg Zank
p. 87, 88 Stadt Homberg(Efze)
p. 89, 90 Stadt Homberg(Efze): Jörg Zank
p. 93 Stadtmarketing Fritzlar e.V.: Katharina Jäger
p. 94 Stadtmarketing Fritzlar e.V.: Katharina Jäger – Heinrichskreuz: Stadtmarketing Fritzlar e.V.
p. 95 Stadtmarketing Fritzlar e.V.: Johannes De Lange
p. 96–99 Stadtmarketing Fritzlar e.V.
p. 100, 101 Staatsbad Bad Wildungen GmbH: Reckhard Pfeil
p. 102, 103 Staatsbad Bad Wildungen GmbH
p. 104 Left: Staatsbad Bad Wildungen GmbH – Right: Prof. McRoberts
p. 105, 106 Staatsbad Bad Wildungen GmbH
p. 107, 108 Ederbergland Touristik e.V.
p. 109, 110 E. Michael Iba
p. 111 Hotel Die SONNE Frankenberg
p. 112 Thonet GmbH Frankenberg
p. 113 Above: E. Michael Iba - Below: Schloss Waldeck Hotelbetriebs GmbH + Co KG
p. 114, 115 Schloss Waldeck Hotelbetriebs GmbH + Co KG
p. 116, 117 Stadt Waldeck GmbH
p. 120–125 Stadt Wolfhagen: Werner Stübe
p. 126 Gemeinde Schauenburg: Rolf Jungermann
p. 127, 128 Förderverein Schauenburger Märchenwache e.V.: Dieter Schwertle
p. 129 Förderverein Schauenburger Märchenwache e.V.
p. 130, 131 Gemeinde Schauenburg: Rolf Jungermann
p. 132–135 Bildarchiv der Stadt Niedenstein: Paavo Blåfield
p. 136, 137 Stadt Gudensberg
p. 138 Stadt Gudensberg: Paavo Blåfield
p. 139 Stadt Gudensberg
p. 140 Stadt Gudensberg: Jürgen Preuß
p. 141 Brauhaus Knallhütte, Baunatal
p. 142 Brauhaus Knallhütte, Baunatal – Below: Brüder Grimm-Sammlung Kassel
p. 143–145 Stadtmarketing Baunatal GmbH
p. 146–149 Kassel Marketing GmbH: Paavo Blåfield
p. 150, 151 Prof. McRoberts
p. 152, 153 Kassel Marketing GmbH: Paavo Blåfield

p. 154, 155 Brüder Grimm-Sammlung Kassel
p. 156, 157 Kassel Marketing GmbH: Paavo Blåfield
p. 158–161 Gemeinde Nieste: Helmut Lippert
p. 162, 163 Gemeinde Kaufungen: Helga Noll-Hartwig
p. 164 Right: Gemeinde Kaufungen: Helga Noll-Hartwig – Left: Prof. McRoberts
p. 165 Gemeinde Kaufungen: Helga Noll-Hartwig
p. 166–170 Prof. McRoberts
p. 171 Gemeinde Helsa
p. 172–176 Stadt Hessisch Lichtenau
p. 177–181 Archiv Stadt Melsungen
p. 182 Stadtmarketing Bad Sooden-Allendorf
p. 183 Prof. McRoberts
p. 184, 185 Stadtmarketing Bad Sooden-Allendorf
p. 186 Prof. McRoberts
p. 187 Pro Witzenhausen GmbH: E. Strauch
p. 188 Pro Witzenhausen GmbH
p. 189 Prof. McRoberts
p. 190 Pro Witzenhausen GmbH: Werner Keller
p. 191 Pro Witzenhausen GmbH: Tina Gassmann
p. 192 Pro Witzenhausen GmbH
p. 193–196 Thomas Heddergott
p. 197–203 Stadtverwaltung Heilbad Heiligenstadt
p. 206 Europäisches Brotmuseum e.V. Ebergötzen
p. 207 Förderkreis Wilhelm-Busch-Stätten in Ebergötzen e.V.
p. 208 Europäisches Brotmuseum e.V. Ebergötzen
p. 212, 213 Flecken Bovenden: Hempel
p. 214 Flecken Bovenden: Left: Lies – Right: Heller
p. 215 Touristik Naturpark Münden e.V.: Photo Burkhardt
p. 216 Touristik Naturpark Münden e.V.: Peter Heitmann
p. 217 Touristik Naturpark Münden e.V.: Photo Burkhardt (two photos)
p. 218, 219 Touristik Naturpark Münden e.V.: Peter Heitmann
p. 220 Touristik Naturpark Münden e.V.
p. 221 Deutsche Märchenstraße e.V.
p. 223, 224 Stadt Grebenstein
p. 225 Prof. McRoberts
p. 226, 227 Stadt Grebenstein
p. 228 Archiv Stadt Hofgeismar: Paavo Blåfield
p. 229, 230 Prof. McRoberts
p. 231 E. Michael Iba
p. 232 Archiv Stadt Hofgeismar: Paavo Blåfield
p. 233, 234 Prof. McRoberts
p. 236–239 Stadt Trendelburg: Harald Schmidt
p. 240–242 Gemeinde Oberweser
p. 243 Gemeinde Oberweser: Hendrik Homburg
p. 244 Gemeinde Oberweser
p. 245–247 Prof. McRoberts

p. 248 Gemeinde Wahlsburg
p. 249–254 Bad Karlshafen GmbH, Gesellschaft für Standort und Marketing
p. 256–259 Porzellanmanusfaktur FÜRSTENBERG GmbH
p. 260, 261 Gemeinde Flecken Polle: Heinz Heil
p. 262 Prof. McRoberts
p. 263 Paavo Blåfield
p. 264 Prof. McRoberts
p. 265, 266 Lügde Marketing e.V.
p. 267 Lügde Marketing e.V.: Falko Sieker
p. 268–271 Lügde Marketing e.V.
p. 272 Above: Samtgemeinde Bodenwerder-Polle – Below: Paavo Blåfield
p. 273 Samtgemeinde Bodenwerder-Polle
p. 274 Above: Samtgemeinde Bodenwerder-Polle – Below: Prof. McRoberts
p. 275, 276 Samtgemeinde Bodenwerder-Polle
p. 278 Hameln Marketing und Tourismus GmbH
p. 279 Prof. McRoberts
p. 280–283 Hameln Marketing und Tourismus GmbH
p. 284 Schlosshotel Münchhausen, Aerzen: Salzmann
p. 285 Schloss Hämelschenburg
p. 289–293 Stadt Hessisch Oldendorf
p. 294 Städtische Museen Bad Oeynhausen: Helmut Saak
p. 295 Städtische Museen Bad Oeynhausen: Sandra Sanchez
p. 296, 297 Ernst-Udo Hartmann
p. 298 Ernst Udo Hartmann – Sültemeyer-Brunnen: Peter Hübbe
p. 299 Bali Therme
p. 300 Städtische Museen Bad Oeynhausen: Helmut Saak
p. 301, 302 Gemeinde Flecken Wiedensahl
p. 303 Above: Gemeinde Flecken Wiedensahl – Drawing below: W. Busch: Ut ôler Welt
p. 304–307 Gemeinde Flecken Wiedensahl
p. 308–312 Mittelweser-Touristik GmbH
p. 314–318 Samtgemeinde Grafschaft Hoya
p. 319 Prof. McRoberts
p. 320 Left: Stadtmarketing Buxtehude e.V. – Right: Prof. Mc Roberts
p. 321 Stadtmarketing Buxtehude e.V.
p. 322 Prof. Mc Roberts
p. 323 Stadtmarketing Buxtehude e.V.
p. 324 Prof. McRoberts
p. 325–327 BTZ Bremer Touristik-Zentrale
p. 328, 329 Prof. McRoberts
p. 330, 331 BTZ Bremer Touristik-Zentrale
p. 333 Above :Erlebnis Bremerhaven. Gesellschaft für Touristik, Marketing und Veranstaltungen mbH – Below: Helmut Gross
p. 334–336 Erlebnis Bremerhaven …

p. 337 Kay Riechers
p. 338, 339 Erlebnis Bremerhaven …
p. 342, 343 Göttingen Tourismus e.V.: Lars Gerhardts
p. 344 Göttingen Tourismus e.V.: Ronald Schmidt
p. 345 Göttingen Tourismus e.V.: Bernd Beuermann
p. 346 Göttingen Tourismus e.V.: Alciro Theodoro da Silva
p. 347 Göttingen Tourismus e.V.: Torsten Krüger
p. 348 Above: Prof. McRoberts - Below: Prof. Johnson
p. 349, 350 Prof. McRoberts
p. 351 Above: Prof. McRoberts - Below: Prof. Johnson
p. 352–403 Deutsche Märchenstraße Paavo Blåfield
p. 409 Manfred Weltermann, Grebenstein
p. 416 Stadtmarketing Buxtehude e.V.
p. 420, 439 Schloss Waldeck Hotelbetriebs GmbH + Co KG
p. 442 GrimmHeimat NordHessen

Map of the German Fairy Tale Route:
With the approval of "Deutsche Märchenstraße e.V.", Kassel

Web-index

Inhabitants: German census 2011

The German Fairy Tale Route, Kassel – www.german-fairytaleroute.com

Alsfeld: ca. 16,300 inhabitants – www.alsfeld.de
Bad Hersfeld: ca. 28,600 inhabitants – www.bad-hersfeld.de
Bad Karlshafen: ca. 3,500 inhabitants – www.bad-karlshafen.de
Bad Oeynhausen: ca. 48,600 inhabitants – www.badoeynhausen.de
Bad Sooden-Allendorf: ca. 8,200 inhabitants – www.bad-sooden-allendorf.de
Bad Wildungen: ca. 16,600 inhabitants – www.bad-wildungen.de
Baunatal: ca. 27,400 inhabitants – www.baunatal.de
Berlin: ca. 3,500,000 inhabitants – www.visitberlin.de
Bodenwerder: ca. 5,700 inhabitants – www.muenchhausenland.de
Bovenden: ca. 13,200 inhabitants – www.bovenden.de
Bremen, Free Hanseatic City: ca. 544,000 inhabitants – www.bremen-tourism.de
Bremerhaven, Sea City: ca. 108,000 inhabitants –
www.bremerhaven-tourism.de
Buxtehude: ca. 39,500 inhabitants - www.buxtehude.de
Ebergötzen: ca. 1,900 inhabitants – www.ebergoetzen.de
www.radolfshausen.de
Frankenberg (Eder): ca. 17,800 inhabitants – ederbergland-touristik.de
Freiensteinau: ca. 3,200 inhabitants - www.freiensteinau.de
Fritzlar: ca. 14,400 inhabitants - www.fritzlar.de
Fürstenberg: ca. 1,100 inhabitants – www.fuerstenberg-porzellan.com
Göttingen: ca. 116,000 inhabitants – www.goettingen-tourismus.de
Grebenstein: ca. 5,800 inhabitants - www.stadt-grebenstein.de
Gudensberg: ca. 9,100 inhabitants - www.gudensberg.de
Hamelin: ca. 56,700 inhabitants - www.hameln.de
Hanau: ca. 88,800 inhabitants – www.hanau.de
Hann. Münden: ca. 23,700 inhabitants – www.hann.muenden-tourismus.de
Heiligenstadt, Heilbad: ca. 16,300 inhabitants – www.heilbad-heiligenstadt.de
Helsa: ca. 5,600 inhabitants – www.gemeinde-helsa.de
Herbstein: ca. 4,800 inhabitants – www.herbstein.de
Hessisch Lichtenau: ca. 12,100 inhabitants – www.hessisch-lichtenau.de
Hessisch Oldendorf: ca. 18,500 inhabitants – www.hessisch-oldendorf.de
Hofgeismar: ca. 15,100 inhabitants – www.hofgeismar.de
Homberg (Efze): ca. 14,000 inhabitants – www.homberg-efze.de
Hoya: ca. 3,800 inhabitants - www.grafschaft-hoya.de
Kassel: ca. 190,000 inhabitants - www.kassel-marketing.de
Kaufungen: ca. 12,500 inhabitants – www.kaufungen.eu
Knüllwald: ca. 4,500 inhabitants - www.knuelltouristik.de
Lahntal: ca. 6,800 inhabitants - www.lahntal.de
Lügde: ca.10,000 inhabitants – www.luegde.de
Mackenrode: ca. 300 inhabitants – www.vg-uder.de
Marburg: ca. 72,000 inhabitants - www.marburg. de
Melsungen: ca. 13,200 inhabitants – www.melsungen.de
Niedenstein: ca. 5,200 inhabitants - www.niedenstein.de
Nienburg: ca. 30,800 inhabitants – www.mittelweser-tourismus.de

Nieste: ca. 1,800 inhabitants - www.nieste.de
Oberweser: ca. 3,300 inhabitants – www.oberweser.de
Polle: ca. 1,200 inhabitants - www.muenchhausenland.de
Schauenburg: ca. 10,000 inhabitants - www.gemeinde.schauenburg.de
Schwalmstadt: ca. 18,300 inhabitants – www.schwalmstadt.de
Steinau an der Straße: ca. 10,500 inhabitants - www.steinau.de
Trendelburg: ca. 5,100 inhabitants – www.trendelburg.de
Wahlsburg: ca. 2,100 inhabitants – www.wahlsburg.de
Waldeck: ca. 7,000 inhabitants – www.waldeck.de
Wiedensahl: ca. 1,000 inhabitants – www.wiedensahl.de
Willingshausen: ca. 5,000 inhabitants - www.willingshausen.de
Witzenhausen: ca. 16,200 inhabitants – www.kirschenland.de
Wolfhagen: ca. 12,600 inhabitants - www.wolfhagen.de

GrimmHeimat NordHessen

Fairy Tale Country of the Brothers Grimm in North Hesse

WELCOME TO THE HOME OF THE BROTHERS GRIMM – situated in the heart of Germany!

More than 200 years ago, Jacob and Wilhelm Grimm spent their Fridays listening to fairy tales in the company of young people in their apartment on the Market Lane (Marktgasse) of Kassel. They wrote the tales down at their own desk or they got written records sent by informants or they pulled texts from rare books. The majority of Grimm's fairy tales and legends come, in any case, from the region of North Hesse. The Children's and Household Tales of the Brothers Grimm became

so popular that they were eventually translated into more than 160 languages. Their working copy of the first edition from 1812 with its handwritten marginal notes is a UNESCO World Heritage Document. It can be viewed at the GRIMM WORLD in Kassel, a recently opened exhibition center with numerous displays focusing on the career and works of the Brothers Grimm and their brother, painter Ludwig Emil Grimm – a very interesting destination for adults and for children.

Discover the world of the Brothers Grimm with fascinating tours in and around Kassel. There are plenty of romantic towns, villages with half-timbered buildings, stylish Baroque houses and legendary castles, romantic hotels, inns and restaurants. The Grimm Fairy Tale Country is so magical and original, that talking animals, dwarfs and mythical creatures still seem alive and Grimm fairy tales and legends are ubiquitous. Visit High Meißner, the mountain of Frau Holle (also called Mother Hulda), during the fairy tale week around Easter in Bad Sooden-Allendorf or Hessisch Lichtenau with its Frau Holle Park and Holleum, a museum dedicated completely to Frau Holle. Other notable fairy tale destinations are Sababurg Castle, home of the Sleeping Beauty in the mysterious forest Reinhardswald near Hofgeismar, the Snow White Village Bergfreiheit near Bad Wildungen, Trendelburg Castle with its Rapunzel Tower, the Little Red Riding Hood Region around Schwalmstadt as well as the district of Kassel-Niederzwehren around Niederzwehren church where the storyteller Dorothea Viehmann and her family lived at Märchenweg 11.

After so much information about fairy tales and the Brothers Grimm, it might be appropriate to ask our visitors a fairy tale question: "At noon, when he came home, the table was set and a good meal was laid out." In which of the fairy tales of the Brothers Grimm does a shepherd come home to such a treat? Answer: In the fairy tale "Sweetheart Roland." Dortchen Wild told Wilhelm Grimm that tale on January 19, 1812 in Kassel; years later she became his wife.

Speaking of good food, in the Grimm Fairy Tale Country of North Hesse there are over fifty specially trained and certified cooks in kitchens, called fairy tale cooks, who make the life and work of the Brothers Grimm into a culinary experience by using regional and seasonal products in their creations.

It is always recommended that one moves around after a good meal. The idyllic and varied fairy tale landscape of the Brothers Grimm with its mountains, valleys, rivers, lakes and enchanted forests is ideal for hikers, Nordic walkers or cyclists, be it mountain biking or E(lectro)-biking. And something rather special! The Grimm Country of North Hesse has two UNESCO World Heritage Sites: UNESCO Mountain Park Kassel-Wilhelmshöhe with its impressive waterfall display and the old beech forest of the Edersee National Park.

Enjoy yourself!

www.grimmheimat.de

Alphabetical Listing of Locations

Alsfeld
Bad Hersfeld
Bad Karlshafen
Bad Oeynhausen
Bad Sooden-Allendorf
Bad Wildungen
Baunatal
Berlin
Bodenwerder
Bovenden
Bremen
Bremerhaven
Buxtehude
Ebergötzen
Frankenberg (Eder)
Freiensteinau
Fritzlar
Fürstenberg (Weser)
Göttingen
Grebenstein
Gudensberg
Hamelin
Hanau
Hann. Münden
Heilbad Heiligenstadt
Helsa
Herbstein
Hessisch Lichtenau
Hessisch Oldendorf
Hofgeismar
Homberg (Efze)
Hoya
Kassel
Kaufungen
Knüllwald
Lahntal
Lügde
Mackenrode
Marburg
Melsungen
Niedenstein
Nienburg (Weser)
Nieste
Oberweser
Polle
Schauenburg
Schwalmstadt
Steinau an der Straße
Trendelburg
Wahlsburg
Waldeck
Wiedensahl
Willingshausen
Witzenhausen
Wolfhagen